HORIZONTAL HARMONY

of the Four Gospels in Parallel Columns

(King James Version)

THOMAS M. MUMFORD

Deseret Book Company
Salt Lake City, Utah

Bible text reproduced by permission,
Cambridge University Press,
Cambridge, England

Third printing November 1982

Library of Congress Catalog Card No. A90-6346

ISBN 0-87747-942-9

Printed in the United States of America 49510
10

TABLE OF CONTENTS

INTRODUCTION

This harmony is based on the idea that the greatest life we can study is that of Jesus Christ. There are only four authentic accounts of his mortal life and these are known as the Four Gospels, i.e., Matthew, Mark, Luke and John.

Since each writer had his own unique style and emphasis, any effort to truly study the life of Christ must include the complete study of all four gospels. One of the tools to help in this study is a harmony.

Harmonies are based upon the Gestalt principle that the whole of anything is greater than the sum of its parts. Since each gospel represents a part, the greater message of the life of Jesus can only be seen when all four are arranged together.

Most harmonies use a variation of parallel columns. That is, they use the number of columns ranging from one to four as they are needed on any given page. I have always found this confusing when trying to keep track of which gospel is being read. For example, a two column page may have Matthew and Mark or Matthew and Luke or Mark and Luke. Also, these harmonies make it difficult to identify each gospel individually and to see how each contributes to the total picture.

This harmony is an attempt to solve the above problems. Each page is divided into four equal-width columns representing the four gospels in the order in which they are found in the New Testament, i.e., Matthew, Mark, Luke and John. By using four continuous equal-width columns, the book becomes not only a reading experience but a visual experience as well, appying the saying, ''A picture is worth a thousand words.'' For example, one can readily see by just turning pages how much in common Matthew, Mark, and Luke have and why they are called the synoptic gospels. Further, it is obvious without reading a word but just by turning pages that John is the only source for much of his gospel. The empty columns fulfill the paradox of saying something by being silent. On any given page then, one can immediately tell which writer(s) included a particular event or teaching. For example, when reading the account of the ''Visit of the Wise Men'' on page nine, it is obvious immediately that Matthew is the only writer to record this visit since the first column is the only one with any printing.

This work, then, is an attempt to place all the events in all four gospels in chronological order and print them in four continuous parallel columns. Those events which are recorded by two or more writers are placed side by side so that the identical or equivalent words are on the same horizontal line across the page, hence the title, ''Horizontal Harmony of the Four Gospels in Parallel Columns.'' With this format the total picture of the life of Christ created by all four gospels can be most easily studied. Also, each individual gospel retains its own identity. Further, those events or teachings recorded by two or more writers can be easily compared.

The Four Gospels are usually divided into two classes: the synoptic gospels and John. The reason Matthew, Mark and Luke are called the synoptic gospels is because they have so much in common. The synoptics primarily tell the events and teachings of the Galilean ministry. John on the other hand centers his writings largely around Jerusalem and the feasts of the Jews.

Following is a brief description of each of the gospels:

MATTHEW — This gospel was written primarily to the Jews to show that Jesus was the literal fulfillment of the Old Testament prophecies concerning the Messiah. All through the gospel the phrase ''that it might be fulfilled'' can be found followed by the Old Testament prophecy. Jesus' nobility is pointed out by the visit of wise men at the birth and the royal lineage showing Jesus a descendant of Abraham and David. The arrangement of the book is by topic rather than chronological and contains many lengthy sermons.

MARK — This gospel is thought to be the earliest written. It is believed that Mark as a companion of Peter wrote his account from the teachings of Peter. The book is written mainly for the gentiles and especially those of Rome. In Mark, Jesus is shown as the Son of God, a man of power and action, performing miracles among men. Mark contains fewer teachings of Jesus than any of the other gospels.

LUKE — Luke was a physician and missionary companion of Paul. His gospel is thought to be the most literary and beautiful of the four. It was written for the Greeks and shows Jesus not only to be the Messiah for the Jews, but the Savior of all mankind. Jesus is the man of compassion who himself started from humble beginnings (the manger birth and shepherds) and goes on to give hope to Samaritans, lepers, the poor, the prodigal son and others. Luke contains many parables as well as much material which is unique to Luke alone.

JOHN — As one begins reading John, it is apparent immediately that this gospel is different from the other three. John is writing to Greeks and Christians in a defense of Jesus as the divine Son of God. He has carefully picked those incidents which will support his purpose. The gospel of John is therefore not so much a history of Jesus' life as it is a profound study of who and what Jesus was. The language is deeply spiritual and filled with symbolisms.

CHRONOLOGICAL INDEX

CHRONOLOGICAL INDEX

CHRONOLOGICAL INDEX

CHRONOLOGICAL INDEX

I. INTRODUCTORY COMMENTS BY THE WRITERS

1. MARK'S TITLE

CHAPTER I

THE beginning of the gospel of Jesus Christ, the Son of God;

2. LUKE'S PREFACE

CHAPTER I

FORASMUCH as many have taken in hand to set forth in order a declaration of those things which are most surely believed among us,

2 Even as they delivered them unto us, which from the beginning were eyewitnesses, and ministers of the word;

3 It seemed good to me also, having had perfect understanding of all things from the very first, to write unto thee in order, most excellent Thē-ŏph′-ĭ-lŭs,

4 That thou mightest know the certainty of those things, wherein thou hast been instructed.

3. JOHN'S TESTIMONY

CHAPTER I

IN the beginning was the Word, and the Word was with God, and the Word was God.

2 The same was in the beginning with God.

3 All things were made by him; and without him was not any thing made that was made.

4 In him was life; and the life was the light of men.

5 And the light shineth in darkness; and the darkness comprehended it not.

6 ¶ There was a man sent from God, whose name *was* John.

7 The same came for a witness, to bear witness of the Light, that all *men* through him might believe.

8 He was not that Light, but *was sent* to bear witness of that Light.

9 *That* was the true Light, which lighteth every man that cometh into the world.

10 He was in the world, and the world was made by him, and the world knew him not.

11 He came unto his own, and his own received him not.

12 But as many as received him, to them gave he power to become the sons of God, *even* to them that believe on his name:

13 Which were born, not of blood, nor of the will of the flesh, nor of the will of man, but of God.

14 And the Word was made flesh, and dwelt among us, (and we beheld his glory, the glory as of the only begotten of the Father,) full of grace and truth.

MATTHEW –	MARK –	LUKE – 1	JOHN – 1
			15 ¶ John bare witness of him, and cried, saying, This was he of whom I spake, He that cometh after me is preferred before me: for he was before me.
			16 And of his fulness have all we received, and grace for grace.
			17 For the law was given by Moses, *but* grace and truth came by Jesus Christ.
			18 No man hath seen God at any time; the only begotten Son, which is in the bosom of the Father, he hath declared *him.*

II.   THE BIRTH AND CHILDHOOD OF JESUS AND JOHN THE BAPTIST

4. ANNUNCIATION TO ZACHARIAS

5 ¶ THERE was in the days of Herod, the king of Judæa, a certain priest named Zăch·ȧ·rī′·ăs, of the course of Ȧ·bī′·ȧ: and his wife *was* of the daughters of Aaron, and her name *was* Elisabeth.

6 And they were both righteous before God, walking in all the commandments and ordinances of the Lord blameless.

7 And they had no child, because that Elisabeth was barren, and they both were *now* well stricken in years.

8 And it came to pass, that while he executed the priest's office before God in the order of his course,

9 According to the custom of the priest's office, his lot was to burn incense when he went into the temple of the Lord.

10 And the whole multitude of the people were praying without at the time of incense.

11 And there appeared unto him an angel of the Lord standing on the right side of the altar of incense.

12 And when Zăch·ȧ·rī′·ăs saw *him,* he was troubled, and fear fell upon him.

13 But the angel said unto him, Fear not, Zăch·ȧ·rī′·ăs: for thy prayer is heard; and thy wife Elisabeth shall bear thee a son, and thou shalt call his name John.

14 And thou shalt have joy and gladness; and many shall rejoice at his birth.

15 For he shall be great in the sight of the Lord, and shall drink neither wine nor strong drink; and he shall be filled with the Holy Ghost, even from his mother's womb.

16 And many of the children of Israel shall he turn to the Lord their God.

17 And he shall go before him in the spirit and power of Ē·lī′·ăs, to turn the hearts of the fathers to the children, and the disobedient to the wisdom of the just; to make ready a people prepared for the Lord.

18 And Zăch·ȧ·rī′·ăs said unto the angel, Whereby shall I know this? for I am an old man, and my wife well stricken in years.

MATTHEW –	MARK –	LUKE – 1	JOHN –
		19 And the angel answering said unto him, I am Gabriel, that stand in the presence of God; and am sent to speak unto thee, and to shew thee these glad tidings.	

20 And, behold, thou shalt be dumb, and not able to speak, until the day that these things shall be performed, because thou believest not my words, which shall be fulfilled in their season.

21 And the people waited for Zăch·ă·rī´·ăs, and marvelled that he tarried so long in the temple.

22 And when he came out, he could not speak unto them: and they perceived that he had seen a vision in the temple: for he beckoned unto them, and remained speechless.

23 And it came to pass, that, as soon as the days of his ministration were accomplished, he departed to his own house.

24 And after those days his wife Elisabeth conceived, and hid herself five months, saying,

25 Thus hath the Lord dealt with me in the days wherein he looked on *me*, to take away my reproach among men.

5. ANNUNCIATION TO MARY

26 And in the sixth month the angel Gabriel was sent from God unto a city of Galilee, named Nazareth,

27 To a virgin espoused to a man whose name was Joseph, of the house of David; and the virgin's name *was* Mary.

28 And the angel came in unto her, and said, Hail, *thou that art* highly favoured, the Lord *is* with thee: blessed *art* thou among women.

29 And when she saw *him*, she was troubled at his saying, and cast in her mind what manner of salutation this should be.

30 And the angel said unto her, Fear not, Mary: for thou hast found favour with God.

31 And, behold, thou shalt conceive in thy womb, and bring forth a son, and shalt call his name JESUS.

32 He shall be great, and shall be called the Son of the Highest: and the Lord God shall give unto him the throne of his father David:

33 And he shall reign over the house of Jacob for ever; and of his kingdom there shall be no end.

34 Then said Mary unto the angel, How shall this be, seeing I know not a man?

35 And the angel answered and said unto her, The Holy Ghost shall come upon thee, and the power of the Highest shall overshadow thee: therefore also that holy thing which shall be born of thee shall be called the Son of God.

36 And, behold, thy cousin Elisabeth, she hath also conceived a son in her old age: and this is the sixth month with her, who was called barren.

37 For with God nothing shall be impossible.

MATTHEW –	MARK –	LUKE – 1	JOHN –
		38 And Mary said, Behold the handmaid of the Lord; be it unto me according to thy word. And the angel departed from her.	

6. MARY VISITS ELIZABETH

MATTHEW –	MARK –	LUKE – 1	JOHN –
		39 And Mary arose in those days, and went into the hill country with haste, into a city of Juda;	

39 And Mary arose in those days, and went into the hill country with haste, into a city of Juda;

40 And entered into the house of Zăch·ă·rī´·ăs, and saluted Elisabeth.

41 And it came to pass, that, when Elisabeth heard the salutation of Mary, the babe leaped in her womb; and Elisabeth was filled with the Holy Ghost:

42 And she spake out with a loud voice, and said, Blessed *art* thou among women, and blessed *is* the fruit of thy womb.

43 And whence *is* this to me, that the mother of my Lord should come to me?

44 For, lo, as soon as the voice of thy salutation sounded in mine ears, the babe leaped in my womb for joy.

45 And blessed *is* she that believed: for there shall be a performance of those things which were told her from the Lord.

46 And Mary said, My soul doth magnify the Lord,

47 And my spirit hath rejoiced in God my Saviour.

48 For he hath regarded the low estate of his handmaiden: for, behold, from henceforth all generations shall call me blessed.

49 For he that is mighty hath done to me great things; and holy *is* his name.

50 And his mercy *is* on them that fear him from generation to generation.

51 He hath shewed strength with his arm; he hath scattered the proud in the imagination of their hearts.

52 He hath put down the mighty from *their* seats, and exalted them of low degree.

53 He hath filled the hungry with good things; and the rich he hath sent empty away.

54 He hath holpen his servant Israel, in remembrance of *his* mercy;

55 As he spake to our fathers, to Abraham, and to his seed for ever.

7. BIRTH OF JOHN THE BAPTIST

57 Now Elisabeth's full time came that she should be delivered; and she brought forth a son.

58 And her neighbours and her cousins heard how the Lord had shewed great mercy upon her; and they rejoiced with her.

59 And it came to pass, that on the eighth day they came to circumcise the child; and they called him Zăch·ă·rī´·ăs, after the name of his father.

60 And his mother answered and said, Not *so;* but he shall be called John.

61 And they said unto her, There is none of thy kindred that is called by this name.

MATTHEW – 1	MARK –	LUKE – 1	JOHN –
		62 And they made signs to his father, how he would have him called. 63 And he asked for a writing table, and wrote, saying, His name is John. And they marvelled all. 64 And his mouth was opened immediately, and his tongue *loosed*, and he spake, and praised God.	

8. PROPHECY OF ZACHARIAS

MATTHEW – 1	MARK –	LUKE – 1	JOHN –
		67 And his father Zăch-ă-rī'-ăs was filled with the Holy Ghost, and prophesied, saying, 68 Blessed *be* the Lord God of Israel; for he hath visited and redeemed his people, 69 And hath raised up an horn of salvation for us in the house of his servant David; 70 As he spake by the mouth of his holy prophets, which have been since the world began: 71 That we should be saved from our enemies, and from the hand of all that hate us; 72 To perform the mercy *promised* to our fathers, and to remember his holy covenant; 73 The oath which he sware to our father Abraham, 74 That he would grant unto us, that we being delivered out of the hand of our enemies might serve him without fear, 75 In holiness and righteousness before him, all the days of our life. 76 And thou, child, shalt be called the prophet of the Highest: for thou shalt go before the face of the Lord to prepare his ways; 77 To give knowledge of salvation unto his people by the remission of their sins, 78 Through the tender mercy of our God; whereby the dayspring from on high hath visited us, 79 To give light to them that sit in darkness and *in* the shadow of death, to guide our feet into the way of peace. 65 And fear came on all that dwelt round about them: and all these sayings were noised abroad throughout all the hill country of Judæa. 66 And all they that heard *them* laid *them* up in their hearts, saying, What manner of child shall this be! And the hand of the Lord was with him.	

9. MARY RETURNS TO NAZARETH

MATTHEW – 1	MARK –	LUKE – 1	JOHN –
		56 And Mary abode with her about three months, and returned to her own house.	

10. ANNUNCIATION TO JOSEPH

MATTHEW – 1	MARK –	LUKE – 1	JOHN –
18 ¶ Now the birth of Jesus Christ was on this wise: When as his mother Mary was espoused to Joseph, before they came together, she was found with child of the Holy Ghost. 19 Then Joseph her husband, being a just *man*, and not willing to make her a publick example, was minded to put her away privily.			

MATTHEW – 1	MARK –	LUKE – 2	JOHN –

MATTHEW – 1

20 But while he thought on these things, behold, the angel of the Lord appeared unto him in a dream, saying, Joseph, thou son of David, fear not to take unto thee Mary thy wife: for that which is conceived in her is of the Holy Ghost.

21 And she shall bring forth a son, and thou shalt call his name JESUS: for he shall save his people from their sins.

22 Now all this was done, that it might be fulfilled which was spoken of the Lord by the prophet, saying,

23 Behold, a virgin shall be with child, and shall bring forth a son, and they shall call his name Ĕm·măn′·ū·ĕl, which being interpreted is, God with us.

24 Then Joseph being raised from sleep did as the angel of the Lord had bidden him, and took unto him his wife:

25a And knew her not till she had brought forth her firstborn son:

11. BIRTH OF JESUS THE CHRIST

LUKE – 2

CHAPTER 2

AND it came to pass in those days, that there went out a decree from Cæsar Augustus, that all the world should be taxed.

2 (And this taxing was first made when Çȳ·rē′·nĭ·ús was governor of Syria.)

3 And all went to be taxed, every one into his own city.

4 And Joseph also went up from Galilee, out of the city of Nazareth, into Judæa, unto the city of David, which is called Bethlehem; (because he was of the house and lineage of David:)

5 To be taxed with Mary his espoused wife, being great with child.

6 And so it was, that, while they were there, the days were accomplished that she should be delivered.

7 And she brought forth her firstborn son, and wrapped him in swaddling clothes, and laid him in a manger; because there was no room for them in the inn.

12. SHEPHERDS WITNESS THE BABE AND MAKE KNOWN HIS BIRTH

8 And there were in the same country shepherds abiding in the field, keeping watch over their flock by night.

9 And, lo, the angel of the Lord came upon them, and the glory of the Lord shone round about them: and they were sore afraid.

10 And the angel said unto them, Fear not: for, behold, I bring you good tidings of great joy, which shall be to all people.

11 For unto you is born this day in the city of David a Saviour, which is Christ the Lord.

12 And this *shall be* a sign unto you; Ye shall find the babe wrapped in swaddling clothes, lying in a manger.

13 And suddenly there was with the angel a multitude of the heavenly host praising God, and saying,

14 Glory to God in the highest, and on earth peace, good will toward men.

15 And it came to pass, as the angels were gone away from them into heaven, the shepherds said one to another, Let us now go even unto Bethlehem, and see this thing which is come to pass, which the Lord hath made known unto us.

16 And they came with haste, and found Mary, and Joseph, and the babe lying in a manger.

17 And when they had seen *it*, they made known abroad the saying which was told them concerning this child.

18 And all they that heard *it* wondered at those things which were told them by the shepherds.

19 But Mary kept all these things, and pondered *them* in her heart.

20 And the shepherds returned, glorifying and praising God for all the things that they had heard and seen, as it was told unto them.

13. CIRCUMCISION AND NAMING OF JESUS

25b and he called his name JESUS.

21 And when eight days were accomplished for the circumcising of the child, his name was called JESUS, which was so named of the angel before he was conceived in the womb.

14. GENEALOGIES OF JESUS *

CHAPTER I

THE book of the generation of Jesus Christ, the son of David, the son of Abraham.

2 Abraham begat Isaac; and Isaac begat Jacob; and Jacob begat Judas and his brethren;

3 And Judas begat Phâr´-ĕś and Zâr´-ă of Thä´-mär; and Phâr´-ĕś begat Ĕś´-rŏm; and Ĕś´-rŏm begat Âr´-ăm;

4 And Âr´-ăm begat Ă-mĭn´-ă-dăb; and Ă-mĭn´-ă-dăb begat Nā-ăs´-sŏn; and Nā-ăs´-sŏn begat Săl´-mŏn;

5 And Săl´-mŏn begat Bō´-ŏz of Rā´-chăb; and Bō´-ŏz begat Ō´-bĕd of Ruth; and Ō´-bĕd begat Jesse;

6 And Jesse begat David the king; and David the king begat Solomon of her *that had been the wife* of Ū-rī´-ăs;

7 And Solomon begat Rō-bō´-ăm; and Rō-bō´-ăm begat Ā-bī´-ă; and Ā-bī´-ă begat Ā´-să;

8 And Ā´-să begat Jŏs´-ă-phăt; and Jŏs´-ă-phăt begat Joram; and Joram begat Ō-zī´-ăs;

9 And Ō-zī´-ăs begat Jō´-ă-thăm; and Jō´-ă-thăm begat Ā´-chăz; and Ā´-chăz begat Ĕz-ē-kī´-ăs;

10 And Ĕz-ē-kī´-ăs begat Mă-năs´-sēś; and Mă-năs´-sēś begat Amon; and Amon begat Jō-sī´-ăs;

11 And Jō-sī´-ăs begat Jĕch-ō-nī´-ăs and his brethren, about the time they were carried away to Babylon:

Ch. 3

23b being (as was supposed) the son of Joseph, which was *the son* of Hē´-lī,

24 Which was *the son* of Măt´-thăt, which was *the son* of Levi, which was *the son* of Mĕl´-chī, which was *the son* of Jăn´-nă, which was *the son* of Joseph,

25 Which was *the son* of Măt-tă-thī´-ăs, which was *the son* of Amos, which was *the son* of Nā´-ŭm, which was *the son* of Ĕś´-lī, which was *the son* of Năg´-gē,

26 Which was *the son* of Mā´-ăth, which was *the son* of Măt-tă-thī´-ăs, which was *the son* of Sĕm´-ĕ-ī, which was *the son* of Joseph, which was *the son* of Juda,

27 Which was *the son* of Jō-ăn´-nă, which was *the son* of Rhē´-să, which was *the son* of Zō-rŏb´-ă-bĕl, which was *the son* of Să-lā´-thī-ĕl, which was *the son* of Nē´-rī,

28 Which was *the son* of Mĕl´-chī, which was *the son* of Ăd´-dī, which was *the son* of Cō´-săm, which was *the son* of Ĕl-mō´-dăm, which was *the son* of Er,

29 Which was *the son* of Jō´-sē, which was *the son* of Ĕl-ĭ-ē-zĕr, which was *the son* of Jō´-rĭm, which was *the son* of Măt´-thăt, which was *the son* of Levi,

30 Which was *the son* of Simeon, which was *the son* of Juda, which was *the son* of Joseph, which was *the son* of Jō´-năn, which was *the son* of Ē-lī´-ă-kĭm,

*Many scholars believe Matthew gives the genealogy of Joseph while Luke gives that of Mary.

MATTHEW – 1

12 And after they were brought to Babylon, Jĕch·ō·nī´·ăs begat Să·lā´·thĭ·ĕl; and Să·lā´·thĭ·ĕl begat Zŏ·rŏb´·ă·bĕl;

13 And Zŏ·rŏb´·ă·bĕl begat Ă·bī´·ŭd; and Ă·bī´·ŭd begat Ē·lī´·ă·kĭm; and Ē·lī´·ă·kĭm begat Ā´·zôr;

14 And Ā´·zôr begat Sā´·dŏc; and Sā´·dŏc begat Ā´·chĭm; and Ā´·chĭm begat Ē·lī´·ŭd;

15 And Ē·lī´·ŭd begat Ĕl·ē·ā´·zär; and Ĕl·ē·ā´·zär begat Măt´·thăn; and Măt´·thăn begat Jacob;

16 And Jacob begat Joseph the husband of Mary, of whom was born Jesus, who is called Christ.

17 So all the generations from Abraham to David *are* fourteen generations; and from David until the carrying away into Babylon *are* fourteen generations; and from the carrying away into Babylon unto Christ *are* fourteen generations.

LUKE – 3,2

31 Which was *the son* of Mĕl´·ĕ·ă, which was *the son* of Mē´·năn, which was *the son* of Măt´·tă·thă, which was *the son* of Nathan, which was *the son* of David,

32 Which was *the son* of Jesse, which was *the son* of Ō´·bĕd, which was *the son* of Bō´·ŏz, which was *the son* of Săl´·mŏn, which was *the son* of Nā·ăs´·sŏn,

33 Which was *the son* of Ă·mĭn´·ă·dăb, which was *the son* of Ăr´·ăm, which was *the son* of Ĕś´·rŏm, which was *the son* of Phăr´·ĕś, which was *the son* of Juda,

34 Which was *the son* of Jacob, which was *the son* of Isaac, which was *the son* of Abraham, which was *the son* of Thâr´·ă, which was *the son* of Nā´·chôr,

35 Which was *the son* of Sâr´·ŭch, which was *the son* of Ră´·gău, which was *the son* of Phă´·lĕc, which was *the son* of Hĕ´·bĕr, which was *the son* of Sā´·lă,

36 Which was *the son* of Că·ī´·năn, which was *the son* of Ăr·phăx´·ăd, which was *the son* of Sem, which was *the son* of Nō´·ē, which was *the son* of Lā´·mĕch,

37 Which was *the son* of Mă·thŭ´·să·lă, which was *the son* of Ē´·nŏch, which was *the son* of Jăr´·ĕd, which was *the son* of Mă̆l´·ĕ·lēĕl, which was *the son* of Că·ī´·năn,

38 Which was *the son* of Ē´·nŏs, which was *the son* of Seth, which was *the son* of Adam, which was *the son* of God.

15. JESUS PRESENTED AT THE TEMPLE

Ch. 2

22 And when the days of her purification according to the law of Moses were accomplished, they brought him to Jerusalem, to present *him* to the Lord;

23 (As it is written in the law of the Lord, Every male that openeth the womb shall be called holy to the Lord;)

24 And to offer a sacrifice according to that which is said in the law of the Lord, A pair of turtledoves, or two young pigeons.

25 And, behold, there was a man in Jerusalem, whose name *was* Simeon; and the same man *was* just and devout, waiting for the consolation of Israel: and the Holy Ghost was upon him.

26 And it was revealed unto him by the Holy Ghost, that he should not see death, before he had seen the Lord's Christ.

27 And he came by the Spirit into the temple: and when the parents brought in the child Jesus, to do for him after the custom of the law,

28 Then took he him up in his arms, and blessed God, and said,

29 Lord, now lettest thou thy servant depart in peace, according to thy word:

30 For mine eyes have seen thy salvation,

31 Which thou hast prepared before the face of all people;

32 A light to lighten the Gentiles, and the glory of thy people Israel.

33 And Joseph and his mother marvelled at those things which were spoken of him.

34 And Simeon blessed them, and said unto Mary his mother, Behold, this *child* is set for the fall and rising again of many in Israel; and for a sign which shall be spoken against;

35 (Yea, a sword shall pierce through thy own soul also,) that the thoughts of many hearts may be revealed.

36 And there was one Anna, a prophetess, the daughter of Phă-nū´-ĕl, of the tribe of Ā´-sĕr: she was of a great age, and had lived with an husband seven years from her virginity;

37 And she *was* a widow of about fourscore and four years, which departed not from the temple, but served *God* with fastings and prayers night and day.

38 And she coming in that instant gave thanks likewise unto the Lord, and spake of him to all them that looked for redemption in Jerusalem.

39a And when they had performed all things according to the law of the Lord,

16. VISIT OF THE WISE MEN

CHAPTER 2

NOW when Jesus was born in Bethlehem of Judæa in the days of Herod the king, behold, there came wise men from the east to Jerusalem,

2 Saying, Where is he that is born King of the Jews? for we have seen his star in the east, and are come to worship him.

3 When Herod the king had heard *these things*, he was troubled, and all Jerusalem with him.

4 And when he had gathered all the chief priests and scribes of the people together, he demanded of them where Christ should be born.

5 And they said unto him, In Bethlehem of Judæa: for thus it is written by the prophet,

6 And thou Bethlehem, *in* the land of Juda, art not the least among the princes of Juda: for out of thee shall come a Governor, that shall rule my people Israel.

7 Then Herod, when he had privily called the wise men, inquired of them diligently what time the star appeared.

8 And he sent them to Bethlehem, and said, Go and search diligently for the young child; and when ye have found *him*, bring me word again, that I may come and worship him also.

9 When they had heard the king, they departed; and, lo, the star, which they saw in the east, went before them, till it came and stood over where the young child was.

9

MATTHEW – 2	MARK –	LUKE – 2	JOHN –
10 When they saw the star, they rejoiced with exceeding great joy. 11 ¶ And when they were come into the house, they saw the young child with Mary his mother, and fell down, and worshipped him: and when they had opened their treasures, they presented unto him gifts; gold, and frankincense, and myrrh. 12 And being warned of God in a dream that they should not return to Herod, they departed into their own country another way.			

17. FLIGHT INTO EGYPT

MATTHEW – 2	MARK –	LUKE – 2	JOHN –
13 And when they were departed, behold, the angel of the Lord appeareth to Joseph in a dream, saying, Arise, and take the young child and his mother, and flee into Egypt, and be thou there until I bring thee word: for Herod will seek the young child to destroy him. 14 When he arose, he took the young child and his mother by night, and departed into Egypt: 15 And was there until the death of Herod: that it might be fulfilled which was spoken of the Lord by the prophet, saying, Out of Egypt have I called my son. 16 ¶ Then Herod, when he saw that he was mocked of the wise men, was exceeding wroth, and sent forth, and slew all the children that were in Bethlehem, and in all the coasts thereof, from two years old and under, according to the time which he had diligently inquired of the wise men. 17 Then was fulfilled that which was spoken by Jeremy the prophet, saying, 18 In Rā'-mă was there a voice heard, lamentation, and weeping, and great mourning, Rachel weeping *for* her children, and would not be comforted, because they are not.			

18. RETURN FROM EGYPT TO NAZARETH

MATTHEW – 2	MARK –	LUKE – 2	JOHN –
19 ¶ But when Herod was dead, behold, an angel of the Lord appeareth in a dream to Joseph in Egypt, 20 Saying, Arise, and take the young child and his mother, and go into the land of Israel: for they are dead which sought the young child's life. 21 And he arose, and took the young child and his mother, and came into the land of Israel. 22 But when he heard that Ăr-chĕ-lā'-ŭs did reign in Judæa in the room of his father Herod, he was afraid to go thither: notwithstanding, being warned of God in a dream, he turned aside into the parts of Galilee: 23 And he came and dwelt in a city called Nazareth: that it might be fulfilled which was spoken by the prophets, He shall be called a Nazarene.		39b they returned into Galilee, to their own city Nazareth.	

19. CHILDHOOD OF JESUS

40 And the child grew, and waxed strong in spirit, filled with wisdom: and the grace of God was upon him.

20. JESUS AT THE TEMPLE, AGE TWELVE

41 Now his parents went to Jerusalem every year at the feast of the passover.

42 And when he was twelve years old, they went up to Jerusalem after the custom of the feast.

43 And when they had fulfilled the days, as they returned, the child Jesus tarried behind in Jerusalem; and Joseph and his mother knew not *of it*.

44 But they, supposing him to have been in the company, went a day's journey; and they sought him among *their* kinsfolk and acquaintance.

45 And when they found him not, they turned back again to Jerusalem, seeking him.

46 And it came to pass, that after three days they found him in the temple, sitting in the midst of the doctors, both hearing them, and asking them questions.

47 And all that heard him were astonished at his understanding and answers.

48 And when they saw him, they were amazed: and his mother said unto him, Son, why hast thou thus dealt with us? behold, thy father and I have sought thee sorrowing.

49 And he said unto them, How is it that ye sought me? wist ye not that I must be about my Father's business?

50 And they understood not the saying which he spake unto them.

51 And he went down with them, and came to Nazareth, and was subject unto them: but his mother kept all these sayings in her heart.

21. YOUNG MANHOOD OF JESUS

52 And Jesus increased in wisdom and stature, and in favour with God and man.

22. PREPARATION OF JOHN THE BAPTIST

Ch. 1

80 And the child grew, and waxed strong in spirit, and was in the deserts till the day of his shewing unto Israel.

III. THE OPENING EVENTS IN JESUS' MINISTRY

23. TIME AND BACKGROUND OF JOHN'S MINISTRY

CHAPTER 3

NOW in the fifteenth year of the reign of Tī-bē´-rǐ-ŭs Cæsar, Pontius Pilate being governor of Judæa, and Herod being tē´-trärch of Galilee, and his brother Philip tē´-trärch of Ī-tū-ræ´-ă and of the region of Trăch-ō-nī´-tǐs, and Lȳ-sā´-nǐ-ăs the tē´-trärch of Ăb-ǐ-lē´-nē,

2 Ăn´-năs and Cāi´-ă-phăs being the high priests, the word of God came unto John the son of Zăch-ă-rī´-ăs in the wilderness.

24. JOHN AND HIS MESSAGE

CHAPTER 3

IN those days came John the Baptist, preaching in the wilderness of Judæa,

2 And saying, Repent ye: for the kingdom of heaven is at hand.

3 For this is he that was spoken of by the prophet Ē-sāi´-ăs, saying, The voice of one crying in the wilderness, Prepare ye the way of the Lord, make his paths straight.

4 John did baptize in the wilderness, and preach the baptism of repentance for the remission of sins.

2 As it is written in the prophets, Behold, I send my messenger before thy face, which shall prepare thy way before thee.

3 The voice of one crying in the wilderness, Prepare ye the way of the Lord, make his paths straight.

3 And he came into all the country about Jordan, preaching the baptism of repentance for the remission of sins;

4 As it is written in the book of the words of Ē-sāi´-ăs the prophet, saying, The voice of one crying in the wilderness, Prepare ye the way of the Lord, make his paths straight.

5 Every valley shall be filled, and every mountain and hill shall be brought low; and the crooked shall be made straight, and the rough ways shall be made smooth;

6 And all flesh shall see the salvation of God.

4 And the same John had his raiment of camel's hair, and a leathern girdle about his loins; and his meat was locusts and wild honey.

5 Then went out to him Jerusalem, and all Judæa, and all the region round about Jordan,

6 And were baptized of him in Jordan, confessing their sins.

7 ¶ But when he saw many of the Pharisees and Săd´-dū-çēěs come to his baptism, he said unto them, O generation of vipers, who hath warned you to flee from the wrath to come?

8 Bring forth therefore fruits meet for repentance:

9 And think not to say within yourselves, We have Abraham to our father: for I say unto you, that God is able of these stones to raise up children unto Abraham.

10 And now also the axe is laid unto the root of the trees: therefore every tree which bringeth not forth good fruit is hewn down, and cast into the fire.

6 And John was clothed with camel's hair, and with a girdle of a skin about his loins; and he did eat locusts and wild honey;

5 And there went out unto him all the land of Judæa, and they of Jerusalem, and were all baptized of him in the river of Jordan, confessing their sins.

7 Then said he to the multitude that came forth to be baptized of him, O generation of vipers, who hath warned you to flee from the wrath to come?

8 Bring forth therefore fruits worthy of repentance, and begin not to say within yourselves, We have Abraham to our father: for I say unto you, That God is able of these stones to raise up children unto Abraham.

9 And now also the axe is laid unto the root of the trees: every tree therefore which bringeth not forth good fruit is hewn down, and cast into the fire.

10 And the people asked him, saying, What shall we do then?

11 He answereth and saith unto them, He that hath two coats, let him impart to him that hath none; and he that hath meat, let him do likewise.

12 Then came also publicans to be baptized, and said unto him, Master, what shall we do?

13 And he said unto them, Exact no more than that which is appointed you.

14 And the soldiers likewise demanded of him, saying, And what shall we do? And he said unto them, Do violence to no man, neither accuse *any* falsely; and be content with your wages.

15 And as the people were in expectation, and all men mused in their hearts of John, whether he were the Christ, or not;

11 I indeed baptize you with water unto repentance: but he that cometh after me is mightier than I, whose shoes I am not worthy to bear: he shall baptize you with the Holy Ghost, and *with* fire:

12 Whose fan *is* in his hand, and he will throughly purge his floor, and gather his wheat into the garner; but he will burn up the chaff with unquenchable fire.

7 And preached, saying, There cometh one mightier than I after me, the latchet of whose shoes I am not worthy to stoop down and unloose.

8 I indeed have baptized you with water: but he shall baptize you with the Holy Ghost.

16 John answered, saying unto *them* all, I indeed baptize you with water; but one mightier than I cometh, the latchet of whose shoes I am not worthy to unloose: he shall baptize you with the Holy Ghost and with fire:

17 Whose fan *is* in his hand, and he will throughly purge his floor, and will gather the wheat into his garner; but the chaff he will burn with fire unquenchable.

18 And many other things in his exhortation preached he unto the people.

25. JESUS IS BAPTIZED BY JOHN

13 ¶ Then cometh Jesus from Galilee to Jordan unto John, to be baptized of him.

14 But John forbad him, saying, I have need to be baptized of thee, and comest thou to me?

15 And Jesus answering said unto him, Suffer *it to be so* now: for thus it becometh us to fulfil all righteousness. Then he suffered him.

16 And Jesus, when he was baptized, went up straightway out of the water: and, lo, the heavens were opened unto him, and he saw the Spirit of God descending like a dove, and lighting upon him:

17 And lo a voice from heaven, saying, This is my beloved Son, in whom I am well pleased.

9 And it came to pass in those days, that Jesus came from Nazareth of Galilee,

and was baptized of John in Jordan.

10 And straightway coming up out of the water, he saw the heavens opened, and the Spirit like a dove descending upon him:

11 And there came a voice from heaven, *saying*, Thou art my beloved Son, in whom I am well pleased.

21 Now when all the people were baptized, it came to pass, that Jesus also being baptized, and praying, the heaven was opened,

22 And the Holy Ghost descended in a bodily shape like a dove upon him, and a voice came from heaven, which said, Thou art my beloved Son; in thee I am well pleased.

23a And Jesus himself began to be about thirty years of age,

26. FAST AND TEMPTATION OF JESUS

CHAPTER 4

THEN was Jesus led up of the Spirit into the wilderness to be tempted of the devil.

2 And when he had fasted forty days and forty nights, he was afterward an hungred.

3 And when the tempter came to him, he said, If thou be the Son of God, command that these stones be made bread.

4 But he answered and said, It is written, Man shall not live by bread alone, but by every word that proceedeth out of the mouth of God.

5 Then the devil taketh him up into the holy city, and setteth him on a pinnacle of the temple,

6 And saith unto him, If thou be the Son of God, cast thyself down: for it is written, He shall give his angels charge concerning thee:

and in *their* hands they shall bear thee up, lest at any time thou dash thy foot against a stone.

12 And immediately the Spirit driveth him into the wilderness.

CHAPTER 4

AND Jesus being full of the Holy Ghost returned from Jordan, and was led by the Spirit into the wilderness,

2 Being forty days tempted of the devil. And in those days he did eat nothing: and when they were ended, he afterward hungered.

3 And the devil said unto him, If thou be the Son of God, command this stone that it be made bread.

4 And Jesus answered him, saying, It is written, That man shall not live by bread alone, but by every word of God.

9 And he brought him to Jerusalem, and set him on a pinnacle of the temple, and said unto him, If thou be the Son of God, cast thyself down from hence:

10 For it is written, He shall give his angels charge over thee, to keep thee:

11 And in *their* hands they shall bear thee up, lest at any time thou dash thy foot against a stone.

MATTHEW – 4	MARK – 1	LUKE – 4	JOHN – 1
7 Jesus said unto him, It is written again, Thou shalt not tempt the Lord thy God. 8 Again, the devil taketh him up into an exceeding high mountain, and sheweth him all the kingdoms of the world, and the glory of them; 9 And saith unto him, All these things will I give thee, if thou wilt fall down and worship me. 10 Then saith Jesus unto him, Get thee hence, Satan: for it is written, Thou shalt worship the Lord thy God, and him only shalt thou serve. 11 Then the devil leaveth him, and, behold, angels came and ministered unto him.	13 And he was there in the wilderness forty days, tempted of Satan; and was with the wild beasts; and the angels ministered unto him.	12 And Jesus answering said unto him, It is said, Thou shalt not tempt the Lord thy God. 5 And the devil, taking him up into an high mountain, shewed unto him all the kingdoms of the world in a moment of time. 6 And the devil said unto him, All this power will I give thee, and the glory of them: for that is delivered unto me; and to whomsoever I will I give it. 7 If thou therefore wilt worship me, all shall be thine. 8 And Jesus answered and said unto him, Get thee behind me, Satan: for it is written, Thou shalt worship the Lord thy God, and him only shalt thou serve. 13 And when the devil had ended all the temptation, he departed from him for a season.	

27. JOHN TESTIFIES OF JESUS

			19 ¶ And this is the record of John, when the Jews sent priests and Levites from Jerusalem to ask him, Who art thou? 20 And he confessed, and denied not; but confessed, I am not the Christ. 21 And they asked him, What then? Art thou Ē-lí-ăs? And he saith, I am not. Art thou that prophet? And he answered, No. 22 Then said they unto him, Who art thou? that we may give an answer to them that sent us. What sayest thou of thyself? 23 He said, I *am* the voice of one crying in the wilderness, Make straight the way of the Lord, as said the prophet Ē-śáī-ăs. 24 And they which were sent were of the Pharisees. 25 And they asked him, and said unto him, Why baptizest thou then, if thou be not that Christ, nor Ē-lí-ăs, neither that prophet? 26 John answered them, saying, I baptize with water: but there standeth one among you, whom ye know not; 27 He it is, who coming after me is preferred before me, whose shoe's latchet I am not worthy to unloose. 28 These things were done in Běth-ăb-á-rä beyond Jordan, where John was baptizing. 29 ¶ The next day John seeth Jesus coming unto him, and saith, Behold the Lamb of God, which taketh away the sin of the world. 30 This is he of whom I said, After me cometh a man which is preferred before me: for he was before me. 31 And I knew him not: but that he should be made manifest to Israel, therefore am I come baptizing with water. 32 And John bare record, saying, I saw the Spirit descending from heaven like a dove, and it abode upon him.

MATTHEW –	MARK –	LUKE –	JOHN – 1
			33 And I knew him not: but he that sent me to baptize with water, the same said unto me, Upon whom thou shalt see the Spirit descending, and remaining on him, the same is he which baptizeth with the Holy Ghost. 34 And I saw, and bare record that this is the Son of God.

28. FIRST CALL OF DISCIPLES

			35 ¶ Again the next day after John stood, and two of his disciples; 36 And looking upon Jesus as he walked, he saith, Behold the Lamb of God! 37 And the two disciples heard him speak, and they followed Jesus. 38 Then Jesus turned, and saw them following, and saith unto them, What seek ye? They said unto him, Rabbi, (which is to say, being interpreted, Master,) where dwellest thou? 39 He saith unto them, Come and see. They came and saw where he dwelt, and abode with him that day: for it was about the tenth hour. 40 One of the two which heard John *speak*, and followed him, was Andrew, Simon Peter's brother. 41 He first findeth his own brother Simon, and saith unto him, We have found the Mĕs-sī´-ăs, which is, being interpreted, the Christ. 42 And he brought him to Jesus. And when Jesus beheld him, he said, Thou art Simon the son of Jona: thou shalt be called Cĕ´-phăs, which is by interpretation, A stone. 43 ¶ The day following Jesus would go forth into Galilee, and findeth Philip, and saith unto him, Follow me. 44 Now Philip was of Bĕth-să´-ĭ-dă, the city of Andrew and Peter. 45 Philip findeth Nă-thăn´-ă-ĕl, and saith unto him, We have found him, of whom Moses in the law, and the prophets, did write, Jesus of Nazareth, the son of Joseph. 46 And Nă-thăn´-ă-ĕl said unto him, Can there any good thing come out of Nazareth? Philip saith unto him, Come and see. 47 Jesus saw Nă-thăn´-ă-ĕl coming to him, and saith of him, Behold an Israelite indeed, in whom is no guile! 48 Nă-thăn´-ă-ĕl saith unto him, Whence knowest thou me? Jesus answered and said unto him, Before that Philip called thee, when thou wast under the fig tree, I saw thee. 49 Nă-thăn´-ă-ĕl answered and saith unto him, Rabbi, thou art the Son of God; thou art the King of Israel. 50 Jesus answered and said unto him, Because I said unto thee, I saw thee under the fig tree, believest thou? thou shalt see greater things than these. 51 And he saith unto him, Verily, verily, I say unto you, Hereafter ye shall see heaven open, and the angels of God ascending and descending upon the Son of man.

29. FIRST MIRACLE: WATER TO WINE AT MARRIAGE IN CANA

CHAPTER 2

AND the third day there was a marriage in Cana of Galilee; and the mother of Jesus was there:

2 And both Jesus was called, and his disciples, to the marriage.

3 And when they wanted wine, the mother of Jesus saith unto him, They have no wine.

4 Jesus saith unto her, Woman, what have I to do with thee? mine hour is not yet come.

5 His mother saith unto the servants, Whatsoever he saith unto you, do *it*.

6 And there were set there six waterpots of stone, after the manner of the purifying of the Jews, containing two or three firkins apiece.

7 Jesus saith unto them, Fill the waterpots with water. And they filled them up to the brim.

8 And he saith unto them, Draw out now, and bear unto the governor of the feast. And they bare *it*.

9 When the ruler of the feast had tasted the water that was made wine, and knew not whence it was: (but the servants which drew the water knew;) the governor of the feast called the bridegroom,

10 And saith unto him, Every man at the beginning doth set forth good wine; and when men have well drunk, then that which is worse: *but* thou hast kept the good wine until now.

11 This beginning of miracles did Jesus in Cana of Galilee, and manifested forth his glory; and his disciples believed on him.

30. JESUS VISITS CAPERNAUM

12 ¶ After this he went down to Că·pĕr′·nă·ŭm, he, and his mother, and his brethren, and his disciples: and they continued there not many days.

IV.   THE EARLY JUDEAN MINISTRY

31. JESUS ATTENDS PASSOVER* AND CLEANSES TEMPLE

13 ¶ And the Jews' passover was at hand, and Jesus went up to Jerusalem,

14 And found in the temple those that sold oxen and sheep and doves, and the changers of money sitting:

15 And when he had made a scourge of small cords, he drove them all out of the temple, and the sheep, and the oxen; and poured out the changers' money, and overthrew the tables;

16 And said unto them that sold doves, Take these things hence; make not my Father's house an house of merchandise.

17 And his disciples remembered that it was written, The zeal of thine house hath eaten me up.

18 ¶ Then answered the Jews and said unto him, What sign shewest thou unto us, seeing that thou doest these things?

19 Jesus answered and said unto them, Destroy this temple, and in three days I will raise it up.

20 Then said the Jews, Forty and six years was this temple in building, and wilt thou rear it up in three days?

21 But he spake of the temple of his body.

22 When therefore he was risen from the dead, his disciples remembered that he had said this unto them; and they believed the scripture, and the word which Jesus had said.

23 ¶ Now when he was in Jerusalem at the passover, in the feast day, many believed in his name, when they saw the miracles which he did.

24 But Jesus did not commit himself unto them, because he knew all men,

25 And needed not that any should testify of man: for he knew what was in man.

32. NICODEMUS, A PHARISEE AND RULER IS TAUGHT BY JESUS

CHAPTER 3

THERE was a man of the Pharisees, named Nĭc-ŏ-dē´-mŭs, a ruler of the Jews:

2 The same came to Jesus by night, and said unto him, Rabbi, we know that thou art a teacher come from God: for no man can do these miracles that thou doest, except God be with him.

3 Jesus answered and said unto him, Verily, verily, I say unto thee, Except a man be born again, he cannot see the kingdom of God.

4 Nĭc-ŏ-dē´-mŭs saith unto him, How can a man be born when he is old? can he enter the second time into his mother's womb, and be born?

*Feast of the Passover, see note 31.

MATTHEW –	MARK –	LUKE –	JOHN – 3
			5 Jesus answered, Verily, verily, I say unto thee, Except a man be born of water and *of* the Spirit, he cannot enter into the kingdom of God.
			6 That which is born of the flesh is flesh; and that which is born of the Spirit is spirit.
			7 Marvel not that I said unto thee, Ye must be born again.
			8 The wind bloweth where it listeth, and thou hearest the sound thereof, but canst not tell whence it cometh, and whither it goeth: so is every one that is born of the Spirit.
			9 Nĭc-ŏ-dē´-mŭs answered and said unto him, How can these things be?
			10 Jesus answered and said unto him, Art thou a master of Israel, and knowest not these things?
			11 Verily, verily, I say unto thee, We speak that we do know, and testify that we have seen; and ye receive not our witness.
			12 If I have told you earthly things, and ye believe not, how shall ye believe, if I tell you *of* heavenly things?
			13 And no man hath ascended up to heaven, but he that came down from heaven, *even* the Son of man which is in heaven.
			14 ¶ And as Moses lifted up the serpent in the wilderness, even so must the Son of man be lifted up:
			15 That whosoever believeth in him should not perish, but have eternal life.
			16 ¶ For God so loved the world, that he gave his only begotten Son, that whosoever believeth in him should not perish, but have everlasting life.
			17 For God sent not his Son into the world to condemn the world; but that the world through him might be saved.
			18 ¶ He that believeth on him is not condemned: but he that believeth not is condemned already, because he hath not believed in the name of the only begotten Son of God.
			19 And this is the condemnation, that light is come into the world, and men loved darkness rather than light, because their deeds were evil.
			20 For every one that doeth evil hateth the light, neither cometh to the light, lest his deeds should be reproved.
			21 But he that doeth truth cometh to the light, that his deeds may be made manifest, that they are wrought in God.

33. JOHN FURTHER TESTIFIES OF JESUS

MATTHEW	MARK	LUKE	JOHN
			22 ¶ After these things came Jesus and his disciples into the land of Judæa; and there he tarried with them, and baptized.
			23 ¶ And John also was baptizing in Æ´-nŏn near to Sā´-lĭm, because there was much water there: and they came, and were baptized.
			24 For John was not yet cast into prison.
			25 ¶ Then there arose a question between *some* of John's disciples and the Jews about purifying.

MATTHEW – 14,4	MARK – 6,1	LUKE – 3,4	JOHN – 3,4
			26 And they came unto John, and said unto him, Rabbi, he that was with thee beyond Jordan, to whom thou barest witness, behold, the same baptizeth, and all *men* come to him. 27 John answered and said, A man can receive nothing, except it be given him from heaven. 28 Ye yourselves bear me witness, that I said, I am not the Christ, but that I am sent before him. 29 He that hath the bride is the bridegroom: but the friend of the bridegroom, which standeth and heareth him, rejoiceth greatly because of the bridegroom's voice: this my joy therefore is fulfilled. 30 He must increase, but I *must* decrease. 31 He that cometh from above is above all: he that is of the earth is earthly, and speaketh of the earth: he that cometh from heaven is above all. 32 And what he hath seen and heard, that he testifieth; and no man receiveth his testimony. 33 He that hath received his testimony hath set to his seal that God is true. 34 For he whom God hath sent speaketh the words of God: for God giveth not the Spirit by measure *unto him.* 35 The Father loveth the Son, and hath given all things into his hand. 36 He that believeth on the Son hath everlasting life: and he that believeth not the Son shall not see life; but the wrath of God abideth on him.

34. JOHN THE BAPTIST IMPRISONED BY HEROD

MATTHEW	MARK	LUKE	JOHN
3 ¶ For Herod had laid hold on John, and bound him, and put *him* in prison for Hĕ·rō′·dĭ·ăs' sake, his brother Philip's wife. 4 For John said unto him, It is not lawful for thee to have her. 5 And when he would have put him to death, he feared the multitude, because they counted him as a prophet.	17 For Herod himself had sent forth and laid hold upon John, and bound him in prison for Hĕ·rō′·dĭ·ăs' sake, his brother Philip's wife: for he had married her. 18 For John had said unto Herod, It is not lawful for thee to have thy brother's wife. 19 Therefore Hĕ·rō′·dĭ·ăs had a quarrel against him, and would have killed him; but she could not: 20 For Herod feared John, knowing that he was a just man and an holy, and observed him; and when he heard him, he did many things, and heard him gladly.	19 But Herod the tĕ′·trärch, being reproved by him for Hĕ·rō′·dĭ·ăs his brother Philip's wife, and for all the evils which Herod had done, 20 Added yet this above all, that he shut up John in prison.	

35. JESUS LEAVES JUDEA FOR GALILEE

MATTHEW	MARK	LUKE	JOHN
Ch. 4	Ch. 1	Ch. 4	CHAPTER 4 WHEN therefore the Lord knew how the Pharisees had heard that Jesus made and baptized more disciples than John, 2 (Though Jesus himself baptized not, but his disciples,) 3 He left Judæa, and departed again into Galilee.
12 ¶ Now when Jesus had heard that John was cast into prison, he departed into Galilee;	14 Now after that John was put in prison, Jesus came into Galilee, preaching the gospel of the kingdom of God,	14 ¶ And Jesus returned in the power of the Spirit into Galilee: and there went out a fame of him through all the region round about.	

36. SAMARIAN WOMAN AT JACOB'S WELL

4 And he must needs go through Să·mâr´·ĭ·ă.

5 Then cometh he to a city of Să·mâr´·ĭ·ă, which is called Sȳ´·chär, near to the parcel of ground that Jacob gave to his son Joseph.

6 Now Jacob's well was there. Jesus therefore, being wearied with *his* journey, sat thus on the well: *and* it was about the sixth hour.

7 There cometh a woman of Să·mâr´·ĭ·ă to draw water: Jesus saith unto her, Give me to drink.

8 (For his disciples were gone away unto the city to buy meat.)

9 Then saith the woman of Să·mâr´·ĭ·ă unto him, How is it that thou, being a Jew, askest drink of me, which am a woman of Să·mâr´·ĭ·ă? for the Jews have no dealings with the Să·măr´·ĭ·tăns.

10 Jesus answered and said unto her, If thou knewest the gift of God, and who it is that saith to thee, Give me to drink; thou wouldest have asked of him, and he would have given thee living water.

11 The woman saith unto him, Sir, thou hast nothing to draw with, and the well is deep: from whence then hast thou that living water?

12 Art thou greater than our father Jacob, which gave us the well, and drank thereof himself, and his children, and his cattle?

13 Jesus answered and said unto her, Whosoever drinketh of this water shall thirst again:

14 But whosoever drinketh of the water that I shall give him shall never thirst; but the water that I shall give him shall be in him a well of water springing up into everlasting life.

15 The woman saith unto him, Sir, give me this water, that I thirst not, neither come hither to draw.

16 Jesus saith unto her, Go, call thy husband, and come hither.

17 The woman answered and said, I have no husband. Jesus said unto her, Thou hast well said, I have no husband:

18 For thou hast had five husbands; and he whom thou now hast is not thy husband: in that saidst thou truly.

19 The woman saith unto him, Sir, I perceive that thou art a prophet.

20 Our fathers worshipped in this mountain; and ye say, that in Jerusalem is the place where men ought to worship.

21 Jesus saith unto her, Woman, believe me, the hour cometh, when ye shall neither in this mountain, nor yet at Jerusalem, worship the Father.

22 Ye worship ye know not what: we know what we worship: for salvation is of the Jews.

23 But the hour cometh, and now is, when the true worshippers shall worship the Father in spirit and in truth: for the Father seeketh such to worship him.

24 God *is* a Spirit: and they that worship him must worship *him* in spirit and in truth.

25 The woman saith unto him, I know that Měs·sī'·ǎs cometh, which is called Christ: when he is come, he will tell us all things.

26 Jesus saith unto her, I that speak unto thee am *he*.

27 ¶ And upon this came his disciples, and marvelled that he talked with the woman: yet no man said, What seekest thou? or, Why talkest thou with her?

28 The woman then left her waterpot, and went her way into the city, and saith to the men,

29 Come, see a man, which told me all things that ever I did: is not this the Christ?

30 Then they went out of the city, and came unto him.

31 ¶ In the mean while his disciples prayed him, saying, Master, eat.

32 But he said unto them, I have meat to eat that ye know not of.

33 Therefore said the disciples one to another, Hath any man brought him *ought* to eat?

34 Jesus saith unto them, My meat is to do the will of him that sent me, and to finish his work.

35 Say not ye, There are yet four months, and *then* cometh harvest? behold, I say unto you, Lift up your eyes, and look on the fields; for they are white already to harvest.

36 And he that reapeth receiveth wages, and gathereth fruit unto life eternal: that both he that soweth and he that reapeth may rejoice together.

37 And herein is that saying true, One soweth, and another reapeth.

38 I sent you to reap that whereon ye bestowed no labour: other men laboured, and ye are entered into their labours.

39 ¶ And many of the Să·măr'·ĭ·tăns of that city believed on him for the saying of the woman, which testified, He told me all that ever I did.

40 So when the Să·măr'·ĭ·tăns were come unto him, they besought him that he would tarry with them: and he abode there two days.

41 And many more believed because of his own word;

42 And said unto the woman, Now we believe, not because of thy saying: for we have heard *him* ourselves, and know that this is indeed the Christ, the Saviour of the world.

V. THE GALILEAN MINISTRY

37. JESUS ENTERS GALILEE

MATTHEW	MARK	LUKE	JOHN
		15 And he taught in their synagogues, being glorified of all.	43 ¶ Now after two days he departed thence, and went into Galilee. 44 For Jesus himself testified, that a prophet hath no honour in his own country. 45 Then when he was come into Galilee, the Galilæans received him, having seen all the things that he did at Jerusalem at the feast: for they also went unto the feast.

38. HEALS NOBLEMAN'S SON

MATTHEW	MARK	LUKE	JOHN
			46 So Jesus came again into Cana of Galilee, where he made the water wine. And there was a certain nobleman, whose son was sick at Că·pĕr′-nă·ŭm. 47 When he heard that Jesus was come out of Judæa into Galilee, he went unto him, and besought him that he would come down, and heal his son: for he was at the point of death. 48 Then said Jesus unto him, Except ye see signs and wonders, ye will not believe. 49 The nobleman saith unto him, Sir, come down ere my child die. 50 Jesus saith unto him, Go thy way; thy son liveth. And the man believed the word that Jesus had spoken unto him, and he went his way. 51 And as he was now going down, his servants met him, and told *him*, saying, Thy son liveth. 52 Then inquired he of them the hour when he began to amend. And they said unto him, Yesterday at the seventh hour the fever left him. 53 So the father knew that *it was* at the same hour, in the which Jesus said unto him, Thy son liveth: and himself believed, and his whole house. 54 This *is* again the second miracle *that* Jesus did, when he was come out of Judæa into Galilee.

39. JESUS IS REJECTED AT NAZARETH

MATTHEW	MARK	LUKE	JOHN
		16 ¶ And he came to Nazareth, where he had been brought up: and, as his custom was, he went into the synagogue on the sabbath day, and stood up for to read. 17 And there was delivered unto him the book of the prophet Ē·śāi′-ăs. And when he had opened the book, he found the place where it was written, 18 The Spirit of the Lord *is* upon me, because he hath anointed me to preach the gospel to the poor; he hath sent me to heal the brokenhearted, to preach deliverance to the captives, and recovering of sight to the blind, to set at liberty them that are bruised, 19 To preach the acceptable year of the Lord.	

MATTHEW – 4	MARK – 1	LUKE – 4	JOHN –
		20 And he closed the book, and he gave *it* again to the minister, and sat down. And the eyes of all them that were in the synagogue were fastened on him. 21 And he began to say unto them, This day is this scripture fulfilled in your ears. 22 And all bare him witness, and wondered at the gracious words which proceeded out of his mouth. And they said, Is not this Joseph's son? 23 And he said unto them, Ye will surely say unto me this proverb, Physician, heal thyself: whatsoever we have heard done in Că·pĕr´·nă·ŭm, do also here in thy country. 24 And he said, Verily I say unto you, No prophet is accepted in his own country. 25 But I tell you of a truth, many widows were in Israel in the days of Ē·lī´·ăs, when the heaven was shut up three years and six months, when great famine was throughout all the land; 26 But unto none of them was Ē·lī´·ăs sent, save unto Să·rĕp´·tă, *a city* of Sī´·dŏn, unto a woman *that was* a widow. 27 And many lepers were in Israel in the time of Ĕl·ĭ·sĕ´·ŭs the prophet; and none of them was cleansed, saving Nā´·ă·măn the Syrian. 28 And all they in the synagogue, when they heard these things, were filled with wrath, 29 And rose up, and thrust him out of the city, and led him unto the brow of the hill whereon their city was built, that they might cast him down headlong. 30 But he passing through the midst of them went his way,	

40. GOES TO CAPERNAUM

MATTHEW – 4	MARK – 1	LUKE – 4	JOHN –
13 And leaving Nazareth, he came and dwelt in Că·pĕr´·nă·ŭm, which is upon the sea coast, in the borders of Ză·bū´·lŏn and Nĕph´·thă·lĭm: 14 That it might be fulfilled which was spoken by Ē·sāi´·ăs the prophet, saying, 15 The land of Ză·bū´·lŏn, and the land of Nĕph´·thă·lĭm, *by* the way of the sea, beyond Jordan, Galilee of the Gentiles; 16 The people which sat in darkness saw great light; and to them which sat in the region and shadow of death light is sprung up. 17 ¶ From that time Jesus began to preach, and to say, Repent: for the kingdom of heaven is at hand.	15 And saying, The time is fulfilled, and the kingdom of God is at hand: repent ye, and believe the gospel.		

41. PETER, ANDREW, JAMES AND JOHN TO BE FISHERS OF MEN

MATTHEW – 4	MARK – 1	LUKE – 4	JOHN –
18 ¶ And Jesus, walking by the sea of Galilee, saw two brethren, Simon called Peter, and Andrew his brother, casting a net into the sea: for they were fishers.	16 Now as he walked by the sea of Galilee, he saw Simon and Andrew his brother casting a net into the sea: for they were fishers.		

CHAPTER 5

AND it came to pass, that, as the people pressed upon him to hear the word of God, he stood by the lake of Gĕn·nĕś′·ă·rĕt,

2 And saw two ships standing by the lake: but the fishermen were gone out of them, and were washing *their* nets.

3 And he entered into one of the ships, which was Simon's, and prayed him that he would thrust out a little from the land. And he sat down, and taught the people out of the ship.

4 Now when he had left speaking, he said unto Simon, Launch out into the deep, and let down your nets for a draught.

5 And Simon answering said unto him, Master, we have toiled all the night, and have taken nothing: nevertheless at thy word I will let down the net.

6 And when they had this done, they inclosed a great multitude of fishes: and their net brake.

7 And they beckoned unto *their* partners, which were in the other ship, that they should come and help them. And they came, and filled both the ships, so that they began to sink.

8 When Simon Peter saw *it*, he fell down at Jesus' knees, saying, Depart from me; for I am a sinful man, O Lord.

9 For he was astonished, and all that were with him, at the draught of the fishes which they had taken:

10 And so *was* also James, and John, the sons of Zĕb′·ĕ·dēē, which were partners with Simon. And Jesus said unto Simon, Fear not; from henceforth thou shalt catch men.

MATTHEW

19 And he saith unto them, Follow me, and I will make you fishers of men.
20 And they straightway left *their* nets, and followed him.

21 And going on from thence, he saw other two brethren, James *the son* of Zĕb′·ĕ·dēē, and John his brother, in a ship with Zĕb′·ĕ·dēē their father, mending their nets; and he called them.

22 And they immediately left the ship and their father, and followed him.

MARK

17 And Jesus said unto them, Come ye after me, and I will make you to become fishers of men.
18 And straightway they forsook their nets, and followed him.
19 And when he had gone a little further thence, he saw James the *son* of Zĕb′·ĕ·dēē, and John his brother, who also were in the ship mending their nets.
20 And straightway he called them: and they left their father Zĕb′·ĕ·dēē in the ship with the hired servants, and went after him.

LUKE

11 And when they had brought their ships to land, they forsook all, and followed him.

42. JESUS TEACHES WITH POWER AND AUTHORITY

MARK

21 And they went into Că·pĕr′·nă·ŭm; and straightway on the sabbath day he entered into the synagogue, and taught.
22 And they were astonished at his doctrine: for he taught them as one that had authority, and not as the scribes.

LUKE

Ch. 4

31 And came down to Că·pĕr′·nă·ŭm, a city of Galilee, and taught them on the sabbath days.
32 And they were astonished at his doctrine: for his word was with power.

43. CASTS OUT AN UNCLEAN SPIRIT

MARK

23 And there was in their synagogue a man with an unclean spirit; and he cried out,

LUKE

33 ¶ And in the synagogue there was a man, which had a spirit of an unclean devil, and cried out with a loud voice,

MATTHEW – 8,4	MARK – 1	LUKE – 4	JOHN –
	24 Saying, Let *us* alone; what have we to do with thee, thou Jesus of Nazareth? art thou come to destroy us? I know thee who thou art, the Holy One of God.	34 Saying, Let *us* alone; what have we to do with thee, *thou* Jesus of Nazareth? art thou come to destroy us? I know thee who thou art; the Holy One of God.	
	25 And Jesus rebuked him, saying, Hold thy peace, and come out of him.	35 And Jesus rebuked him, saying, Hold thy peace, and come out of him. And when the devil had thrown him in the midst, he came out of him, and hurt him not.	
	26 And when the unclean spirit had torn him, and cried with a loud voice, he came out of him.		
	27 And they were all amazed, insomuch that they questioned among themselves, saying, What thing is this? what new doctrine *is* this? for with authority commandeth he even the unclean spirits, and they do obey him.	36 And they were all amazed, and spake among themselves, saying, What a word *is* this! for with authority and power he commandeth the unclean spirits, and they come out.	
	28 And immediately his fame spread abroad throughout all the region round about Galilee.	37 And the fame of him went out into every place of the country round about.	

44. HEALS PETER'S MOTHER-IN-LAW AND OTHERS

MATTHEW	MARK	LUKE	JOHN
	29 And forthwith, when they were come out of the synagogue, they entered into the house of Simon and Andrew, with James and John.	38 ¶ And he arose out of the synagogue, and entered into Simon's house. And Simon's wife's mother was taken with a great fever; and they besought him for her.	
14 ¶ And when Jesus was come into Peter's house, he saw his wife's mother laid, and sick of a fever.	30 But Simon's wife's mother lay sick of a fever, and anon they tell him of her.		
15 And he touched her hand, and the fever left her: and she arose, and ministered unto them.	31 And he came and took her by the hand, and lifted her up; and immediately the fever left her, and she ministered unto them.	39 And he stood over her, and rebuked the fever; and it left her: and immediately she arose and ministered unto them.	
16 ¶ When the even was come, they brought unto him many that were possessed with devils: and he cast out the spirits with *his* word, and healed all that were sick:	32 And at even, when the sun did set, they brought unto him all that were diseased, and them that were possessed with devils.	40 ¶ Now when the sun was setting, all they that had any sick with divers diseases brought them unto him; and he laid his hands on every one of them, and healed them.	
	33 And all the city was gathered together at the door.		
	34 And he healed many that were sick of divers diseases, and cast out many devils; and suffered not the devils to speak, because they knew him.	41 And devils also came out of many, crying out, and saying, Thou art Christ the Son of God. And he rebuking *them* suffered them not to speak: for they knew that he was Christ.	
17 That it might be fulfilled which was spoken by Ē-śāī-ăs the prophet, saying, Himself took our infirmities, and bare *our* sicknesses.			

45. PREACHES AND HEALS IN GALILEE

MATTHEW	MARK	LUKE	JOHN
	35 And in the morning, rising up a great while before day, he went out, and departed into a solitary place, and there prayed.	42 And when it was day, he departed and went into a desert place: and the people sought him, and came unto him, and stayed him, that he should not depart from them.	
	36 And Simon and they that were with him followed after him.		
	37 And when they had found him, they said unto him, All *men* seek for thee.		
Ch. 4	38 And he said unto them, Let us go into the next towns, that I may preach there also: for therefore came I forth.	43 And he said unto them, I must preach the kingdom of God to other cities also: for therefore am I sent.	
23 ¶ And Jesus went about all Galilee, teaching in their synagogues, and preaching the gospel of the kingdom, and healing all manner of sickness and all manner of disease among the people.	39 And he preached in their synagogues throughout all Galilee, and cast out devils.	44 And he preached in the synagogues of Galilee.	
24 And his fame went throughout all Syria: and they brought unto him all sick people that were taken with divers diseases and torments, and those which were possessed with devils, and those which were lunatick, and those that had the palsy; and he healed them.			

25 And there followed him great multitudes of people from Galilee, and *from* Dĕ-căp'-ŏ-lĭs, and *from* Jerusalem, and *from* Judæa, and *from* beyond Jordan.

46. CLEANSES LEPER

Ch. 8

2 And, behold, there came a leper and worshipped him, saying, Lord, if thou wilt, thou canst make me clean.

3 And Jesus put forth *his* hand, and touched him, saying, I will; be thou clean. And immediately his leprosy was cleansed.

4 And Jesus saith unto him, See thou tell no man; but go thy way, shew thyself to the priest, and offer the gift that Moses commanded, for a testimony unto them.

40 And there came a leper to him, beseeching him, and kneeling down to him, and saying unto him, If thou wilt, thou canst make me clean.
41 And Jesus, moved with compassion, put forth *his* hand, and touched him, and saith unto him, I will; be thou clean.
42 And as soon as he had spoken, immediately the leprosy departed from him, and he was cleansed.
43 And he straitly charged him, and forthwith sent him away;
44 And saith unto him, See thou say nothing to any man: but go thy way, shew thyself to the priest, and offer for thy cleansing those things which Moses commanded, for a testimony unto them.
45 But he went out, and began to publish *it* much, and to blaze abroad the matter,

insomuch that Jesus could no more openly enter into the city, but was without in desert places: and they came to him from every quarter.

12 ¶ And it came to pass, when he was in a certain city, behold a man full of leprosy: who seeing Jesus fell on *his* face, and besought him, saying, Lord, if thou wilt, thou canst make me clean.

13 And he put forth *his* hand, and touched him, saying, I will: be thou clean. And immediately the leprosy departed from him.

14 And he charged him to tell no man: but go, and shew thyself to the priest, and offer

for thy cleansing, according as Moses commanded, for a testimony unto them.
15 But so much the more went there a fame abroad of him: and great multitudes came together to hear, and to be healed by him of their infirmities.

16 ¶ And he withdrew himself into the wilderness, and prayed.

47. HEALS A MAN SICK OF THE PALSY

CHAPTER 2

AND again he entered into Că-pĕr'-nă-ŭm, after *some* days; and it was noised that he was in the house.
2 And straightway many were gathered together, insomuch that there was no room to receive *them*, no, not so much as about the door: and he preached the word unto them.
3 And they come unto him, bringing one sick of the palsy, which was borne of four.

Ch. 9

2 And, behold, they brought to him a man sick of the palsy, lying on a bed:

and Jesus seeing their faith said unto the sick of the palsy; Son, be of good cheer; thy sins be forgiven thee.

3 And, behold, certain of the scribes said within themselves, This *man* blasphemeth.

4 And Jesus knowing their thoughts said, Wherefore think ye evil in your hearts?

4 And when they could not come nigh unto him for the press, they uncovered the roof where he was: and when they had broken *it* up, they let down the bed wherein the sick of the palsy lay.
5 When Jesus saw their faith, he said unto the sick of the palsy, Son, thy sins be forgiven thee.
6 But there were certain of the scribes sitting there, and reasoning in their hearts,
7 Why doth this *man* thus speak blasphemies? who can forgive sins but God only?
8 And immediately when Jesus perceived in his spirit that they so reasoned within themselves, he said unto them, Why reason ye these things in your hearts?

17 And it came to pass on a certain day, as he was teaching, that there were Pharisees and doctors of the law sitting by, which were come out of every town of Galilee, and Judæa, and Jerusalem: and the power of the Lord was *present* to heal them.
18 ¶ And, behold, men brought in a bed a man which was taken with a palsy: and they sought *means* to bring him in, and to lay *him* before him.
19 And when they could not find by what *way* they might bring him in because of the multitude, they went upon the housetop, and let him down through the tiling with *his* couch into the midst before Jesus.
20 And when he saw their faith, he said unto him, Man, thy sins are forgiven thee.
21 And the scribes and the Pharisees began to reason, saying, Who is this which speaketh blasphemies? Who can forgive sins, but God alone?
22 But when Jesus perceived their thoughts, he answering said unto them, What reason ye in your hearts?

5 For whether is easier, to say, *Thy* sins be forgiven thee; or to say, Arise, and walk?

6 But that ye may know that the Son of man hath power on earth to forgive sins, (then saith he to the sick of the palsy,) Arise, take up thy bed, and go unto thine house.

7 And he arose, and departed to his house.

8 But when the multitudes saw *it*, they marvelled, and glorified God, which had given such power unto men.

---

9 Whether is it easier to say to the sick of the palsy, *Thy* sins be forgiven thee; or to say, Arise, and take up thy bed, and walk?

10 But that ye may know that the Son of man hath power on earth to forgive sins, (he saith to the sick of the palsy,)

11 I say unto thee, Arise, and take up thy bed, and go thy way into thine house.

12 And immediately he arose, took up the bed, and went forth before them all; insomuch that they were all amazed, and glorified God, saying, We never saw it on this fashion.

---

23 Whether is easier, to say, Thy sins be forgiven thee; or to say, Rise up and walk?

24 But that ye may know that the Son of man hath power upon earth to forgive sins, (he said unto the sick of the palsy,) I say unto thee, Arise, and take up thy couch, and go into thine house.

25 And immediately he rose up before them, and took up that whereon he lay, and departed to his own house, glorifying God.

26 And they were all amazed, and they glorified God, and were filled with fear, saying, We have seen strange things to day.

48. MATTHEW FOLLOWS JESUS

9 ¶ And as Jesus passed forth from thence, he saw a man, named Matthew, sitting at the receipt of custom: and he saith unto him, Follow me. And he arose, and followed him.

---

13 And he went forth again by the sea side; and all the multitude resorted unto him, and he taught them.

14 And as he passed by, he saw Levi the *son* of Ăl-phǽ-ŭs sitting at the receipt of custom, and said unto him, Follow me. And he arose and followed him.

---

27 ¶ And after these things he went forth, and saw a publican, named Levi, sitting at the receipt of custom: and he said unto him, Follow me.

28 And he left all, rose up, and followed him.

49. JESUS CAME TO CALL SINNERS TO REPENTANCE

10 ¶ And it came to pass, as Jesus sat at meat in the house, behold, many publicans and sinners came and sat down with him and his disciples.

11 And when the Pharisees saw *it*, they said unto his disciples, Why eateth your Master with publicans and sinners?

12 But when Jesus heard *that*, he said unto them, They that be whole need not a physician, but they that are sick.

13 But go ye and learn what *that* meaneth, I will have mercy, and not sacrifice: for I am not come to call the righteous, but sinners to repentance.

---

15 And it came to pass, that, as Jesus sat at meat in his house, many publicans and sinners sat also together with Jesus and his disciples: for there were many, and they followed him.

16 And when the scribes and Pharisees saw him eat with publicans and sinners, they said unto his disciples, How is it that he eateth and drinketh with publicans and sinners?

17 When Jesus heard *it*, he saith unto them, They that are whole have no need of the physician, but they that are sick:

I came not to call the righteous, but sinners to repentance.

---

29 And Levi made him a great feast in his own house: and there was a great company of publicans and of others that sat down with them.

30 But their scribes and Pharisees murmured against his disciples, saying, Why do ye eat and drink with publicans and sinners?

31 And Jesus answering said unto them, They that are whole need not a physician; but they that are sick.

32 I came not to call the righteous, but sinners to repentance.

50. JESUS IS THE NEW LAW

14 ¶ Then came to him the disciples of John, saying, Why do we and the Pharisees fast oft, but thy disciples fast not?

15 And Jesus said unto them, Can the children of the bridechamber mourn, as long as the bridegroom is with them? but the days will come, when the bridegroom shall be taken from them, and then shall they fast.

16 No man putteth a piece of new cloth unto an old garment, for that which is put in to fill it up taketh from the garment, and the rent is made worse.

---

18 And the disciples of John and of the Pharisees used to fast: and they come and say unto him, Why do the disciples of John and of the Pharisees fast, but thy disciples fast not?

19 And Jesus said unto them, Can the children of the bridechamber fast, while the bridegroom is with them? as long as they have the bridegroom with them, they cannot fast.

20 But the days will come, when the bridegroom shall be taken away from them, and then shall they fast in those days.

21 No man also seweth a piece of new cloth on an old garment: else the new piece that filled it up taketh away from the old, and the rent is made worse.

---

33 ¶ And they said unto him, Why do the disciples of John fast often, and make prayers, and likewise *the disciples* of the Pharisees; but thine eat and drink?

34 And he said unto them, Can ye make the children of the bridechamber fast, while the bridegroom is with them?

35 But the days will come, when the bridegroom shall be taken away from them, and then shall they fast in those days.

36 ¶ And he spake also a parable unto them; No man putteth a piece of a new garment upon an old; if otherwise, then both the new maketh a rent, and the piece that was *taken* out of the new agreeth not with the old.

17 Neither do men put new wine into old bottles: else the bottles break, and the wine runneth out, and the bottles perish: but they put new wine into new bottles, and both are preserved.	22 And no man putteth new wine into old bottles: else the new wine doth burst the bottles, and the wine is spilled, and the bottles will be marred: but new wine must be put into new bottles.	37 And no man putteth new wine into old bottles; else the new wine will burst the bottles, and be spilled, and the bottles shall perish. 38 But new wine must be put into new bottles; and both are preserved. 39 No man also having drunk old *wine* straightway desireth new: for he saith, The old is better.	

51. JESUS ATTENDS A FEAST AT JERUSALEM *

CHAPTER 5

AFTER this there was a feast of the Jews; and Jesus went up to Jerusalem.

52. HEALS A MAN ON THE SABBATH

2 Now there is at Jerusalem by the sheep *market* a pool, which is called in the Hebrew tongue Bĕth-ĕś'-dă, having five porches.

3 In these lay a great multitude of impotent folk, of blind, halt, withered, waiting for the moving of the water.

4 For an angel went down at a certain season into the pool, and troubled the water: whosoever then first after the troubling of the water stepped in was made whole of whatsoever disease he had.

5 And a certain man was there, which had an infirmity thirty and eight years.

6 When Jesus saw him lie, and knew that he had been now a long time *in that case*, he saith unto him, Wilt thou be made whole?

7 The impotent man answered him, Sir, I have no man, when the water is troubled, to put me into the pool: but while I am coming, another steppeth down before me.

8 Jesus saith unto him, Rise, take up thy bed, and walk.

9 And immediately the man was made whole, and took up his bed, and walked: and on the same day was the sabbath.

10 ¶ The Jews therefore said unto him that was cured, It is the sabbath day: it is not lawful for thee to carry *thy* bed.

11 He answered them, He that made me whole, the same said unto me, Take up thy bed, and walk.

12 Then asked they him, What man is that which said unto thee, Take up thy bed, and walk?

13 And he that was healed wist not who it was: for Jesus had conveyed himself away, a multitude being in *that* place.

14 Afterward Jesus findeth him in the temple, and said unto him, Behold, thou art made whole: sin no more, lest a worse thing come unto thee.

15 The man departed, and told the Jews that it was Jesus, which had made him whole.

16 And therefore did the Jews persecute Jesus, and sought to slay him, because he had done these things on the sabbath day.

*Which feast did Jesus attend? How long was the ministry of Jesus? See note 51.

53. JESUS TO DO THE WORK OF HIS FATHER

17 ¶ But Jesus answered them, My Father worketh hitherto, and I work.

18 Therefore the Jews sought the more to kill him, because he not only had broken the sabbath, but said also that God was his Father, making himself equal with God.

19 Then answered Jesus and said unto them, Verily, verily, I say unto you, The Son can do nothing of himself, but what he seeth the Father do: for what things soever he doeth, these also doeth the Son likewise.

20 For the Father loveth the Son, and sheweth him all things that himself doeth: and he will shew him greater works than these, that ye may marvel.

21 For as the Father raiseth up the dead, and quickeneth *them;* even so the Son quickeneth whom he will.

22 For the Father judgeth no man, but hath committed all judgment unto the Son:

23 That all *men* should honour the Son, even as they honour the Father. He that honoureth not the Son honoureth not the Father which hath sent him.

24 Verily, verily, I say unto you, He that heareth my word, and believeth on him that sent me, hath everlasting life, and shall not come into condemnation; but is passed from death unto life.

25 Verily, verily, I say unto you, The hour is coming, and now is, when the dead shall hear the voice of the Son of God: and they that hear shall live.

26 For as the Father hath life in himself; so hath he given to the Son to have life in himself;

27 And hath given him authority to execute judgment also, because he is the Son of man.

28 Marvel not at this: for the hour is coming, in the which all that are in the graves shall hear his voice,

29 And shall come forth; they that have done good, unto the resurrection of life; and they that have done evil, unto the resurrection of damnation.

30 I can of mine own self do nothing: as I hear, I judge: and my judgment is just; because I seek not mine own will, but the will of the Father which hath sent me.

31 If I bear witness of myself, my witness is not true.

32 ¶ There is another that beareth witness of me; and I know that the witness which he witnesseth of me is true.

33 Ye sent unto John, and he bare witness unto the truth.

34 But I receive not testimony from man: but these things I say, that ye might be saved.

35 He was a burning and a shining light: and ye were willing for a season to rejoice in his light.

36 ¶ But I have greater witness than *that* of John: for the works which the Father hath given me to finish, the same works that I do, bear witness of me, that the Father hath sent me.

37 And the Father himself, which hath sent me, hath borne witness of me. Ye have neither heard his voice at any time, nor seen his shape.

38 And ye have not his word abiding in you: for whom he hath sent, him ye believe not.

39 ¶ Search the scriptures; for in them ye think ye have eternal life: and they are they which testify of me.

40 And ye will not come to me, that ye might have life.

41 I receive not honour from men.

42 But I know you, that ye have not the love of God in you.

43 I am come in my Father's name, and ye receive me not: if another shall come in his own name, him ye will receive.

44 How can ye believe, which receive honour one of another, and seek not the honour that *cometh* from God only?

45 Do not think that I will accuse you to the Father: there is *one* that accuseth you, *even* Moses, in whom ye trust.

46 For had ye believed Moses, ye would have believed me: for he wrote of me.

47 But if ye believe not his writings, how shall ye believe my words?

54. JESUS IS LORD OF THE SABBATH

CHAPTER 12

AT that time Jesus went on the sabbath day through the corn; and his disciples were an hungred, and began to pluck the ears of corn, and to eat.

2 But when the Pharisees saw *it*, they said unto him, Behold, thy disciples do that which is not lawful to do upon the sabbath day.

3 But he said unto them, Have ye not read what David did, when he was an hungred, and they that were with him;

4 How he entered into the house of God, and did eat the shewbread, which was not lawful for him to eat, neither for them which were with him, but only for the priests?

5 Or have ye not read in the law, how that on the sabbath days the priests in the temple profane the sabbath, and are blameless?

6 But I say unto you, That in this place is *one* greater than the temple.

7 But if ye had known what *this* meaneth, I will have mercy, and not sacrifice, ye would not have condemned the guiltless.

8 For the Son of man is Lord even of the sabbath day.

---

23 And it came to pass, that he went through the corn fields on the sabbath day; and his disciples began, as they went, to pluck the ears of corn.

24 And the Pharisees said unto him, Behold, why do they on the sabbath day that which is not lawful?

25 And he said unto them, Have ye never read what David did, when he had need, and was an hungred, he, and they that were with him?

26 How he went into the house of God in the days of Ă-bī′-ă-thär the high priest, and did eat the shewbread, which is not lawful to eat but for the priests, and gave also to them which were with him?

27 And he said unto them, The sabbath was made for man, and not man for the sabbath:

28 Therefore the Son of man is Lord also of the sabbath.

CHAPTER 6

AND it came to pass on the second sabbath after the first, that he went through the corn fields; and his disciples plucked the ears of corn, and did eat, rubbing *them* in *their* hands.

2 And certain of the Pharisees said unto them, Why do ye that which is not lawful to do on the sabbath days?

3 And Jesus answering them said, Have ye not read so much as this, what David did, when himself was an hungred, and they which were with him;

4 How he went into the house of God, and did take and eat the shewbread, and gave also to them that were with him; which it is not lawful to eat but for the priests alone?

5 And he said unto them, That the Son of man is Lord also of the sabbath.

55. MAN WITH WITHERED HAND HEALED ON THE SABBATH

MATTHEW – 12

9 And when he was departed thence, he went into their synagogue:

10 ¶ And, behold, there was a man which had *his* hand withered. And they asked him, saying, Is it lawful to heal on the sabbath days? that they might accuse him.

11 And he said unto them, What man shall there be among you, that shall have one sheep, and if it fall into a pit on the sabbath day, will he not lay hold on it, and lift *it* out?

12 How much then is a man better than a sheep? Wherefore it is lawful to do well on the sabbath days.

13 Then saith he to the man, Stretch forth thine hand. And he stretched *it* forth; and it was restored whole, like as the other.

14 ¶ Then the Pharisees went out, and held a council against him, how they might destroy him.

MARK – 3

CHAPTER 3

AND he entered again into the synagogue; and there was a man there which had a withered hand.

2 And they watched him, whether he would heal him on the sabbath day; that they might accuse him.

3 And he saith unto the man which had the withered hand, Stand forth.

4 And he saith unto them, Is it lawful to do good on the sabbath days, or to do evil? to save life, or to kill? But they held their peace.

5 And when he had looked round about on them with anger, being grieved for the hardness of their hearts, he saith unto the man, Stretch forth thine hand. And he stretched *it* out: and his hand was restored whole as the other.

6 And the Pharisees went forth, and straightway took counsel with the Hĕ-rō´-dĭ-ăns against him, how they might destroy him.

LUKE – 6

6 And it came to pass also on another sabbath, that he entered into the synagogue and taught: and there was a man whose right hand was withered.

7 And the scribes and Pharisees watched him, whether he would heal on the sabbath day; that they might find an accusation against him.

8 But he knew their thoughts, and said to the man which had the withered hand, Rise up, and stand forth in the midst. And he arose and stood forth.

9 Then said Jesus unto them, I will ask you one thing; Is it lawful on the sabbath days to do good, or to do evil? to save life, or to destroy *it*?

10 And looking round about upon them all, he said unto the man, Stretch forth thy hand. And he did so: and his hand was restored whole as the other.

11 And they were filled with madness; and communed one with another what they might do to Jesus.

56. MULTITUDES THRONG JESUS

MATTHEW – 12

15 But when Jesus knew *it*, he withdrew himself from thence: and great multitudes followed him, and he healed them all;

16 And charged them that they should not make him known:

17 That it might be fulfilled which was spoken by E̅-śā́-ăs the prophet, saying,

18 Behold my servant, whom I have chosen; my beloved, in whom my soul is well pleased: I will put my spirit upon him, and he shall shew judgment to the Gentiles.

19 He shall not strive, nor cry; neither shall any man hear his voice in the streets.

MARK – 3

7 But Jesus withdrew himself with his disciples to the sea: and a great multitude from Galilee followed him, and from Judæa,

8 And from Jerusalem, and from Ĭ-dū-mǣ´-ă, and *from* beyond Jordan; and they about Tyre and Śĭ´-dŏn, a great multitude, when they had heard what great things he did, came unto him.

9 And he spake to his disciples, that a small ship should wait on him because of the multitude, lest they should throng him.

10 For he had healed many; insomuch that they pressed upon him for to touch him, as many as had plagues.

11 And unclean spirits, when they saw him, fell down before him, and cried, saying, Thou art the Son of God.

12 And he straitly charged them that they should not make him known.

MATTHEW	MARK	LUKE	JOHN
20 A bruised reed shall he not break, and smoking flax shall he not quench, till he send forth judgment unto victory. 21 And in his name shall the Gentiles trust.			

57. CALL AND ORDINATION OF THE TWELVE APOSTLES

MATTHEW	MARK	LUKE	JOHN
		12 And it came to pass in those days, that he went out into a mountain to pray, and continued all night in prayer to God.	
	13 And he goeth up into a mountain, and calleth *unto him* whom he would: and they came unto him. 14 And he ordained twelve, that they should be with him, and that he might send them forth to preach, 15 And to have power to heal sicknesses, and to cast out devils:	13 ¶ And when it was day, he called *unto him* his disciples: and of them he chose twelve, whom also he named apostles;	
Ch. 10 2 Now the names of the twelve apostles are these; The first, Simon, who is called Peter, and Andrew his brother; James *the son* of Zĕb´-ĕ-dĕĕ, and John his brother; 3 Philip, and Bartholomew; Thomas, and Matthew the publican; James *the son* of Ăl-phæ´-ŭs, and Lĕb-bæ´-ŭs, whose surname was Thăd-dæ´-ŭs; 4 Simon the Canaanite, and Judas Iscariot, who also betrayed him.	16 And Simon he surnamed Peter; 17 And James the *son* of Zĕb´-ĕ-dĕĕ, and John the brother of James; and he surnamed them Bō-ăn-ĕr´-ġĕŝ, which is, The sons of thunder: 18 And Andrew, and Philip, and Bartholomew, and Matthew, and Thomas, and James the *son* of Ăl-phæ´-ŭs, and Thăd-dæ´-ŭs, and Simon the Canaanite, 19a And Judas Iscariot, which also betrayed him:	14 Simon, (whom he also named Peter,) and Andrew his brother, James and John, Philip and Bartholomew, 15 Matthew and Thomas, James the *son* of Ăl-phæ´-ŭs, and Simon called Zē-lō´-tĕŝ, 16 And Judas *the brother* of James, and Judas Iscariot, which also was the traitor.	

58. THE SERMON ON THE MOUNT *

MATTHEW	MARK	LUKE	JOHN
		17 ¶ And he came down with them, and stood in the plain, and the company of his disciples, and a great multitude of people out of all Judæa and Jerusalem, and from the sea coast of Tyre and Sī´-dŏn, which came to hear him, and to be healed of their diseases; 18 And they that were vexed with unclean spirits: and they were healed. 19 And the whole multitude sought to touch him: for there went virtue out of him, and healed *them* all.	
CHAPTER 5 AND seeing the multitudes, he went up into a mountain: and when he was set, his disciples came unto him: 2 And he opened his mouth, and taught them, saying, 3 Blessed *are* the poor in spirit: for theirs is the kingdom of heaven. 4 Blessed *are* they that mourn: for they shall be comforted. 5 Blessed *are* the meek: for they shall inherit the earth. 6 Blessed *are* they which do hunger and thirst after righteousness: for they shall be filled. 7 Blessed *are* the merciful: for they shall obtain mercy. 8 Blessed *are* the pure in heart: for they shall see God. 9 Blessed *are* the peacemakers: for they shall be called the children of God.		20 ¶ And he lifted up his eyes on his disciples, and said, Blessed *be ye* poor: for yours is the kingdom of God. 21 Blessed *are ye* that hunger now: for ye shall be filled. Blessed *are ye* that weep now: for ye shall laugh.	

*Most Harmonies show Matthew 5-7 and Luke 6:17-49 as two accounts of the same sermon.

MATTHEW – 5

10 Blessed *are* they which are persecuted for righteousness' sake: for theirs is the kingdom of heaven.

11 Blessed are ye, when *men* shall revile you, and persecute *you*, and shall say all manner of evil against you falsely, for my sake.

12 Rejoice, and be exceeding glad: for great *is* your reward in heaven: for so persecuted they the prophets which were before you.

13 ¶ Ye are the salt of the earth: but if the salt have lost his savour, wherewith shall it be salted? it is thenceforth good for nothing, but to be cast out, and to be trodden under foot of men.

14 Ye are the light of the world. A city that is set on an hill cannot be hid.

15 Neither do men light a candle, and put it under a bushel, but on a candlestick; and it giveth light unto all that are in the house.

16 Let your light so shine before men, that they may see your good works, and glorify your Father which is in heaven.

17 ¶ Think not that I am come to destroy the law, or the prophets: I am not come to destroy, but to fulfil.

18 For verily I say unto you, Till heaven and earth pass, one jot or one tittle shall in no wise pass from the law, till all be fulfilled.

19 Whosoever therefore shall break one of these least commandments, and shall teach men so, he shall be called the least in the kingdom of heaven: but whosoever shall do and teach *them*, the same shall be called great in the kingdom of heaven.

20 For I say unto you, That except your righteousness shall exceed *the righteousness* of the scribes and Pharisees, ye shall in no case enter into the kingdom of heaven.

21 ¶ Ye have heard that it was said by them of old time, Thou shalt not kill; and whosoever shall kill shall be in danger of the judgment:

22 But I say unto you, That whosoever is angry with his brother without a cause shall be in danger of the judgment: and whosoever shall say to his brother, Rā'·că, shall be in danger of the council: but whosoever shall say, Thou fool, shall be in danger of hell fire.

23 Therefore if thou bring thy gift to the altar, and there rememberest that thy brother hath ought against thee;

24 Leave there thy gift before the altar, and go thy way; first be reconciled to thy brother, and then come and offer thy gift.

LUKE – 6

22 Blessed are ye, when men shall hate you, and when they shall separate you *from their company*, and shall reproach *you*, and cast out your name as evil, for the Son of man's sake.

23 Rejoice ye in that day, and leap for joy: for, behold, your reward *is* great in heaven: for in the like manner did their fathers unto the prophets.

24 But woe unto you that are rich! for ye have received your consolation.

25 Woe unto you that are full! for ye shall hunger. Woe unto you that laugh now! for ye shall mourn and weep.

26 Woe unto you, when all men shall speak well of you! for so did their fathers to the false prophets.

MATTHEW – 5	MARK –	LUKE – 6	JOHN –
25 Agree with thine adversary quickly, whiles thou art in the way with him; lest at any time the adversary deliver thee to the judge, and the judge deliver thee to the officer, and thou be cast into prison. 26 Verily I say unto thee, Thou shalt by no means come out thence, till thou hast paid the uttermost farthing. 27 ¶ Ye have heard that it was said by them of old time, Thou shalt not commit adultery: 28 But I say unto you, That whosoever looketh on a woman to lust after her hath committed adultery with her already in his heart. 29 And if thy right eye offend thee, pluck it out, and cast *it* from thee: for it is profitable for thee that one of thy members should perish, and not *that* thy whole body should be cast into hell. 30 And if thy right hand offend thee, cut it off, and cast *it* from thee: for it is profitable for thee that one of thy members should perish, and not *that* thy whole body should be cast into hell. 31 It hath been said, Whosoever shall put away his wife, let him give her a writing of divorcement: 32 But I say unto you, That whosoever shall put away his wife, saving for the cause of fornication, causeth her to commit adultery: and whosoever shall marry her that is divorced committeth adultery. 33 ¶ Again, ye have heard that it hath been said by them of old time, Thou shalt not forswear thyself, but shalt perform unto the Lord thine oaths: 34 But I say unto you, Swear not at all; neither by heaven; for it is God's throne: 35 Nor by the earth; for it is his footstool: neither by Jerusalem; for it is the city of the great King. 36 Neither shalt thou swear by thy head, because thou canst not make one hair white or black. 37 But let your communication be, Yea, yea; Nay, nay: for whatsoever is more than these cometh of evil. 38 ¶ Ye have heard that it hath been said, An eye for an eye, and a tooth for a tooth: 39 But I say unto you, That ye resist not evil: but whosoever shall smite thee on thy right cheek, turn to him the other also. 40 And if any man will sue thee at the law, and take away thy coat, let him have *thy* cloke also. 41 And whosoever shall compel thee to go a mile, go with him twain. 42 Give to him that asketh thee, and from him that would borrow of thee turn not thou away. 43 ¶ Ye have heard that it hath been said, Thou shalt love thy neighbour, and hate thine enemy.		29 And unto him that smiteth thee on the *one* cheek offer also the other; and him that taketh away thy cloke forbid not *to take thy* coat also. 30 Give to every man that asketh of thee; and of him that taketh away thy goods ask *them* not again. 31 And as ye would that men should do to you, do ye also to them likewise.	

34

MATTHEW – 5,6

44 But I say unto you, Love your enemies, bless them that curse you, do good to them that hate you, and pray for them which despitefully use you, and persecute you;

45 That ye may be the children of your Father which is in heaven: for he maketh his sun to rise on the evil and on the good, and sendeth rain on the just and on the unjust.

46 For if ye love them which love you, what reward have ye? do not even the publicans the same?

47 And if ye salute your brethren only, what do ye more *than others?* do not even the publicans so?

48 Be ye therefore perfect, even as your Father which is in heaven is perfect.

CHAPTER 6

TAKE heed that ye do not your alms before men, to be seen of them: otherwise ye have no reward of your Father which is in heaven.

2 Therefore when thou doest *thine* alms, do not sound a trumpet before thee, as the hypocrites do in the synagogues and in the streets, that they may have glory of men. Verily I say unto you, They have their reward.

3 But when thou doest alms, let not thy left hand know what thy right hand doeth:

4 That thine alms may be in secret: and thy Father which seeth in secret himself shall reward thee openly.

5 ¶ And when thou prayest, thou shalt not be as the hypocrites *are:* for they love to pray standing in the synagogues and in the corners of the streets, that they may be seen of men. Verily I say unto you, They have their reward.

6 But thou, when thou prayest, enter into thy closet, and when thou hast shut thy door, pray to thy Father which is in secret; and thy Father which seeth in secret shall reward thee openly.

7 But when ye pray, use not vain repetitions, as the heathen *do:* for they think that they shall be heard for their much speaking.

8 Be not ye therefore like unto them: for your Father knoweth what things ye have need of, before ye ask him.

9 After this manner therefore pray ye: Our Father which art in heaven, Hallowed be thy name.

LUKE – 6

27 ¶ But I say unto you which hear, Love your enemies, do good to them which hate you,

28 Bless them that curse you, and pray for them which despitefully use you.

32 For if ye love them which love you, what thank have ye? for sinners also love those that love them.

33 And if ye do good to them which do good to you, what thank have ye? for sinners also do even the same.

34 And if ye lend *to them* of whom ye hope to receive, what thank have ye? for sinners also lend to sinners, to receive as much again.

35 But love ye your enemies, and do good, and lend, hoping for nothing again; and your reward shall be great, and ye shall be the children of the Highest: for he is kind unto the unthankful and *to* the evil.

36 Be ye therefore merciful, as your Father also is merciful.

10 Thy kingdom come. Thy will be done in earth, as *it is* in heaven.

11 Give us this day our daily bread.

12 And forgive us our debts, as we forgive our debtors.

13 And lead us not into temptation, but deliver us from evil: For thine is the kingdom, and the power, and the glory, for ever. Ä´-mĕn.

14 For if ye forgive men their trespasses, your heavenly Father will also forgive you:

15 But if ye forgive not men their trespasses, neither will your Father forgive your trespasses.

16 ¶ Moreover when ye fast, be not, as the hypocrites, of a sad countenance: for they disfigure their faces, that they may appear unto men to fast. Verily I say unto you, They have their reward.

17 But thou, when thou fastest, anoint thine head, and wash thy face;

18 That thou appear not unto men to fast, but unto thy Father which is in secret: and thy Father, which seeth in secret, shall reward thee openly.

19 ¶ Lay not up for yourselves treasures upon earth, where moth and rust doth corrupt, and where thieves break through and steal:

20 But lay up for yourselves treasures in heaven, where neither moth nor rust doth corrupt, and where thieves do not break through nor steal:

21 For where your treasure is, there will your heart be also.

22 The light of the body is the eye: if therefore thine eye be single, thy whole body shall be full of light.

23 But if thine eye be evil, thy whole body shall be full of darkness. If therefore the light that is in thee be darkness, how great *is* that darkness!

24 ¶ No man can serve two masters: for either he will hate the one, and love the other; or else he will hold to the one, and despise the other. Ye cannot serve God and mammon.

25 Therefore I say unto you, Take no thought for your life, what ye shall eat, or what ye shall drink; nor yet for your body, what ye shall put on. Is not the life more than meat, and the body than raiment?

26 Behold the fowls of the air: for they sow not, neither do they reap, nor gather into barns; yet your heavenly Father feedeth them. Are ye not much better than they?

27 Which of you by taking thought can add one cubit unto his stature?

28 And why take ye thought for raiment? Consider the lilies of the field, how they grow; they toil not, neither do they spin:

29 And yet I say unto you, That even Solomon in all his glory was not arrayed like one of these.

30 Wherefore, if God so clothe the grass of the field, which to day is, and to morrow is cast into the oven, *shall he* not much more *clothe* you, O ye of little faith?

31 Therefore take no thought, saying, What shall we eat? or, What shall we drink? or, Wherewithal shall we be clothed?

32 (For after all these things do the Gentiles seek:) for your heavenly Father knoweth that ye have need of all these things.

33 But seek ye first the kingdom of God, and his righteousness; and all these things shall be added unto you.

34 Take therefore no thought for the morrow: for the morrow shall take thought for the things of itself. Sufficient unto the day *is* the evil thereof.

CHAPTER 7

JUDGE not, that ye be not judged.

2 For with what judgment ye judge, ye shall be judged: and with what measure ye mete, it shall be measured to you again.

3 And why beholdest thou the mote that is in thy brother's eye, but considerest not the beam that is in thine own eye?

4 Or how wilt thou say to thy brother, Let me pull out the mote out of thine eye; and, behold, a beam *is* in thine own eye?

5 Thou hypocrite, first cast out the beam out of thine own eye; and then shalt thou see clearly to cast out the mote out of thy brother's eye.

6 ¶ Give not that which is holy unto the dogs, neither cast ye your pearls before swine, lest they trample them under their feet, and turn again and rend you.

7 ¶ Ask, and it shall be given you; seek, and ye shall find; knock, and it shall be opened unto you:

8 For every one that asketh receiveth; and he that seeketh findeth; and to him that knocketh it shall be opened.

9 Or what man is there of you, whom if his son ask bread, will he give him a stone?

10 Or if he ask a fish, will he give him a serpent?

11 If ye then, being evil, know how to give good gifts unto your children, how much more shall your Father which is in heaven give good things to them that ask him?

37 Judge not, and ye shall not be judged: condemn not, and ye shall not be condemned: forgive, and ye shall be forgiven:

38 Give, and it shall be given unto you; good measure, pressed down, and shaken together, and running over, shall men give into your bosom. For with the same measure that ye mete withal it shall be measured to you again.

39 And he spake a parable unto them, Can the blind lead the blind? shall they not both fall into the ditch?

40 The disciple is not above his master: but every one that is perfect shall be as his master.

41 And why beholdest thou the mote that is in thy brother's eye, but perceivest not the beam that is in thine own eye?

42 Either how canst thou say to thy brother, Brother, let me pull out the mote that is in thine eye, when thou thyself beholdest not the beam that is in thine own eye? Thou hypocrite, cast out first the beam out of thine own eye, and then shalt thou see clearly to pull out the mote that is in thy brother's eye.

12 Therefore all things whatsoever ye would that men should do to you, do ye even so to them: for this is the law and the prophets.

13 ¶ Enter ye in at the strait gate: for wide *is* the gate, and broad *is* the way, that leadeth to destruction, and many there be which go in thereat:

14 Because strait *is* the gate, and narrow *is* the way, which leadeth unto life, and few there be that find it.

15 ¶ Beware of false prophets, which come to you in sheep's clothing, but inwardly they are ravening wolves.

16 Ye shall know them by their fruits. Do men gather grapes of thorns, or figs of thistles?

44 For every tree is known by his own fruit. For of thorns men do not gather figs, nor of a bramble bush gather they grapes.

17 Even so every good tree bringeth forth good fruit; but a corrupt tree bringeth forth evil fruit.

18 A good tree cannot bring forth evil fruit, neither *can* a corrupt tree bring forth good fruit.

43 For a good tree bringeth not forth corrupt fruit; neither doth a corrupt tree bring forth good fruit.

19 Every tree that bringeth not forth good fruit is hewn down, and cast into the fire.

20 Wherefore by their fruits ye shall know them.

45 A good man out of the good treasure of his heart bringeth forth that which is good; and an evil man out of the evil treasure of his heart bringeth forth that which is evil: for of the abundance of the heart his mouth speaketh.

46 ¶ And why call ye me, Lord, Lord, and do not the things which I say?

21 ¶ Not every one that saith unto me, Lord, Lord, shall enter into the kingdom of heaven; but he that doeth the will of my Father which is in heaven.

22 Many will say to me in that day, Lord, Lord, have we not prophesied in thy name? and in thy name have cast out devils? and in thy name done many wonderful works?

23 And then will I profess unto them, I never knew you: depart from me, ye that work iniquity.

24 ¶ Therefore whosoever heareth these sayings of mine, and doeth them, I will liken him unto a wise man, which built his house upon a rock:

47 Whosoever cometh to me, and heareth my sayings, and doeth them, I will shew you to whom he is like:

48 He is like a man which built an house, and digged deep, and laid the foundation on a rock: and when the flood arose, the stream beat vehemently upon that house, and could not shake it: for it was founded upon a rock.

25 And the rain descended, and the floods came, and the winds blew, and beat upon that house; and it fell not: for it was founded upon a rock.

26 And every one that heareth these sayings of mine, and doeth them not, shall be likened unto a foolish man, which built his house upon the sand:

49 But he that heareth, and doeth not, is like a man that without a foundation built an house upon the earth; against which the stream did beat vehemently, and immediately it fell; and the ruin of that house was great.

27 And the rain descended, and the floods came, and the winds blew, and beat upon that house; and it fell: and great was the fall of it.

28 And it came to pass, when Jesus had ended these sayings, the people were astonished at his doctrine:

29 For he taught them as *one* having authority, and not as the scribes.

59. JESUS GOES TO CAPERNAUM AND HEALS CENTURION'S SERVANT

CHAPTER 8

WHEN he was come down from the mountain, great multitudes followed him.

5 ¶ And when Jesus was entered into Că·pĕr´·nă·ŭm, there came unto him a centurion, beseeching him,

6 And saying, Lord, my servant lieth at home sick of the palsy, grievously tormented.

7 And Jesus saith unto him, I will come and heal him.

8 The centurion answered and said, Lord, I am not worthy that thou shouldest come under my roof: but speak the word only, and my servant shall be healed.

9 For I am a man under authority, having soldiers under me: and I say to this *man*, Go, and he goeth; and to another, Come, and he cometh; and to my servant, Do this, and he doeth *it*.

10 When Jesus heard *it*, he marvelled, and said to them that followed, Verily I say unto you, I have not found so great faith, no, not in Israel.

11 And I say unto you, That many shall come from the east and west, and shall sit down with Abraham, and Isaac, and Jacob, in the kingdom of heaven.

12 But the children of the kingdom shall be cast out into outer darkness: there shall be weeping and gnashing of teeth.

13 And Jesus said unto the centurion, Go thy way; and as thou hast believed, *so* be it done unto thee. And his servant was healed in the selfsame hour.

CHAPTER 7

NOW when he had ended all his sayings in the audience of the people, he entered into Că·pĕr´·nă·ŭm.

2 And a certain centurion's servant, who was dear unto him, was sick, and ready to die.

3 And when he heard of Jesus, he sent unto him the elders of the Jews, beseeching him that he would come and heal his servant.

4 And when they came to Jesus, they besought him instantly, saying,

That he was worthy for whom he should do this:

5 For he loveth our nation, and he hath built us a synagogue.

6 Then Jesus went with them. And when he was now not far from the house, the centurion sent friends to him, saying unto him, Lord, trouble not thyself: for I am not worthy that thou shouldest enter under my roof:

7 Wherefore neither thought I myself worthy to come unto thee: but say in a word, and my servant shall be healed.

8 For I also am a man set under authority, having under me soldiers, and I say unto one, Go, and he goeth; and to another, Come, and he cometh; and to my servant, Do this, and he doeth *it*.

9 When Jesus heard these things, he marvelled at him, and turned him about, and said unto the people that followed him, I say unto you, I have not found so great faith, no, not in Israel.

10 And they that were sent, returning to the house, found the servant whole that had been sick.

60. RAISES A WIDOW'S SON FROM THE DEAD

11 ¶ And it came to pass the day after, that he went into a city called Nā´·ĭn; and many of his disciples went with him, and much people.

12 Now when he came nigh to the gate of the city, behold, there was a dead man carried out, the only son of his mother, and she was a widow: and much people of the city was with her.

13 And when the Lord saw her, he had compassion on her, and said unto her, Weep not.

14 And he came and touched the bier: and they that bare *him* stood still. And he said, Young man, I say unto thee, Arise.

15 And he that was dead sat up, and began to speak. And he delivered him to his mother.

16 And there came a fear on all: and they glorified God, saying, That a great prophet is risen up among us; and, That God hath visited his people.

17 And this rumour of him went forth throughout all Judæa, and throughout all the region round about.

61. JOHN SENDS MESSENGERS TO JESUS

18 And the disciples of John shewed him of all these things.

2 Now when John had heard in the prison the works of Christ, he sent two of his disciples,

19 ¶ And John calling *unto him* two of his disciples sent *them* to Jesus, saying, Art thou he that should come? or look we for another?

20 When the men were come unto him, they said, John Baptist hath sent us unto thee, saying, Art thou he that should come? or look we for another?

3 And said unto him, Art thou he that should come, or do we look for another?

21 And in that same hour he cured many of *their* infirmities and plagues, and of evil spirits; and unto many *that were* blind he gave sight.

4 Jesus answered and said unto them, Go and shew John again those things which ye do hear and see:

5 The blind receive their sight, and the lame walk, the lepers are cleansed, and the deaf hear, the dead are raised up, and the poor have the gospel preached to them.

22 Then Jesus answering said unto them, Go your way, and tell John what things ye have seen and heard; how that the blind see, the lame walk, the lepers are cleansed, the deaf hear, the dead are raised, to the poor the gospel is preached.

6 And blessed is *he*, whosoever shall not be offended in me.

23 And blessed is *he*, whosoever shall not be offended in me.

62. JESUS TESTIFIES OF JOHN'S GREATNESS

7 ¶ And as they departed, Jesus began to say unto the multitudes concerning John, What went ye out into the wilderness to see? A reed shaken with the wind?

8 But what went ye out for to see? A man clothed in soft raiment? behold, they that wear soft *clothing* are in kings' houses.

9 But what went ye out for to see? A prophet? yea, I say unto you, and more than a prophet.

10 For this is *he*, of whom it is written, Behold, I send my messenger before thy face, which shall prepare thy way before thee.

11 Verily I say unto you, Among them that are born of women there hath not risen a greater than John the Baptist: notwithstanding he that is least in the kingdom of heaven is greater than he.

12 And from the days of John the Baptist until now the kingdom of heaven suffereth violence, and the violent take it by force.

24 ¶ And when the messengers of John were departed, he began to speak unto the people concerning John, What went ye out into the wilderness for to see? A reed shaken with the wind?

25 But what went ye out for to see? A man clothed in soft raiment? Behold, they which are gorgeously apparelled, and live delicately, are in kings' courts.

26 But what went ye out for to see? A prophet? Yea, I say unto you, and much more than a prophet.

27 This is *he*, of whom it is written, Behold, I send my messenger before thy face, which shall prepare thy way before thee.

28 For I say unto you, Among those that are born of women there is not a greater prophet than John the Baptist: but he that is least in the kingdom of God is greater than he.

MATTHEW – 11	MARK –	LUKE – 7	JOHN –
13 For all the prophets and the law prophesied until John. 14 And if ye will receive *it*, this is Ē-lī́-ȧs, which was for to come. 15 He that hath ears to hear, let him hear.			
		29 And all the people that heard *him*, and the publicans, justified God, being baptized with the baptism of John. 30 But the Pharisees and lawyers rejected the counsel of God against themselves, being not baptized of him. 31 ¶ And the Lord said, Whereunto then shall I liken the men of this generation? and to what are they like?	
16 ¶ But whereunto shall I liken this generation? It is like unto children sitting in the markets, and calling unto their fellows,		32 They are like unto children sitting in the marketplace, and calling one to another, and saying, We have piped unto you, and ye have not danced; we have mourned to you, and ye have not wept.	
17 And saying, We have piped unto you, and ye have not danced; we have mourned unto you, and ye have not lamented. 18 For John came neither eating nor drinking, and they say, He hath a devil.		33 For John the Baptist came neither eating bread nor drinking wine; and ye say, He hath a devil.	
19 The Son of man came eating and drinking, and they say, Behold a man gluttonous, and a winebibber, a friend of publicans and sinners. But wisdom is justified of her children.		34 The Son of man is come eating and drinking; and ye say, Behold a gluttonous man, and a winebibber, a friend of publicans and sinners! 35 But wisdom is justified of all her children.	

63. WOMAN ANOINTS JESUS' FEET WITH OIL

MATTHEW – 11	MARK –	LUKE – 7	JOHN –
		36 ¶ And one of the Pharisees desired him that he would eat with him. And he went into the Pharisee's house, and sat down to meat. 37 And, behold, a woman in the city, which was a sinner, when she knew that *Jesus* sat at meat in the Pharisee's house, brought an alabaster box of ointment, 38 And stood at his feet behind *him* weeping, and began to wash his feet with tears, and did wipe *them* with the hairs of her head, and kissed his feet, and anointed *them* with the ointment. 39 Now when the Pharisee which had bidden him saw *it*, he spake within himself, saying, This man, if he were a prophet, would have known who and what manner of woman *this is* that toucheth him: for she is a sinner. 40 And Jesus answering said unto him, Simon, I have somewhat to say unto thee. And he saith, Master, say on. 41 There was a certain creditor which had two debtors: the one owed five hundred pence, and the other fifty. 42 And when they had nothing to pay, he frankly forgave them both. Tell me therefore, which of them will love him most? 43 Simon answered and said, I suppose that *he*, to whom he forgave most. And he said unto him, Thou hast rightly judged. 44 And he turned to the woman, and said unto Simon, Seest thou this woman? I entered into thine house, thou gavest me no water for my feet: but she hath washed my feet with tears, and wiped *them* with the hairs of her head.	

LUKE – 7

45 Thou gavest me no kiss: but this woman since the time I came in hath not ceased to kiss my feet.

46 My head with oil thou didst not anoint: but this woman hath anointed my feet with ointment.

47 Wherefore I say unto thee, Her sins, which are many, are forgiven; for she loved much: but to whom little is forgiven, *the same* loveth little.

48 And he said unto her, Thy sins are forgiven.

49 And they that sat at meat with him began to say within themselves, Who is this that forgiveth sins also?

50 And he said to the woman, Thy faith hath saved thee; go in peace.

64. PREACHING IN GALILEE WITH THE TWELVE

LUKE – 7

CHAPTER 8

AND it came to pass afterward, that he went throughout every city and village, preaching and shewing the glad tidings of the kingdom of God: and the twelve *were* with him,

2 And certain women, which had been healed of evil spirits and infirmities, Mary called Măg'-dä-lēne, out of whom went seven devils,

3 And Jō-ăn'-nä the wife of Chû'-zä Herod's steward, and Susanna, and many others, which ministered unto him of their substance.

65. JESUS ACCUSED OF WORKING WITH BEELZEBUB

MARK – 3

19b and they went into an house.

20 And the multitude cometh together again, so that they could not so much as eat bread.

21 And when his friends heard *of it*, they went out to lay hold on him: for they said, He is beside himself.

MATTHEW – 12

22 ¶ Then was brought unto him one possessed with a devil, blind, and dumb: and he healed him, insomuch that the blind and dumb both spake and saw.

23 And all the people were amazed, and said, Is not this the son of David?

24 But when the Pharisees heard *it*, they said, This *fellow* doth not cast out devils, but by Bĕ-ĕl'-zĕ-bŭb the prince of the devils.

25 And Jesus knew their thoughts, and said unto them,

Every kingdom divided against itself is brought to desolation; and every city or house divided against itself shall not stand:

26 And if Satan cast out Satan, he is divided against himself; how shall then his kingdom stand?

27 And if I by Bĕ-ĕl'-zĕ-bŭb cast out devils, by whom do your children cast *them* out? therefore they shall be your judges.

28 But if I cast out devils by the Spirit of God, then the kingdom of God is come unto you.

MARK – 3

22 ¶ And the scribes which came down from Jerusalem said, He hath Bĕ-ĕl'-zĕ-bŭb, and by the prince of the devils casteth he out devils.

23 And he called them *unto him*, and said unto them in parables, How can Satan cast out Satan?

24 And if a kingdom be divided against itself, that kingdom cannot stand.

25 And if a house be divided against itself, that house cannot stand.

26 And if Satan rise up against himself, and be divided, he cannot stand, but hath an end.

MATTHEW – 12	MARK – 3	LUKE –	JOHN –
29 Or else how can one enter into a strong man's house, and spoil his goods, except he first bind the strong man? and then he will spoil his house. 30 He that is not with me is against me; and he that gathereth not with me scattereth abroad.	27 No man can enter into a strong man's house, and spoil his goods, except he will first bind the strong man; and then he will spoil his house.		

66. NO FORGIVENESS FOR BLASPHEMY AGAINST HOLY GHOST

MATTHEW – 12	MARK – 3	LUKE –	JOHN –
31 ¶ Wherefore I say unto you, All manner of sin and blasphemy shall be forgiven unto men: but the blasphemy *against* the *Holy* Ghost shall not be forgiven unto men. 32 And whosoever speaketh a word against the Son of man, it shall be forgiven him: but whosoever speaketh against the Holy Ghost, it shall not be forgiven him, neither in this world, neither in the *world* to come. 33 Either make the tree good, and his fruit good; or else make the tree corrupt, and his fruit corrupt: for the tree is known by *his* fruit. 34 O generation of vipers, how can ye, being evil, speak good things? for out of the abundance of the heart the mouth speaketh. 35 A good man out of the good treasure of the heart bringeth forth good things: and an evil man out of the evil treasure bringeth forth evil things. 36 But I say unto you, That every idle word that men shall speak, they shall give account thereof in the day of judgment. 37 For by thy words thou shalt be justified, and by thy words thou shalt be condemned.	28 Verily I say unto you, All sins shall be forgiven unto the sons of men, and blasphemies wherewith soever they shall blaspheme: 29 But he that shall blaspheme against the Holy Ghost hath never forgiveness, but is in danger of eternal damnation: 30 Because they said, He hath an unclean spirit.		

67. DISCOURSE ON SIGNS

MATTHEW – 12	MARK – 3	LUKE –	JOHN –
38 ¶ Then certain of the scribes and of the Pharisees answered, saying, Master, we would see a sign from thee. 39 But he answered and said unto them, An evil and adulterous generation seeketh after a sign; and there shall no sign be given to it, but the sign of the prophet Jonas: 40 For as Jonas was three days and three nights in the whale's belly; so shall the Son of man be three days and three nights in the heart of the earth. 41 The men of Nĭn·ĕ·vĕh shall rise in judgment with this generation, and shall condemn it: because they repented at the preaching of Jonas; and, behold, a greater than Jonas *is* here. 42 The queen of the south shall rise up in the judgment with this generation, and shall condemn it: for she came from the uttermost parts of the earth to hear the wisdom of Solomon; and, behold, a greater than Solomon *is* here. 43 When the unclean spirit is gone out of a man, he walketh through dry places, seeking rest, and findeth none. 44 Then he saith, I will return into my house from whence I came out; and when he is come, he findeth *it* empty, swept, and garnished.			

45 Then goeth he, and taketh with himself seven other spirits more wicked than himself, and they enter in and dwell there: and the last *state* of that man is worse than the first. Even so shall it be also unto this wicked generation.

68. JESUS' MOTHER AND BRETHREN SEEK HIM

46 ¶ While he yet talked to the people, behold, *his* mother and his brethren stood without, desiring to speak with him.

47 Then one said unto him, Behold, thy mother and thy brethren stand without, desiring to speak with thee.

48 But he answered and said unto him that told him, Who is my mother? and who are my brethren?

49 And he stretched forth his hand toward his disciples, and said, Behold my mother and my brethren!

50 For whosoever shall do the will of my Father which is in heaven, the same is my brother, and sister, and mother.

31 ¶ There came then his brethren and his mother, and, standing without, sent unto him, calling him.

32 And the multitude sat about him, and they said unto him, Behold, thy mother and thy brethren without seek for thee.

33 And he answered them, saying, Who is my mother, or my brethren?

34 And he looked round about on them which sat about him, and said, Behold my mother and my brethren!

35 For whosoever shall do the will of God, the same is my brother, and my sister, and mother.

19 ¶ Then came to him *his* mother and his brethren, and could not come at him for the press.

20 And it was told him *by certain* which said, Thy mother and thy brethren stand without, desiring to see thee.

21 And he answered and said unto them, My mother and my brethren are these which hear the word of God, and do it.

69. PARABLE OF THE SOWER, OR DIFFERENT KINDS OF SOIL

CHAPTER 13

THE same day went Jesus out of the house, and sat by the sea side.

2 And great multitudes were gathered together unto him, so that he went into a ship, and sat; and the whole multitude stood on the shore.

3 And he spake many things unto them in parables, saying, Behold, a sower went forth to sow;

4 And when he sowed, some *seeds* fell by the way side, and the fowls came and devoured them up:

5 Some fell upon stony places, where they had not much earth: and forthwith they sprung up, because they had no deepness of earth:

6 And when the sun was up, they were scorched; and because they had no root, they withered away.

7 And some fell among thorns; and the thorns sprung up, and choked them:

8 But other fell into good ground, and brought forth fruit, some an hundredfold, some sixtyfold, some thirtyfold.

9 Who hath ears to hear, let him hear.

10 And the disciples came, and said unto him, Why speakest thou unto them in parables?

11 He answered and said unto them, Because it is given unto you to know the mysteries of the kingdom of heaven, but to them it is not given.

12 For whosoever hath, to him shall be given, and he shall have more abundance: but whosoever hath not, from him shall be taken away even that he hath.

CHAPTER 4

AND he began again to teach by the sea side: and there was gathered unto him a great multitude, so that he entered into a ship, and sat in the sea; and the whole multitude was by the sea on the land.

2 And he taught them many things by parables, and said unto them in his doctrine,

3 Hearken; Behold, there went out a sower to sow:

4 And it came to pass, as he sowed, some fell by the way side, and the fowls of the air came and devoured it up.

5 And some fell on stony ground, where it had not much earth; and immediately it sprang up, because it had no depth of earth:

6 But when the sun was up, it was scorched; and because it had no root, it withered away.

7 And some fell among thorns, and the thorns grew up, and choked it, and it yielded no fruit.

8 And other fell on good ground, and did yield fruit that sprang up and increased; and brought forth, some thirty, and some sixty, and some an hundred.

9 And he said unto them, He that hath ears to hear, let him hear.

10 And when he was alone, they that were about him with the twelve asked of him the parable.

11 And he said unto them, Unto you it is given to know the mystery of the kingdom of God: but unto them that are without, all *these* things are done in parables:

4 ¶ And when much people were gathered together, and were come to him out of every city, he spake by a parable:

5 A sower went out to sow his seed: and as he sowed, some fell by the way side; and it was trodden down, and the fowls of the air devoured it.

6 And some fell upon a rock; and as soon as it was sprung up, it withered away, because it lacked moisture.

7 And some fell among thorns; and the thorns sprang up with it, and choked it.

8 And other fell on good ground, and sprang up, and bare fruit an hundredfold. And when he had said these things, he cried, He that hath ears to hear, let him hear.

9 And his disciples asked him, saying, What might this parable be?

10a And he said, Unto you it is given to know the mysteries of the kingdom of God: but to others in parables;

44

MATTHEW – 13

13 Therefore speak I to them in parables: because they seeing see not; and hearing they hear not, neither do they understand.

14 And in them is fulfilled the prophecy of Ē-śāī'-ăs, which saith, By hearing ye shall hear, and shall not understand; and seeing ye shall see, and shall not perceive:

15 For this people's heart is waxed gross, and *their* ears are dull of hearing, and their eyes they have closed; lest at any time they should see with *their* eyes, and hear with *their* ears, and should understand with *their* heart, and should be converted, and I should heal them.

16 But blessed *are* your eyes, for they see: and your ears, for they hear.

17 For verily I say unto you, That many prophets and righteous *men* have desired to see *those things* which ye see, and have not seen *them;* and to hear *those things* which ye hear, and have not heard *them.*

18 ¶ Hear ye therefore the parable of the sower.

19 When any one heareth the word of the kingdom, and understandeth *it* not, then cometh the wicked *one,* and catcheth away that which was sown in his heart. This is he which received seed by the way side.

20 But he that received the seed into stony places, the same is he that heareth the word, and anon with joy receiveth it;

21 Yet hath he not root in himself, but dureth for a while: for when tribulation or persecution ariseth because of the word, by and by he is offended.

22 He also that received seed among the thorns is he that heareth the word; and the care of this world, and the deceitfulness of riches, choke the word, and he becometh unfruitful.

23 But he that received seed into the good ground is he that heareth the word, and understandeth *it;* which also beareth fruit, and bringeth forth, some an hundredfold, some sixty, some thirty.

MARK – 4

12 That seeing they may see, and not perceive; and hearing they may hear, and not understand;

lest at any time they should be converted, and *their* sins should be forgiven them.

13 And he said unto them, Know ye not this parable? and how then will ye know all parables?

14 ¶ The sower soweth the word.

15 And these are they by the way side, where the word is sown; but when they have heard, Satan cometh immediately, and taketh away the word that was sown in their hearts.

16 And these are they likewise which are sown on stony ground; who, when they have heard the word, immediately receive it with gladness;

17 And have no root in themselves, and so endure but for a time: afterward, when affliction or persecution ariseth for the word's sake, immediately they are offended.

18 And these are they which are sown among thorns; such as hear the word,

19 And the cares of this world, and the deceitfulness of riches, and the lusts of other things entering in, choke the word, and it becometh unfruitful.

20 And these are they which are sown on good ground; such as hear the word, and receive *it,* and bring forth fruit, some thirtyfold, some sixty, and some an hundred.

21 ¶ And he said unto them, Is a candle brought to be put under a bushel, or under a bed? and not to be set on a candlestick?

22 For there is nothing hid, which shall not be manifested; neither was any thing kept secret, but that it should come abroad.

23 If any man have ears to hear, let him hear.

LUKE – 8

10b   that seeing they might not see, and hearing they might not understand.

11 Now the parable is this: The seed is the word of God.

12 Those by the way side are they that hear; then cometh the devil, and taketh away the word out of their hearts, lest they should believe and be saved.

13 They on the rock *are they,* which, when they hear, receive the word with joy; and these have no root, which for a while believe, and in time of temptation fall away.

14 And that which fell among thorns are they, which, when they have heard, go forth, and are choked with cares and riches and pleasures of *this* life, and bring no fruit to perfection.

15 But that on the good ground are they, which in an honest and good heart, having heard the word, keep *it,* and bring forth fruit with patience.

16 ¶ No man, when he hath lighted a candle, covereth it with a vessel, or putteth *it* under a bed; but setteth *it* on a candlestick, that they which enter in may see the light.

17 For nothing is secret, that shall not be made manifest; neither *any thing* hid, that shall not be known and come abroad.

JOHN –

MATTHEW – 13	MARK – 4	LUKE – 8	JOHN –
	24 And he said unto them, Take heed what ye hear: with what measure ye mete, it shall be measured to you: and unto you that hear shall more be given.	18 Take heed therefore how ye hear:	
	25 For he that hath, to him shall be given: and he that hath not, from him shall be taken even that which he hath.	for whosoever hath, to him shall be given; and whosoever hath not, from him shall be taken even that which he seemeth to have.	

70. PARABLE OF SEED GROWING BY ITSELF

MATTHEW – 13	MARK – 4	LUKE – 8	JOHN –
	26 ¶ And he said, So is the kingdom of God, as if a man should cast seed into the ground; 27 And should sleep, and rise night and day, and the seed should spring and grow up, he knoweth not how. 28 For the earth bringeth forth fruit of herself; first the blade, then the ear, after that the full corn in the ear. 29 But when the fruit is brought forth, immediately he putteth in the sickle, because the harvest is come.		

71. PARABLE OF WHEAT AND TARES

MATTHEW – 13	MARK – 4	LUKE – 8	JOHN –
24 ¶ Another parable put he forth unto them, saying, The kingdom of heaven is likened unto a man which sowed good seed in his field: 25 But while men slept, his enemy came and sowed tares among the wheat, and went his way. 26 But when the blade was sprung up, and brought forth fruit, then appeared the tares also. 27 So the servants of the householder came and said unto him, Sir, didst not thou sow good seed in thy field? from whence then hath it tares? 28 He said unto them, An enemy hath done this. The servants said unto him, Wilt thou then that we go and gather them up? 29 But he said, Nay; lest while ye gather up the tares, ye root up also the wheat with them. 30 Let both grow together until the harvest: and in the time of harvest I will say to the reapers, Gather ye together first the tares, and bind them in bundles to burn them: but gather the wheat into my barn.			

72. PARABLES OF MUSTARD SEED AND LEAVEN

MATTHEW – 13	MARK – 4	LUKE – 8	JOHN –
	30 ¶ And he said, Whereunto shall we liken the kingdom of God? or with what comparison shall we compare it?		
31 ¶ Another parable put he forth unto them, saying, The kingdom of heaven is like to a grain of mustard seed, which a man took, and sowed in his field: 32 Which indeed is the least of	31 It is like a grain of mustard seed, which, when it is sown in the earth, is less than all the seeds that be in the earth:		
all seeds: but when it is grown, it is the greatest among herbs, and becometh a tree, so that the birds of the air come and lodge in the branches thereof.	32 But when it is sown, it groweth up, and becometh greater than all herbs, and shooteth out great branches; so that the fowls of the air may lodge under the shadow of it.		

MATTHEW – 13	MARK – 4	LUKE –	JOHN –
33 ¶ Another parable spake he unto them; The kingdom of heaven is like unto leaven, which a woman took, and hid in three measures of meal, till the whole was leavened.			
34 All these things spake Jesus unto the multitude in parables; and without a parable spake he not unto them:	33 And with many such parables spake he the word unto them, as they were able to hear *it*. 34 But without a parable spake he not unto them:		
35 That it might be fulfilled which was spoken by the prophet, saying, I will open my mouth in parables; I will utter things which have been kept secret from the foundation of the world.	and when they were alone, he expounded all things to his disciples.		

73. INTERPRETATION OF THE WHEAT AND TARES

MATTHEW – 13	MARK – 4	LUKE –	JOHN –
36 Then Jesus sent the multitude away, and went into the house: and his disciples came unto him, saying, Declare unto us the parable of the tares of the field. 37 He answered and said unto them, He that soweth the good seed is the Son of man; 38 The field is the world; the good seed are the children of the kingdom; but the tares are the children of the wicked *one;* 39 The enemy that sowed them is the devil; the harvest is the end of the world; and the reapers are the angels. 40 As therefore the tares are gathered and burned in the fire; so shall it be in the end of this world. 41 The Son of man shall send forth his angels, and they shall gather out of his kingdom all things that offend, and them which do iniquity; 42 And shall cast them into a furnace of fire: there shall be wailing and gnashing of teeth. 43 Then shall the righteous shine forth as the sun in the kingdom of their Father. Who hath ears to hear, let him hear.			

74. OTHER PARABLES ABOUT THE KINGDOM OF HEAVEN

MATTHEW – 13	MARK – 4	LUKE –	JOHN –
44 ¶ Again, the kingdom of heaven is like unto treasure hid in a field; the which when a man hath found, he hideth, and for joy thereof goeth and selleth all that he hath, and buyeth that field. 45 ¶ Again, the kingdom of heaven is like unto a merchant man, seeking goodly pearls: 46 Who, when he had found one pearl of great price, went and sold all that he had, and bought it. 47 ¶ Again, the kingdom of heaven is like unto a net, that was cast into the sea, and gathered of every kind: 48 Which, when it was full, they drew to shore, and sat down, and gathered the good into vessels, but cast the bad away.			

49 So shall it be at the end of the world: the angels shall come forth, and sever the wicked from among the just,			
50 And shall cast them into the furnace of fire: there shall be wailing and gnashing of teeth.			
51 Jesus saith unto them, Have ye understood all these things? They say unto him, Yea, Lord.			
52 Then said he unto them, Therefore every scribe *which is* instructed unto the kingdom of heaven is like unto a man *that is* an householder, which bringeth forth out of his treasure *things* new and old.			
53 ¶ And it came to pass, *that* when Jesus had finished these parables, he departed thence.			

75. JESUS CALMS THE STORM AT SEA

Ch. 8			
18 ¶ Now when Jesus saw great multitudes about him, he gave commandment to depart unto the other side.	35 And the same day, when the even was come, he saith unto them, Let us pass over unto the other side.	22 ¶ Now it came to pass on a certain day, that he went into a ship with his disciples: and he said unto them, Let us go over unto the other side of the lake. And they launched forth.	
23 ¶ And when he was entered into a ship, his disciples followed him.	36 And when they had sent away the multitude, they took him even as he was in the ship. And there were also with him other little ships.		
24 And, behold, there arose a great tempest in the sea, insomuch that the ship was covered with the waves: but he was asleep.	37 And there arose a great storm of wind, and the waves beat into the ship, so that it was now full.	23 But as they sailed he fell asleep: and there came down a storm of wind on the lake; and they were filled *with water*, and were in jeopardy.	
25 And his disciples came to *him*, and awoke him, saying, Lord, save us: we perish.	38 And he was in the hinder part of the ship, asleep on a pillow: and they awake him, and say unto him, Master, carest thou not that we perish?		
26 And he saith unto them, Why are ye fearful, O ye of little faith? Then he arose, and rebuked the winds and the sea; and there was a great calm.	39 And he arose, and rebuked the wind, and said unto the sea, Peace, be still. And the wind ceased, and there was a great calm.	24 And they came to him, and awoke him, saying, Master, master, we perish. Then he arose, and rebuked the wind and the raging of the water: and they ceased, and there was a calm.	
	40 And he said unto them, Why are ye so fearful? how is it that ye have no faith?	25 And he said unto them, Where is your faith? And they being afraid wondered, saying one to another, What manner of man is this! for he commandeth even the winds and water, and they obey him.	
27 But the men marvelled, saying, What manner of man is this, that even the winds and the sea obey him!	41 And they feared exceedingly, and said one to another, What manner of man is this, that even the wind and the sea obey him?		

76. CASTS LEGION OF DEVILS INTO SWINE

	CHAPTER 5		
28 ¶ And when he was come to the other side into the country of the Gĕr'-gĕ-sēnes̀, there met him two possessed with devils, coming out of the tombs, exceeding fierce, so that no man might pass by that way.	AND they came over unto the other side of the sea, into the country of the Găd'-ă-rēnes̀.	26 ¶ And they arrived at the country of the Găd'-ă-rēnes̀, which is over against Galilee.	
	2 And when he was come out of the ship, immediately there met him out of the tombs a man with an unclean spirit,	27 And when he went forth to land, there met him out of the city a certain man, which had devils long time, and ware no clothes, neither abode in *any* house, but in the tombs.	
	3 Who had *his* dwelling among the tombs; and no man could bind him, no, not with chains:		
	4 Because that he had been often bound with fetters and chains, and the chains had been plucked asunder by him, and the fetters broken in pieces: neither could any *man* tame him.		
	5 And always, night and day, he was in the mountains, and in the tombs, crying, and cutting himself with stones.		
	6 But when he saw Jesus afar off, he ran and worshipped him,		

48

MATTHEW – 8,9	MARK – 5	LUKE – 8	JOHN –
29 And, behold, they cried out, saying, What have we to do with thee, Jesus, thou Son of God? art thou come hither to torment us before the time?	7 And cried with a loud voice, and said, What have I to do with thee, Jesus, *thou* Son of the most high God? I adjure thee by God, that thou torment me not. 8 For he said unto him, Come out of the man, *thou* unclean spirit.	28 When he saw Jesus, he cried out, and fell down before him, and with a loud voice said, What have I to do with thee, Jesus, *thou* Son of God most high? I beseech thee, torment me not. 29 (For he had commanded the unclean spirit to come out of the man. For oftentimes it had caught him: and he was kept bound with chains and in fetters; and he brake the bands, and was driven of the devil into the wilderness.)	
	9 And he asked him, What *is* thy name? And he answered, saying, My name *is* Legion: for we are many. 10 And he besought him much that he would not send them away out of the country.	30 And Jesus asked him, saying, What is thy name? And he said, Legion: because many devils were entered into him. 31 And they besought him that he would not command them to go out into the deep.	
30 And there was a good way off from them an herd of many swine feeding. 31 So the devils besought him, saying, If thou cast us out, suffer us to go away into the herd of swine. 32 And he said unto them, Go. And when they were come out, they went into the herd of swine: and, behold, the whole herd of swine ran violently down a steep place into the sea, and perished in the waters.	11 Now there was there nigh unto the mountains a great herd of swine feeding. 12 And all the devils besought him, saying, Send us into the swine, that we may enter into them. 13 And forthwith Jesus gave them leave. And the unclean spirits went out, and entered into the swine: and the herd ran violently down a steep place into the sea, (they were about two thousand;) and were choked in the sea.	32 And there was there an herd of many swine feeding on the mountain: and they besought him that he would suffer them to enter into them. And he suffered them. 33 Then went the devils out of the man, and entered into the swine: and the herd ran violently down a steep place into the lake, and were choked.	
33 And they that kept them fled, and went their ways into the city, and told every thing, and what was befallen to the possessed of the devils. 34 And, behold, the whole city came out to meet Jesus:	14 And they that fed the swine fled, and told *it* in the city, and in the country. And they went out to see what it was that was done. 15 And they come to Jesus, and see him that was possessed with the devil, and had the legion, sitting, and clothed, and in his right mind: and they were afraid. 16 And they that saw *it* told them how it befell to him that was possessed with the devil, and *also* concerning the swine.	34 When they that fed *them* saw what was done, they fled, and went and told *it* in the city and in the country. 35 Then they went out to see what was done; and came to Jesus, and found the man, out of whom the devils were departed, sitting at the feet of Jesus, clothed, and in his right mind: and they were afraid. 36 They also which saw *it* told them by what means he that was possessed of the devils was healed.	
and when they saw him, they besought *him* that he would depart out of their coasts.	17 And they began to pray him to depart out of their coasts. 18 And when he was come into the ship, he that had been possessed with the devil prayed him that he might be with him. 19 Howbeit Jesus suffered him not, but saith unto him, Go home to thy friends, and tell them how great things the Lord hath done for thee, and hath had compassion on thee. 20 And he departed, and began to publish in Dĕ·căp′·ŏ·lĭs how great things Jesus had done for him: and all *men* did marvel.	37 ¶ Then the whole multitude of the country of the Găd′·ă·rēneš round about besought him to depart from them; for they were taken with great fear: and he went up into the ship, and returned back again. 38 Now the man out of whom the devils were departed besought him that he might be with him: but Jesus sent him away, saying, 39 Return to thine own house, and shew how great things God hath done unto thee. And he went his way, and published throughout the whole city how great things Jesus had done unto him.	

77. RETURNS TO CAPERNAUM

CHAPTER 9 AND he entered into a ship, and passed over, and came into his own city.	21 And when Jesus was passed over again by ship unto the other side, much people gathered unto him: and he was nigh unto the sea.	40 And it came to pass, that, when Jesus was returned, the people *gladly* received him: for they were all waiting for him.	

78. JAIRUS SEEKS JESUS TO HEAL HIS DYING DAUGHTER

MATTHEW – 9	MARK – 5	LUKE – 8
18 ¶ While he spake these things unto them, behold, there came a certain ruler, and worshipped him, saying, My daughter is even now dead: but come and lay thy hand upon her, and she shall live. 19 And Jesus arose, and followed him, and *so did* his disciples.	22 And, behold, there cometh one of the rulers of the synagogue, Jă-ī'-rŭs by name; and when he saw him, he fell at his feet, 23 And besought him greatly, saying, My little daughter lieth at the point of death: *I pray thee*, come and lay thy hands on her, that she may be healed; and she shall live. 24 And *Jesus* went with him; and much people followed him, and thronged him.	41 ¶ And, behold, there came a man named Jă-ī'-rŭs, and he was a ruler of the synagogue: and he fell down at Jesus' feet, and besought him that he would come into his house: 42 For he had one only daughter, about twelve years of age, and she lay a dying. But as he went the people thronged him.

79. WOMAN TOUCHES JESUS AND IS HEALED

MATTHEW – 9	MARK – 5	LUKE – 8
20 ¶ And, behold, a woman, which was diseased with an issue of blood twelve years, came behind *him*, and touched the hem of his garment: 21 For she said within herself, If I may but touch his garment, I shall be whole.	25 And a certain woman, which had an issue of blood twelve years, 26 And had suffered many things of many physicians, and had spent all that she had, and was nothing bettered, but rather grew worse, 27 When she had heard of Jesus, came in the press behind, and touched his garment. 28 For she said, If I may touch but his clothes, I shall be whole. 29 And straightway the fountain of her blood was dried up; and she felt in *her* body that she was healed of that plague. 30 And Jesus, immediately knowing in himself that virtue had gone out of him, turned him about in the press, and said, Who touched my clothes? 31 And his disciples said unto him, Thou seest the multitude thronging thee, and sayest thou, Who touched me? 32 And he looked round about to see her that had done this thing. 33 But the woman fearing and trembling, knowing what was done in her, came and fell down before him, and told him all the truth.	43 ¶ And a woman having an issue of blood twelve years, which had spent all her living upon physicians, neither could be healed of any, 44 Came behind *him*, and touched the border of his garment: and immediately her issue of blood stanched. 45 And Jesus said, Who touched me? When all denied, Peter and they that were with him said, Master, the multitude throng thee and press *thee*, and sayest thou, Who touched me? 46 And Jesus said, Somebody hath touched me: for I perceive that virtue is gone out of me. 47 And when the woman saw that she was not hid, she came trembling, and falling down before him, she declared unto him before all the people for what cause she had touched him, and how she was healed immediately.
22 But Jesus turned him about, and when he saw her, he said, Daughter, be of good comfort; thy faith hath made thee whole. And the woman was made whole from that hour.	34 And he said unto her, Daughter, thy faith hath made thee whole; go in peace, and be whole of thy plague.	48 And he said unto her, Daughter, be of good comfort: thy faith hath made thee whole; go in peace.

80. JAIRUS' DAUGHTER RAISED FROM DEATH

MATTHEW – 9	MARK – 5	LUKE – 8
	35 While he yet spake, there came from the ruler of the synagogue's *house certain* which said, Thy daughter is dead: why troublest thou the Master any further? 36 As soon as Jesus heard the word that was spoken, he saith unto the ruler of the synagogue, Be not afraid, only believe. 37 And he suffered no man to follow him, save Peter, and James, and John the brother of James. 38 And he cometh to the house of the ruler of the synagogue, and seeth the tumult, and them that wept and wailed greatly.	49 ¶ While he yet spake, there cometh one from the ruler of the synagogue's *house*, saying to him, Thy daughter is dead; trouble not the Master. 50 But when Jesus heard *it*, he answered him, saying, Fear not: believe only, and she shall be made whole. 51 And when he came into the house, he suffered no man to go in, save Peter, and James, and John, and the father and the mother of the maiden.
23 And when Jesus came into the ruler's house, and saw the minstrels and the people making a noise,		

MATTHEW – 9,13	MARK – 5,6	LUKE – 8	JOHN –
24 He said unto them, Give place: for the maid is not dead, but sleepeth. And they laughed him to scorn.	39 And when he was come in, he saith unto them, Why make ye this ado, and weep? the damsel is not dead, but sleepeth. 40 And they laughed him to scorn. But when he had put them all out, he taketh the father and the mother of the damsel, and them that were with him, and entereth in where the damsel was lying.	52 And all wept, and bewailed her: but he said, Weep not; she is not dead, but sleepeth. 53 And they laughed him to scorn, knowing that she was dead.	
25 But when the people were put forth, he went in, and took her by the hand, and the maid arose.	41 And he took the damsel by the hand, and said unto her, Tăl′-ĭ-thă cŭ′-mĭ; which is, being interpreted, Damsel, I say unto thee, arise. 42 And straightway the damsel arose, and walked; for she was *of the age* of twelve years. And they were astonished with a great astonishment. 43 And he charged them straitly that no man should know it; and commanded that something should be given her to eat.	54 And he put them all out, and took her by the hand, and called, saying, Maid, arise. 55 And her spirit came again, and she arose straightway: and he commanded to give her meat. 56 And her parents were astonished: but he charged them that they should tell no man what was done.	
26 And the fame hereof went abroad into all that land.			

81. TWO BLIND MEN HEALED

MATTHEW	MARK	LUKE	JOHN
27 ¶ And when Jesus departed thence, two blind men followed him, crying, and saying, *Thou Son of David, have mercy on us.* 28 And when he was come into the house, the blind men came to him: and Jesus saith unto them, Believe ye that I am able to do this? They said unto him, Yea, Lord. 29 Then touched he their eyes, saying, According to your faith be it unto you. 30 And their eyes were opened; and Jesus straitly charged them, saying, See *that* no man know *it.* 31 But they, when they were departed, spread abroad his fame in all that country.			

82. CASTS DEVIL OUT OF DUMB MAN

MATTHEW	MARK	LUKE	JOHN
32 ¶ As they went out, behold, they brought to him a dumb man possessed with a devil. 33 And when the devil was cast out, the dumb spake: and the multitudes marvelled, saying, It was never so seen in Israel. 34 But the Pharisees said, He casteth out devils through the prince of the devils.			

83. REJECTED AT NAZARETH ONCE AGAIN

MATTHEW	MARK	LUKE	JOHN
Ch. 13 54 And when he was come into his own country, he taught them in their synagogue, insomuch that they were astonished, and said, Whence hath this *man* this wisdom, and *these* mighty works?	CHAPTER 6 AND he went out from thence, and came into his own country; and his disciples follow him. 2 And when the sabbath day was come, he began to teach in the synagogue: and many hearing *him* were astonished, saying, From whence hath this *man* these things? and what wisdom *is* this which is given unto him, that even such mighty works are wrought by his hands?		

MATTHEW – 13,9,10	MARK – 6	LUKE – 9	JOHN –
55 Is not this the carpenter's son? is not his mother called Mary? and his brethren, James, and Jŏ´-ṡĕṡ, and Simon, and Judas?	3 Is not this the carpenter, the son of Mary, the brother of James, and Jŏ´-ṡĕṡ, and of Juda, and Simon? and are not his sisters here with us? And they were offended at him.		
56 And his sisters, are they not all with us? Whence then hath this *man* all these things?			
57 And they were offended in him. But Jesus said unto them, A prophet is not without honour, save in his own country, and in his own house.	4 But Jesus said unto them, A prophet is not without honour, but in his own country, and among his own kin, and in his own house.		
58 And he did not many mighty works there because of their unbelief.	5 And he could there do no mighty work, save that he laid his hands upon a few sick folk, and healed *them*.		
	6a And he marvelled because of their unbelief.		

84. JESUS AGAIN TOURS GALILEE

MATTHEW	MARK	LUKE	JOHN
Ch. 9	6b And he went round about the villages, teaching.		
35 And Jesus went about all the cities and villages, teaching in their synagogues, and preaching the gospel of the kingdom, and healing every sickness and every disease among the people.			
36 ¶ But when he saw the multitudes, he was moved with compassion on them, because they fainted, and were scattered abroad, as sheep having no shepherd.			
37 Then saith he unto his disciples, The harvest truly *is* plenteous, but the labourers *are* few;			
38 Pray ye therefore the Lord of the harvest, that he will send forth labourers into his harvest.			

85. APOSTLES SENT ON MISSIONS

MATTHEW	MARK	LUKE	JOHN
CHAPTER 10	7 ¶ And he called *unto him* the twelve, and began to send them forth by two and two; and gave them power over unclean spirits;	**CHAPTER 9**	
AND when he had called unto *him* his twelve disciples, he gave them power *against* unclean spirits, to cast them out, and to heal all manner of sickness and all manner of disease.		THEN he called his twelve disciples together, and gave them power and authority over all devils, and to cure diseases.	
5 These twelve Jesus sent forth, and commanded them, saying, Go not into the way of the Gentiles, and into *any* city of the Să-măr´-ĭ-tăns enter ye not:		2 And he sent them to preach the kingdom of God, and to heal the sick.	
6 But go rather to the lost sheep of the house of Israel.			
7 And as ye go, preach, saying, The kingdom of heaven is at hand.			
8 Heal the sick, cleanse the lepers, raise the dead, cast out devils: freely ye have received, freely give.			
9 Provide neither gold, nor silver, nor brass in your purses,	8 And commanded them that they should take nothing for *their* journey, save a staff only; no scrip, no bread, no money in *their* purse:	3 And he said unto them, Take nothing for *your* journey, neither staves, nor scrip, neither bread, neither money; neither have two coats apiece.	
10 Nor scrip for *your* journey, neither two coats, neither shoes, nor yet staves: for the workman is worthy of his meat.	9 But *be* shod with sandals; and not put on two coats.		
11 And into whatsoever city or town ye shall enter, inquire who in it is worthy; and there abide till ye go thence.	10 And he said unto them, In what place soever ye enter into an house, there abide till ye depart from that place.	4 And whatsoever house ye enter into, there abide, and thence depart.	
12 And when ye come into an house, salute it.			
13 And if the house be worthy, let your peace come upon it: but if it be not worthy, let your peace return to you.			

MATTHEW – 10	MARK – 6	LUKE – 9	JOHN –
14 And whosoever shall not receive you, nor hear your words, when ye depart out of that house or city, shake off the dust of your feet. 15 Verily I say unto you, It shall be more tolerable for the land of Sodom and Gō-mŏr´-rhă in the day of judgment, than for that city. 16 ¶ Behold, I send you forth as sheep in the midst of wolves: be ye therefore wise as serpents, and harmless as doves. 17 But beware of men: for they will deliver you up to the councils, and they will scourge you in their synagogues; 18 And ye shall be brought before governors and kings for my sake, for a testimony against them and the Gentiles. 19 But when they deliver you up, take no thought how or what ye shall speak: for it shall be given you in that same hour what ye shall speak. 20 For it is not ye that speak, but the Spirit of your Father which speaketh in you. 21 And the brother shall deliver up the brother to death, and the father the child: and the children shall rise up against *their* parents, and cause them to be put to death. 22 And ye shall be hated of all *men* for my name's sake: but he that endureth to the end shall be saved. 23 But when they persecute you in this city, flee ye into another: for verily I say unto you, Ye shall not have gone over the cities of Israel, till the Son of man be come. 24 The disciple is not above *his* master, nor the servant above his lord. 25 It is enough for the disciple that he be as his master, and the servant as his lord. If they have called the master of the house Bē-ĕl´-zĕ-bŭb, how much more *shall they call* them of his household? 26 Fear them not therefore: for there is nothing covered, that shall not be revealed; and hid, that shall not be known. 27 What I tell you in darkness, *that* speak ye in light: and what ye hear in the ear, *that* preach ye upon the housetops. 28 And fear not them which kill the body, but are not able to kill the soul: but rather fear him which is able to destroy both soul and body in hell. 29 Are not two sparrows sold for a farthing? and one of them shall not fall on the ground without your Father. 30 But the very hairs of your head are all numbered. 31 Fear ye not therefore, ye are of more value than many sparrows. 32 Whosoever therefore shall confess me before men, him will I confess also before my Father which is in heaven. 33 But whosoever shall deny me before men, him will I also deny before my Father which is in heaven. 34 Think not that I am come to send peace on earth: I came not to send peace, but a sword.	11 And whosoever shall not receive you, nor hear you, when ye depart thence, shake off the dust under your feet for a testimony against them. Verily I say unto you, It shall be more tolerable for Sodom and Gō-mŏr´-rhă in the day of judgment, than for that city.	5 And whosoever will not receive you, when ye go out of that city, shake off the very dust from your feet for a testimony against them.	

MATTHEW	MARK	LUKE	JOHN
35 For I am come to set a man at variance against his father, and the daughter against her mother, and the daughter in law against her mother in law. 36 And a man's foes *shall be* they of his own household. 37 He that loveth father or mother more than me is not worthy of me: and he that loveth son or daughter more than me is not worthy of me. 38 And he that taketh not his cross, and followeth after me, is not worthy of me. 39 He that findeth his life shall lose it: and he that loseth his life for my sake shall find it. 40 ¶ He that receiveth you receiveth me, and he that receiveth me receiveth him that sent me. 41 He that receiveth a prophet in the name of a prophet shall receive a prophet's reward; and he that receiveth a righteous man in the name of a righteous man shall receive a righteous man's reward. 42 And whosoever shall give to drink unto one of these little ones a cup of cold *water* only in the name of a disciple, verily I say unto you, he shall in no wise lose his reward.	12 And they went out, and preached that men should repent. 13 And they cast out many devils, and anointed with oil many that were sick, and healed *them.*	6 And they departed, and went through the towns, preaching the gospel, and healing every where.	

86. JESUS CONTINUES TOUR IN GALILEE

MATTHEW	MARK	LUKE	JOHN
CHAPTER 11 AND it came to pass, when Jesus had made an end of commanding his twelve disciples, he departed thence to teach and to preach in their cities.			

87. HEROD ANTIPAS HAS JOHN THE BAPTIST BEHEADED

MATTHEW	MARK	LUKE	JOHN
Ch. 14 6 But when Herod's birthday was kept, the daughter of Hĕ-rō′-dĭ-ăs danced before them, and pleased Herod. 7 Whereupon he promised with an oath to give her whatsoever she would ask. 8 And she, being before instructed of her mother, said, Give me here John Baptist's head in a charger. 9 And the king was sorry: nevertheless for the oath's sake, and them which sat with him at meat, he commanded *it* to be given *her.*	21 And when a convenient day was come, that Herod on his birthday made a supper to his lords, high captains, and chief *estates* of Galilee; 22 And when the daughter of the said Hĕ-rō′-dĭ-ăs came in, and danced, and pleased Herod and them that sat with him, the king said unto the damsel, Ask of me whatsoever thou wilt, and I will give *it* thee. 23 And he sware unto her, Whatsoever thou shalt ask of me, I will give *it* thee, unto the half of my kingdom. 24 And she went forth, and said unto her mother, What shall I ask? And she said, The head of John the Baptist. 25 And she came in straightway with haste unto the king, and asked, saying, I will that thou give me by and by in a charger the head of John the Baptist. 26 And the king was exceeding sorry; *yet* for his oath's sake, and for their sakes which sat with him, he would not reject her.		

MATTHEW – 14	MARK – 6	LUKE – 9	JOHN – 6
	27 And immediately the king sent an executioner, and commanded his head to be brought: and he went and beheaded him in the prison,		
10 And he sent, and beheaded John in the prison.			
11 And his head was brought in a charger, and given to the damsel: and she brought *it* to her mother.	28 And brought his head in a charger, and gave it to the damsel: and the damsel gave it to her mother.		
12 And his disciples came, and took up the body, and buried it, and went and told Jesus.	29 And when his disciples heard *of it*, they came and took up his corpse, and laid it in a tomb.		

88. TWELVE APOSTLES RETURN AND DEPART WITH JESUS FOR A REST

MATTHEW – 14	MARK – 6	LUKE – 9	JOHN – 6
	30 And the apostles gathered themselves together unto Jesus, and told him all things, both what they had done, and what they had taught.	10 ¶ And the apostles, when they were returned, told him all that they had done.	
13 ¶ When Jesus heard *of it*,	31 And he said unto them, Come ye yourselves apart into a desert place, and rest a while: for there were many coming and going, and they had no leisure so much as to eat.	And he took them, and went aside privately into a desert place belonging to the city called Bĕth·sā´·ĭ·dă.	CHAPTER 6 AFTER these things Jesus went over the sea of Galilee, which is *the sea* of Tĭ·bē´·rĭ·ăs.
he departed thence by ship into a desert place apart: and when the people had heard *thereof*, they followed him on foot out of the cities.	32 And they departed into a desert place by ship privately. 33 And the people saw them departing, and many knew him, and ran afoot thither out of all cities, and outwent them, and came together unto him.		2 And a great multitude followed him, because they saw his miracles which he did on them that were diseased.

89. JESUS FEEDS THE FIVE THOUSAND

MATTHEW – 14	MARK – 6	LUKE – 9	JOHN – 6
			3 And Jesus went up into a mountain, and there he sat with his disciples. 4 And the passover, a feast of the Jews, was nigh.
14 And Jesus went forth, and saw a great multitude, and was moved with compassion toward them, and he healed their sick.	34 And Jesus, when he came out, saw much people, and was moved with compassion toward them, because they were as sheep not having a shepherd: and he began to teach them many things.	11 And the people, when they knew *it*, followed him: and he received them, and spake unto them of the kingdom of God, and healed them that had need of healing.	
15 ¶ And when it was evening, his disciples came to him, saying, This is a desert place, and the time is now past; send the multitude away, that they may go into the villages, and buy themselves victuals.	35 And when the day was now far spent, his disciples came unto him, and said, This is a desert place, and now the time *is* far passed: 36 Send them away, that they may go into the country round about, and into the villages, and buy themselves bread: for they have nothing to eat.	12 And when the day began to wear away, then came the twelve, and said unto him, Send the multitude away, that they may go into the towns and country round about, and lodge, and get victuals: for we are here in a desert place.	
			5 ¶ When Jesus then lifted up *his* eyes, and saw a great company come unto him, he saith unto Philip, Whence shall we buy bread, that these may eat? 6 And this he said to prove him: for he himself knew what he would do.
16 But Jesus said unto them, They need not depart; give ye them to eat.	37 He answered and said unto them, Give ye them to eat. And they say unto him, Shall we go and buy two hundred pennyworth of bread, and give them to eat? 38 He saith unto them, How many loaves have ye? go and see.	13 But he said unto them, Give ye them to eat.	7 Philip answered him, Two hundred pennyworth of bread is not sufficient for them, that every one of them may take a little. 8 One of his disciples, Andrew, Simon Peter's brother, saith unto him,
17 And they say unto him, We have here but five loaves, and two fishes. 18 He said, Bring them hither to me.	And when they knew, they say, Five, and two fishes.	And they said, We have no more but five loaves and two fishes; except we should go and buy meat for all this people. 14 For they were about five thousand men. And he said to his disciples, Make them sit down by fifties in a company.	9 There is a lad here, which hath five barley loaves, and two small fishes: but what are they among so many?
19a And he commanded the multitude to sit down on the grass,	39 And he commanded them to make all sit down by companies upon the green grass. 40 And they sat down in ranks, by hundreds, and by fifties.	15 And they did so, and made them all sit down.	10 And Jesus said, Make the men sit down. Now there was much grass in the place. So the men sat down, in number about five thousand.

MATTHEW – 14	MARK – 6	LUKE – 9	JOHN – 6
19b and took the five loaves, and the two fishes, and looking up to heaven, he blessed, and brake, and gave the loaves to *his* disciples, and the disciples to the multitude. 20 And they did all eat, and were filled: and they took up of the fragments that remained twelve baskets full. 21 And they that had eaten were about five thousand men, beside women and children.	41 And when he had taken the five loaves and the two fishes, he looked up to heaven, and blessed, and brake the loaves, and gave *them* to his disciples to set before them; and the two fishes divided he among them all. 42 And they did all eat, and were filled. 43 And they took up twelve baskets full of the fragments, and of the fishes. 44 And they that did eat of the loaves were about five thousand men.	16 Then he took the five loaves and the two fishes, and looking up to heaven, he blessed them, and brake, and gave to the disciples to set before the multitude. 17 And they did eat, and were all filled: and there was taken up of fragments that remained to them twelve baskets.	11 And Jesus took the loaves; and when he had given thanks, he distributed to the disciples, and the disciples to them that were set down; and likewise of the fishes as much as they would. 12 When they were filled, he said unto his disciples, Gather up the fragments that remain, that nothing be lost. 13 Therefore they gathered *them* together, and filled twelve baskets with the fragments of the five barley loaves, which remained over and above unto them that had eaten. 14 Then those men, when they had seen the miracle that Jesus did, said, This is of a truth that prophet that should come into the world.

90. JESUS DEPARTS UP INTO A MOUNTAIN TO AVOID THEIR MAKING HIM A KING

			15 ¶ When Jesus therefore perceived that they would come and take him by force, to make him a king,
22 ¶ And straightway Jesus constrained his disciples to get into a ship, and to go before him unto the other side, while he sent the multitudes away. 23 And when he had sent the multitudes away, he went up into a mountain apart to pray: and when the evening was come, he was there alone.	45 And straightway he constrained his disciples to get into the ship, and to go to the other side before unto Bĕth-sā′-ĭ-dă, while he sent away the people. 46 And when he had sent them away, he departed into a mountain to pray.		he departed again into a mountain himself alone.

91. JESUS WALKS ON WATER

			16 And when even was *now* come, his disciples went down unto the sea, 17 And entered into a ship, and went over the sea toward Că-pĕr′-nă-ŭm. And it was now dark, and Jesus was not come to them. 18 And the sea arose by reason of a great wind that blew.
	47 And when even was come, the ship was in the midst of the sea, and he alone on the land.		
24 But the ship was now in the midst of the sea, tossed with waves: for the wind was contrary. 25 And in the fourth watch of the night Jesus went unto them, walking on the sea. 26 And when the disciples saw him walking on the sea, they were troubled, saying, It is a spirit; and they cried out for fear. 27 But straightway Jesus spake unto them, saying, Be of good cheer; it is I; be not afraid. 28 And Peter answered him and said, Lord, if it be thou, bid me come unto thee on the water. 29 And he said, Come. And when Peter was come down out of the ship, he walked on the water, to go to Jesus. 30 But when he saw the wind boisterous, he was afraid; and beginning to sink, he cried, saying, Lord, save me. 31 And immediately Jesus stretched forth *his* hand, and caught him, and said unto him, O thou of little faith, wherefore didst thou doubt?	48 And he saw them toiling in rowing; for the wind was contrary unto them: and about the fourth watch of the night he cometh unto them, walking upon the sea, and would have passed by them. 49 But when they saw him walking upon the sea, they supposed it had been a spirit, and cried out: 50 For they all saw him, and were troubled. And immediately he talked with them, and saith unto them, Be of good cheer: it is I; be not afraid.		19 So when they had rowed about five and twenty or thirty furlongs, they see Jesus walking on the sea, and drawing nigh unto the ship: and they were afraid. 20 But he saith unto them, It is I; be not afraid.

MATTHEW – 14	MARK – 6	LUKE –	JOHN – 6
32 And when they were come into the ship, the wind ceased. 33 Then they that were in the ship came and worshipped him, saying, Of a truth thou art the Son of God.	51 And he went up unto them into the ship; and the wind ceased: and they were sore amazed in themselves beyond measure, and wondered. 52 For they considered not *the miracle* of the loaves: for their heart was hardened.		21 Then they willingly received him into the ship: and immediately the ship was at the land whither they went.

92. JESUS HEALS PEOPLE OF GENNESARET

MATTHEW – 14	MARK – 6	LUKE –	JOHN – 6
34 ¶ And when they were gone over, they came into the land of Gĕn·nĕs′·à·rĕt. 35 And when the men of that place had knowledge of him, they sent out into all that country round about, and brought unto him all that were diseased; 36 And besought him that they might only touch the hem of his garment: and as many as touched were made perfectly whole.	53 And when they had passed over, they came into the land of Gĕn·nĕs′·à·rĕt, and drew to the shore. 54 And when they were come out of the ship, straightway they knew him, 55 And ran through that whole region round about, and began to carry about in beds those that were sick, where they heard he was. 56 And whithersoever he entered, into villages, or cities, or country, they laid the sick in the streets, and besought him that they might touch if it were but the border of his garment: and as many as touched him were made whole.		

93. JESUS DECLARES HE IS THE BREAD OF LIFE

MATTHEW – 14	MARK – 6	LUKE –	JOHN – 6
			22 ¶ The day following, when the people which stood on the other side of the sea saw that there was none other boat there, save that one whereinto his disciples were entered, and that Jesus went not with his disciples into the boat, but *that* his disciples were gone away alone; 23 (Howbeit there came other boats from Tī·bē′·rĭ·ăs nigh unto the place where they did eat bread, after that the Lord had given thanks:) 24 When the people therefore saw that Jesus was not there, neither his disciples, they also took shipping, and came to Că·pĕr′·nă·ŭm, seeking for Jesus. 25 And when they had found him on the other side of the sea, they said unto him, Rabbi, when camest thou hither? 26 Jesus answered them and said, Verily, verily, I say unto you, Ye seek me, not because ye saw the miracles, but because ye did eat of the loaves, and were filled. 27 Labour not for the meat which perisheth, but for that meat which endureth unto everlasting life, which the Son of man shall give unto you: for him hath God the Father sealed. 28 Then said they unto him, What shall we do, that we might work the works of God? 29 Jesus answered and said unto them, This is the work of God, that ye believe on him whom he hath sent.

30 They said therefore unto him, What sign shewest thou then, that we may see, and believe thee? what dost thou work?

31 Our fathers did eat măn'-nă in the desert; as it is written, He gave them bread from heaven to eat.

32 Then Jesus said unto them, Verily, verily, I say unto you, Moses gave you not that bread from heaven; but my Father giveth you the true bread from heaven.

33 For the bread of God is he which cometh down from heaven, and giveth life unto the world.

34 Then said they unto him, Lord, evermore give us this bread.

35 And Jesus said unto them, I am the bread of life: he that cometh to me shall never hunger; and he that believeth on me shall never thirst.

36 But I said unto you, That ye also have seen me, and believe not.

37 All that the Father giveth me shall come to me; and him that cometh to me I will in no wise cast out.

38 For I came down from heaven, not to do mine own will, but the will of him that sent me.

39 And this is the Father's will which hath sent me, that of all which he hath given me I should lose nothing, but should raise it up again at the last day.

40 And this is the will of him that sent me, that every one which seeth the Son, and believeth on him, may have everlasting life: and I will raise him up at the last day.

41 The Jews then murmured at him, because he said, I am the bread which came down from heaven.

42 And they said, Is not this Jesus, the son of Joseph, whose father and mother we know? how is it then that he saith, I came down from heaven?

43 Jesus therefore answered and said unto them, Murmur not among yourselves.

44 No man can come to me, except the Father which hath sent me draw him: and I will raise him up at the last day.

45 It is written in the prophets, And they shall be all taught of God. Every man therefore that hath heard, and hath learned of the Father, cometh unto me.

46 Not that any man hath seen the Father, save he which is of God, he hath seen the Father.

47 Verily, verily, I say unto you, He that believeth on me hath everlasting life.

48 I am that bread of life.

49 Your fathers did eat măn'-nă in the wilderness, and are dead.

50 This is the bread which cometh down from heaven, that a man may eat thereof, and not die.

51 I am the living bread which came down from heaven: if any man eat of this bread, he shall live for ever: and the bread that I will give is my flesh, which I will give for the life of the world.

52 The Jews therefore strove among themselves, saying, How can this man give us *his* flesh to eat?

53 Then Jesus said unto them, Verily, verily, I say unto you, Except ye eat the flesh of the Son of man, and drink his blood, ye have no life in you.

54 Whoso eateth my flesh, and drinketh my blood, hath eternal life; and I will raise him up at the last day.

55 For my flesh is meat indeed, and my blood is drink indeed.

56 He that eateth my flesh, and drinketh my blood, dwelleth in me, and I in him.

57 As the living Father hath sent me, and I live by the Father: so he that eateth me, even he shall live by me.

58 This is that bread which came down from heaven: not as your fathers did eat măn′-nă, and are dead: he that eateth of this bread shall live for ever.

59 These things said he in the synagogue, as he taught in Că-pĕr′-nă-ŭm.

94. MANY REJECT JESUS

60 Many therefore of his disciples, when they had heard *this*, said, This is an hard saying; who can hear it?

61 When Jesus knew in himself that his disciples murmured at it, he said unto them, Doth this offend you?

62 *What* and if ye shall see the Son of man ascend up where he was before?

63 It is the spirit that quickeneth; the flesh profiteth nothing: the words that I speak unto you, *they* are spirit, and *they* are life.

64 But there are some of you that believe not. For Jesus knew from the beginning who they were that believed not, and who should betray him.

65 And he said, Therefore said I unto you, that no man can come unto me, except it were given unto him of my Father.

66 ¶ From that *time* many of his disciples went back, and walked no more with him.

67 Then said Jesus unto the twelve, Will ye also go away?

68 Then Simon Peter answered him, Lord, to whom shall we go? thou hast the words of eternal life.

69 And we believe and are sure that thou art that Christ, the Son of the living God.

70 Jesus answered them, Have not I chosen you twelve, and one of you is a devil?

71 He spake of Judas Iscariot *the son* of Simon: for he it was that should betray him, being one of the twelve.

95. JEWS SEEK TO KILL JESUS

CHAPTER 7

AFTER these things Jesus walked in Galilee: for he would not walk in Jewry, because the Jews sought to kill him.

96. CONFLICT WITH SCRIBES AND PHARISEES OVER CLEANLINESS

CHAPTER 15

THEN came to Jesus scribes and Pharisees, which were of Jerusalem, saying,

2 Why do thy disciples transgress the tradition of the elders? for they wash not their hands when they eat bread.

7 *Ye* hypocrites, well did Ē·śāī´·ăs prophesy of you, saying,

8 This people draweth nigh unto me with their mouth, and honoureth me with *their* lips; but their heart is far from me.

9 But in vain they do worship me, teaching *for* doctrines the commandments of men.

3 But he answered and said unto them, Why do ye also transgress the commandment of God by your tradition?

4 For God commanded, saying, Honour thy father and mother: and, He that curseth father or mother, let him die the death.

5 But ye say, Whosoever shall say to *his* father or *his* mother, *It is* a gift, by whatsoever thou mightest be profited by me;

6 And honour not his father or his mother, *he shall be free.*

Thus have ye made the commandment of God of none effect by your tradition.

CHAPTER 7

THEN came together unto him the Pharisees, and certain of the scribes, which came from Jerusalem.

2 And when they saw some of his disciples eat bread with defiled, that is to say, with unwashen, hands, they found fault.

3 For the Pharisees, and all the Jews, except they wash *their* hands oft, eat not, holding the tradition of the elders.

4 And *when they come* from the market, except they wash, they eat not. And many other things there be, which they have received to hold, *as* the washing of cups, and pots, brasen vessels, and of tables.

5 Then the Pharisees and scribes asked him, Why walk not thy disciples according to the tradition of the elders, but eat bread with unwashen hands?

6 He answered and said unto them, Well hath Ē·śāī´·ăs prophesied of you hypocrites, as it is written, This people honoureth me with *their* lips, but their heart is far from me.

7 Howbeit in vain do they worship me, teaching *for* doctrines the commandments of men.

8 For laying aside the commandment of God, ye hold the tradition of men, *as* the washing of pots and cups: and many other such like things ye do.

9 And he said unto them, Full well ye reject the commandment of God, that ye may keep your own tradition.

10 For Moses said, Honour thy father and thy mother; and, Whoso curseth father or mother, let him die the death:

11 But ye say, If a man shall say to his father or mother, *It is* Cŏr´·băn, that is to say, a gift, by whatsoever thou mightest be profited by me; *he shall be free.*

12 And ye suffer him no more to do ought for his father or his mother;

13 Making the word of God of none effect through your tradition, which ye have delivered: and many such like things do ye.

MATTHEW – 15	MARK – 7	LUKE –	JOHN –
10 ¶ And he called the multitude, and said unto them, Hear, and understand: 11 Not that which goeth into the mouth defileth a man; but that which cometh out of the mouth, this defileth a man.	14 ¶ And when he had called all the people *unto him*, he said unto them, Hearken unto me every one *of you*, and understand: 15 There is nothing from without a man, that entering into him can defile him: but the things which come out of him, those are they that defile the man. 16 If any man have ears to hear, let him hear.		
12 Then came his disciples, and said unto him, Knowest thou that the Pharisees were offended, after they heard this saying? 13 But he answered and said, Every plant, which my heavenly Father hath not planted, shall be rooted up. 14 Let them alone: they be blind leaders of the blind. And if the blind lead the blind, both shall fall into the ditch.			
15 Then answered Peter and said unto him, Declare unto us this parable. 16 And Jesus said, Are ye also yet without understanding? 17 Do not ye yet understand, that whatsoever entereth in at the mouth goeth into the belly, and is cast out into the draught?	17 And when he was entered into the house from the people, his disciples asked him concerning the parable. 18 And he saith unto them, Are ye so without understanding also? Do ye not perceive, that whatsoever thing from without entereth into the man, *it* cannot defile him; 19 Because it entereth not into his heart, but into the belly, and goeth out into the draught, purging all meats?		
18 But those things which proceed out of the mouth come forth from the heart; and they defile the man. 19 For out of the heart proceed evil thoughts, murders, adulteries, fornications, thefts, false witness, blasphemies:	20 And he said, That which cometh out of the man, that defileth the man. 21 For from within, out of the heart of men, proceed evil thoughts, adulteries, fornications, murders, 22 Thefts, covetousness, wickedness, deceit, lasciviousness, an evil eye, blasphemy, pride, foolishness:		
20 These are *the things* which defile a man: but to eat with unwashen hands defileth not a man.	23 All these evil things come from within, and defile the man.		

97. JESUS HEALS A GENTILE'S DAUGHTER

MATTHEW – 15	MARK – 7	LUKE –	JOHN –
21 ¶ Then Jesus went thence, and departed into the coasts of Tyre and Sī́·dŏn.	24 ¶ And from thence he arose, and went into the borders of Tyre and Sī́·dŏn, and entered into an house, and would have no man know *it*: but he could not be hid. 25 For a *certain* woman, whose young daughter had an unclean spirit, heard of him, and came and fell at his feet:		
22 And, behold, a woman of Canaan came out of the same coasts, and cried unto him, saying, Have mercy on me, O Lord, *thou* Son of David; my daughter is grievously vexed with a devil. 23 But he answered her not a word. And his disciples came and besought him, saying, Send her away; for she crieth after us. 24 But he answered and said, I am not sent but unto the lost sheep of the house of Israel. 25 Then came she and worshipped him, saying, Lord, help me.	26 The woman was a Greek, a Sȳ·rō·phē·nĭç'·ĭ·ăn by nation; and she besought him that he would cast forth the devil out of her daughter.		

MATTHEW – 15	MARK – 7	LUKE –	JOHN –
26 But he answered and said, It is not meet to take the children's bread, and to cast *it* to dogs. 27 And she said, Truth, Lord: yet the dogs eat of the crumbs which fall from their masters' table. 28 Then Jesus answered and said unto her, O woman, great *is* thy faith: be it unto thee even as thou wilt. And her daughter was made whole from that very hour.	27 But Jesus said unto her, Let the children first be filled: for it is not meet to take the children's bread, and to cast *it* unto the dogs. 28 And she answered and said unto him, Yes, Lord: yet the dogs under the table eat of the children's crumbs. 29 And he said unto her, For this saying go thy way; the devil is gone out of thy daughter. 30 And when she was come to her house, she found the devil gone out, and her daughter laid upon the bed.		

98. RETURNS TO THE SEA OF GALILEE AND HEALS MANY

MATTHEW – 15	MARK – 7	LUKE –	JOHN –
29 And Jesus departed from thence, and came nigh unto the sea of Galilee; and went up into a mountain, and sat down there. 30 And great multitudes came unto him, having with them *those that were* lame, blind, dumb, maimed, and many others, and cast them down at Jesus' feet; and he healed them:	31 ¶ And again, departing from the coasts of Tyre and Sī′-dŏn, he came unto the sea of Galilee, through the midst of the coasts of Dĕ-căp′-ŏ-lĭs.		
	32 And they bring unto him one that was deaf, and had an impediment in his speech; and they beseech him to put his hand upon him. 33 And he took him aside from the multitude, and put his fingers into his ears, and he spit, and touched his tongue; 34 And looking up to heaven, he sighed, and saith unto him, Ĕph′-phă-thă, that is, Be opened. 35 And straightway his ears were opened, and the string of his tongue was loosed, and he spake plain. 36 And he charged them that they should tell no man: but the more he charged them, so much the more a great deal they published *it;*		
31 Insomuch that the multitude wondered, when they saw the dumb to speak, the maimed to be whole, the lame to walk, and the blind to see: and they glorified the God of Israel.	37 And were beyond measure astonished, saying, He hath done all things well: he maketh both the deaf to hear, and the dumb to speak.		

99. JESUS FEEDS FOUR THOUSAND

MATTHEW – 15	MARK – 7	LUKE –	JOHN –
32 ¶ Then Jesus called his disciples *unto him,* and said, I have compassion on the multitude, because they continue with me now three days, and have nothing to eat: and I will not send them away fasting, lest they faint in the way. 33 And his disciples say unto him, Whence should we have so much bread in the wilderness, as to fill so great a multitude? 34 And Jesus saith unto them, How many loaves have ye? And they said, Seven, and a few little fishes.	**CHAPTER 8** IN those days the multitude being very great, and having nothing to eat, Jesus called his disciples *unto him,* and saith unto them, 2 I have compassion on the multitude, because they have now been with me three days, and have nothing to eat: 3 And if I send them away fasting to their own houses, they will faint by the way: for divers of them came from far. 4 And his disciples answered him, From whence can a man satisfy these *men* with bread here in the wilderness? 5 And he asked them, How many loaves have ye? And they said, Seven.		

MATTHEW – 15,16	MARK – 8	LUKE –	JOHN –
35 And he commanded the multitude to sit down on the ground. 36 And he took the seven loaves and the fishes, and gave thanks, and brake *them,* and gave to his disciples, and the disciples to the multitude.	6 And he commanded the people to sit down on the ground: and he took the seven loaves, and gave thanks, and brake, and gave to his disciples to set before *them;* and they did set *them* before the people. 7 And they had a few small fishes: and he blessed, and commanded to set them also before *them.*		
37 And they did all eat, and were filled: and they took up of the broken *meat* that was left seven baskets full. 38 And they that did eat were four thousand men, beside women and children.	8 So they did eat, and were filled: and they took up of the broken *meat* that was left seven baskets. 9 And they that had eaten were about four thousand: and he sent them away.		

100. JESUS GOES TO MAGDALA

39 And he sent away the multitude, and took ship, and came into the coasts of Măg'-dă-lä.	10 ¶ And straightway he entered into a ship with his disciples, and came into the parts of Dăl-mă-nū'-thă.		

101. DISCOURSE ON SIGNS

CHAPTER 16 THE Pharisees also with the Săd'-dū-çẹes came, and tempting desired him that he would shew them a sign from heaven. 2 He answered and said unto them, When it is evening, ye say, *It will be* fair weather: for the sky is red. 3 And in the morning, *It will be* foul weather to day: for the sky is red and lowring. O *ye* hypocrites, ye can discern the face of the sky; but can ye not *discern* the signs of the times?	11 And the Pharisees came forth, and began to question with him, seeking of him a sign from heaven, tempting him.		
4 A wicked and adulterous generation seeketh after a sign; and there shall no sign be given unto it, but the sign of the prophet Jonas. And he left them, and departed.	12 And he sighed deeply in his spirit, and saith, Why doth this generation seek after a sign? verily I say unto you, There shall no sign be given unto this generation. 13 And he left them, and entering into the ship again departed to the other side.		

102. BEWARE OF THE LEAVEN OF THE PHARISEES

5 And when his disciples were come to the other side, they had forgotten to take bread. 6 ¶ Then Jesus said unto them, Take heed and beware of the leaven of the Pharisees and of the Săd'-dū-çẹes. 7 And they reasoned among themselves, saying, *It is* because we have taken no bread. 8 *Which* when Jesus perceived, he said unto them, O ye of little faith, why reason ye among yourselves, because ye have brought no bread?	14 ¶ Now *the disciples* had forgotten to take bread, neither had they in the ship with them more than one loaf. 15 And he charged them, saying, Take heed, beware of the leaven of the Pharisees, and *of* the leaven of Herod. 16 And they reasoned among themselves, saying, *It is* because we have no bread. 17 And when Jesus knew *it,* he saith unto them, Why reason ye, because ye have no bread? perceive ye not yet, neither understand? have ye your heart yet hardened? 18 Having eyes, see ye not? and having ears, hear ye not? and do ye not remember?		
9 Do ye not yet understand, neither remember the five loaves of the five thousand, and how many baskets ye took up? 10 Neither the seven loaves of the four thousand, and how many baskets ye took up?	19 When I brake the five loaves among five thousand, how many baskets full of fragments took ye up? They say unto him, Twelve. 20 And when the seven among four thousand, how many baskets full of fragments took ye up? And they said, Seven.		

MATTHEW	MARK	LUKE	JOHN
11 How is it that ye do not understand that I spake *it* not to you concerning bread, that ye should beware of the leaven of the Pharisees and of the Săd′-dū-çēėś? 12 Then understood they how that he bade *them* not beware of the leaven of bread, but of the doctrine of the Pharisees and of the Săd′-dū-çēėś.	21 And he said unto them, How is it that ye do not understand?		

103. BLIND MAN HEALED

MATTHEW	MARK	LUKE	JOHN
	22 ¶ And he cometh to Běth-sā′-ĭ-dă; and they bring a blind man unto him, and besought him to touch him. 23 And he took the blind man by the hand, and led him out of the town; and when he had spit on his eyes, and put his hands upon him, he asked him if he saw ought. 24 And he looked up, and said, I see men as trees, walking. 25 After that he put *his* hands again upon his eyes, and made him look up: and he was restored, and saw every man clearly. 26 And he sent him away to his house, saying, Neither go into the town, nor tell *it* to any in the town.		

104. HEROD WONDERS IF JESUS IS JOHN THE BAPTIST RAISED FROM THE DEAD

MATTHEW	MARK	LUKE	JOHN
CHAPTER 14 AT that time Herod the tĕ′-trärch heard of the fame of Jesus, 2 And said unto his servants, This is John the Baptist; he is risen from the dead; and therefore mighty works do shew forth themselves in him.	Ch. 6 14 And king Herod heard *of him;* (for his name was spread abroad:) and he said, That John the Baptist was risen from the dead, and therefore mighty works do shew forth themselves in him. 15 Others said, That it is Ē-lī′-ăs. And others said, That it is a prophet, or as one of the prophets. 16 But when Herod heard *thereof,* he said, It is John, whom I beheaded: he is risen from the dead.	7 ¶ Now Herod the tĕ′-trärch heard of all that was done by him: and he was perplexed, because that it was said of some, that John was risen from the dead; 8 And of some, that Ē-lī′-ăs had appeared; and of others, that one of the old prophets was risen again. 9 And Herod said, John have I beheaded: but who is this, of whom I hear such things? And he desired to see him.	

105. PETER TESTIFIES THAT JESUS IS THE CHRIST

MATTHEW	MARK	LUKE	JOHN
Ch. 16 13 ¶ When Jesus came into the coasts of Çāē-să-rē′-ă Philippi, he asked his disciples, saying, Whom do men say that I the Son of man am? 14 And they said, Some *say that thou art* John the Baptist: some, Ē-lī′-ăs; and others, Jeremias, or one of the prophets. 15 He saith unto them, But whom say ye that I am? 16 And Simon Peter answered and said, Thou art the Christ, the Son of the living God. 17 And Jesus answered and said unto him, Blessed art thou, Simon Băr-jŏ′-nă: for flesh and blood hath not revealed *it* unto thee, but my Father which is in heaven. 18 And I say also unto thee, That thou art Peter, and upon this rock I will build my church; and the gates of hell shall not prevail against it.	Ch. 8 27 ¶ And Jesus went out, and his disciples, into the towns of Çāē-să-rē′-ă Philippi: and by the way he asked his disciples, saying unto them, Whom do men say that I am? 28 And they answered, John the Baptist: but some *say,* Ē-lī′-ăs; and others, One of the prophets. 29 And he saith unto them, But whom say ye that I am? And Peter answereth and saith unto him, Thou art the Christ.	18 ¶ And it came to pass, as he was alone praying, his disciples were with him: and he asked them, saying, Whom say the people that I am? 19 They answering said, John the Baptist; but some *say,* Ē-lī′-ăs; and others *say,* that one of the old prophets is risen again. 20 He said unto them, But whom say ye that I am? Peter answering said, The Christ of God.	

MATTHEW	MARK	LUKE	JOHN
19 And I will give unto thee the keys of the kingdom of heaven: and whatsoever thou shalt bind on earth shall be bound in heaven: and whatsoever thou shalt loose on earth shall be loosed in heaven. 20 Then charged he his disciples that they should tell no man that he was Jesus the Christ.	30 And he charged them that they should tell no man of him.	21 And he straitly charged them, and commanded *them* to tell no man that thing;	

106. JESUS FORETELLS HIS DEATH AND RESURRECTION

MATTHEW	MARK	LUKE	JOHN
21 ¶ From that time forth began Jesus to shew unto his disciples, how that he must go unto Jerusalem, and suffer many things of the elders and chief priests and scribes, and be killed, and be raised again the third day. 22 Then Peter took him, and began to rebuke him, saying, Be it far from thee, Lord: this shall not be unto thee. 23 But he turned, and said unto Peter, Get thee behind me, Satan: thou art an offence unto me: for thou savourest not the things that be of God, but those that be of men. 24 ¶ Then said Jesus unto his disciples, If any *man* will come after me, let him deny himself, and take up his cross, and follow me. 25 For whosoever will save his life shall lose it: and whosoever will lose his life for my sake shall find it. 26 For what is a man profited, if he shall gain the whole world, and lose his own soul? or what shall a man give in exchange for his soul? 27 For the Son of man shall come in the glory of his Father with his angels; and then he shall reward every man according to his works. 28 Verily I say unto you, There be some standing here, which shall not taste of death, till they see the Son of man coming in his kingdom.	31 And he began to teach them, that the Son of man must suffer many things, and be rejected of the elders, and *of* the chief priests, and scribes, and be killed, and after three days rise again. 32 And he spake that saying openly. And Peter took him, and began to rebuke him. 33 But when he had turned about and looked on his disciples, he rebuked Peter, saying, Get thee behind me, Satan: for thou savourest not the things that be of God, but the things that be of men. 34 ¶ And when he had called the people *unto him* with his disciples also, he said unto them, Whosoever will come after me, let him deny himself, and take up his cross, and follow me. 35 For whosoever will save his life shall lose it; but whosoever shall lose his life for my sake and the gospel's, the same shall save it. 36 For what shall it profit a man, if he shall gain the whole world, and lose his own soul? 37 Or what shall a man give in exchange for his soul? 38 Whosoever therefore shall be ashamed of me and of my words in this adulterous and sinful generation; of him also shall the Son of man be ashamed, when he cometh in the glory of his Father with the holy angels. CHAPTER 9 AND he said unto them, Verily I say unto you, That there be some of them that stand here, which shall not taste of death, till they have seen the kingdom of God come with power.	22 Saying, The Son of man must suffer many things, and be rejected of the elders and chief priests and scribes, and be slain, and be raised the third day. 23 ¶ And he said to *them* all, If any *man* will come after me, let him deny himself, and take up his cross daily, and follow me. 24 For whosoever will save his life shall lose it: but whosoever will lose his life for my sake, the same shall save it. 25 For what is a man advantaged, if he gain the whole world, and lose himself, or be cast away? 26 For whosoever shall be ashamed of me and of my words, of him shall the Son of man be ashamed, when he shall come in his own glory, and *in his* Father's, and of the holy angels. 27 But I tell you of a truth, there be some standing here, which shall not taste of death, till they see the kingdom of God.	

107. THE TRANSFIGURATION

MATTHEW	MARK	LUKE	JOHN
CHAPTER 17 AND after six days Jesus taketh Peter, James, and John his brother, and bringeth them up into an high mountain apart, 2 And was transfigured before them: and his face did shine as the sun, and his raiment was white as the light. 3 And, behold, there appeared unto them Moses and E·lī′·ăs talking with him.	2 ¶ And after six days Jesus taketh *with him* Peter, and James, and John, and leadeth them up into an high mountain apart by themselves: and he was transfigured before them. 3 And his raiment became shining, exceeding white as snow; so as no fuller on earth can white them. 4 And there appeared unto them E·lī′·ăs with Moses: and they were talking with Jesus.	28 ¶ And it came to pass about an eight days after these sayings, he took Peter and John and James, and went up into a mountain to pray. 29 And as he prayed, the fashion of his countenance was altered, and his raiment *was* white *and* glistering. 30 And, behold, there talked with him two men, which were Moses and E·lī′·ăs: 31 Who appeared in glory, and spake of his decease which he should accomplish at Jerusalem.	

| | | 32 But Peter and they that were with him were heavy with sleep: and when they were a- wake, they saw his glory, and the two men that stood with him. | |

LUKE

32 But Peter and they that were with him were heavy with sleep: and when they were awake, they saw his glory, and the two men that stood with him.

33 And it came to pass, as they departed from him, Peter said unto Jesus, Master, it is good for us to be here: and let us make three tabernacles; one for thee, and one for Moses, and one for Ē·lī'·ăs: not knowing what he said.

MATTHEW

4 Then answered Peter, and said unto Jesus, Lord, it is good for us to be here: if thou wilt, let us make here three taber- nacles; one for thee, and one for Moses, and one for Ē·lī'·ăs.

5 While he yet spake, behold, a bright cloud overshadowed them: and behold a voice out of the cloud, which said, This is my beloved Son, in whom I am well pleased; hear ye him.

6 And when the disciples heard *it*, they fell on their face, and were sore afraid.

7 And Jesus came and touched them, and said, Arise, and be not afraid.

8 And when they had lifted up their eyes, they saw no man, save Jesus only.

9 And as they came down from the mountain, Jesus charged them, saying, Tell the vision to no man, until the Son of man be risen again from the dead.

10 And his disciples asked him, saying, Why then say the scribes that Ē·lī'·ăs must first come?

11 And Jesus answered and said unto them, Ē·lī'·ăs truly shall first come, and restore all things.

12 But I say unto you, That Ē·lī'·ăs is come already, and they knew him not, but have done unto him whatsoever they listed. Likewise shall also the Son of man suffer of them.

13 Then the disciples under- stood that he spake unto them of John the Baptist.

MARK

5 And Peter answered and said to Jesus, Master, it is good for us to be here: and let us make three tabernacles; one for thee, and one for Moses, and one for Ē·lī'·ăs.

6 For he wist not what to say; for they were sore afraid.

7 And there was a cloud that overshadowed them: and a voice came out of the cloud, saying, This is my beloved Son: hear him.

8 And suddenly, when they had looked round about, they saw no man any more, save Jesus only with themselves.

9 And as they came down from the mountain, he charged them that they should tell no man what things they had seen, till the Son of man were risen from the dead.

10 And they kept that saying with themselves, questioning one with another what the rising from the dead should mean.

11 ¶ And they asked him, say- ing, Why say the scribes that Ē·lī'·ăs must first come?

12 And he answered and told them, Ē·lī'·ăs verily cometh first, and restoreth all things; and how it is written of the Son of man, that he must suffer many things, and be set at nought.

13 But I say unto you, That Ē·lī'·ăs is indeed come, and they have done unto him what- soever they listed, as it is written of him.

LUKE (continued)

34 While he thus spake, there came a cloud, and overshadow- ed them: and they feared as they entered into the cloud.

35 And there came a voice out of the cloud, saying, This is my beloved Son: hear him.

36 And when the voice was past, Jesus was found alone.

And they kept *it* close, and told no man in those days any of those things which they had seen.

108. DEMONIC BOY HEALED

MATTHEW

14 ¶ And when they were come to the multitude,

there came to him a *certain* man, kneeling down to him, and say- ing,

15 Lord, have mercy on my son: for he is lunatick, and sore vexed: for ofttimes he fall- eth into the fire, and oft into the water.

16 And I brought him to thy disciples, and they could not cure him.

MARK

14 ¶ And when he came to *his* disciples, he saw a great multitude about them, and the scribes questioning with them.

15 And straightway all the people, when they beheld him, were greatly amazed, and run- ning to *him* saluted him.

16 And he asked the scribes, What question ye with them?

17 And one of the multitude answered and said, Master, I have brought unto thee my son, which hath a dumb spirit;

18 And wheresoever he taketh him, he teareth him: and he foameth, and gnasheth with his teeth, and pineth away: and I spake to thy disciples that they should cast him out; and they could not.

LUKE

37 ¶ And it came to pass, that on the next day, when they were come down from the hill, much people met him.

38 And, behold, a man of the company cried out, saying, Master, I beseech thee, look upon my son: for he is mine only child.

39 And, lo, a spirit taketh him, and he suddenly crieth out; and it teareth him that he foameth again, and bruising him hardly departeth from him.

40 And I besought thy disciples to cast him out; and they could not.

MATTHEW – 17	MARK – 9	LUKE – 9	JOHN –
17 Then Jesus answered and said, O faithless and perverse generation, how long shall I be with you? how long shall I suffer you? bring him hither to me.	19 He answereth him, and saith, O faithless generation, how long shall I be with you? how long shall I suffer you? bring him unto me.	41 And Jesus answering said, O faithless and perverse generation, how long shall I be with you, and suffer you? Bring thy son hither.	
	20 And they brought him unto him: and when he saw him, straightway the spirit tare him; and he fell on the ground, and wallowed foaming.		
	21 And he asked his father, How long is it ago since this came unto him? And he said, Of a child.		
	22 And ofttimes it hath cast him into the fire, and into the waters, to destroy him: but if thou canst do any thing, have compassion on us, and help us.		
	23 Jesus said unto him, If thou canst believe, all things *are* possible to him that believeth.		
	24 And straightway the father of the child cried out, and said with tears, Lord, I believe; help thou mine unbelief.		
	25 When Jesus saw that the people came running together, he rebuked the foul spirit, saying unto him, *Thou* dumb and deaf spirit, I charge thee, come out of him, and enter no more into him.		
18 And Jesus rebuked the devil; and he departed out of him: and the child was cured from that very hour.	26 And *the spirit* cried, and rent him sore, and came out of him: and he was as one dead; insomuch that many said, He is dead.	42 And as he was yet a coming, the devil threw him down, and tare *him*. And Jesus rebuked the unclean spirit,	
	27 But Jesus took him by the hand, and lifted him up; and he arose.	and healed the child, and delivered him again to his father. 43a ¶ And they were all amazed at the mighty power of God.	
19 Then came the disciples to Jesus apart, and said, Why could not we cast him out?	28 And when he was come into the house, his disciples asked him privately, Why could not we cast him out?		
20 And Jesus said unto them, Because of your unbelief: for verily I say unto you, If ye have faith as a grain of mustard seed, ye shall say unto this mountain, Remove hence to yonder place; and it shall remove; and nothing shall be impossible unto you.			
21 Howbeit this kind goeth not out but by prayer and fasting.	29 And he said unto them, This kind can come forth by nothing, but by prayer and fasting.		

109. AGAIN FORETELLS HIS DEATH AND RESURRECTION

MATTHEW – 17	MARK – 9	LUKE – 9	JOHN –
	30 ¶ And they departed thence, and passed through Galilee; and he would not that any man should know *it*.	43b But while they wondered every one at all things which Jesus did, he said unto his disciples,	
22 ¶ And while they abode in Galilee, Jesus said unto them, The Son of man shall be betrayed into the hands of men:	31 For he taught his disciples, and said unto them, The Son of man is delivered into the hands of men, and they shall kill him; and after that he is killed, he shall rise the third day.	44 Let these sayings sink down into your ears: for the Son of man shall be delivered into the hands of men.	
23 And they shall kill him, and the third day he shall be raised again. And they were exceeding sorry.	32 But they understood not that saying, and were afraid to ask him.	45 But they understood not this saying, and it was hid from them, that they perceived it not: and they feared to ask him of that saying.	

110. TRIBUTE MONEY

24 ¶ And when they were come to Că·pĕr′·nă·ŭm, they that received tribute *money* came to Peter, and said, Doth not your master pay tribute?

25 He saith, Yes. And when he was come into the house, Jesus prevented him, saying, What thinkest thou, Simon? of whom do the kings of the earth take custom or tribute? of their own children, or of strangers?

26 Peter saith unto him, Of strangers. Jesus saith unto him, Then are the children free.

27 Notwithstanding, lest we should offend them, go thou to the sea, and cast an hook, and take up the fish that first cometh up; and when thou hast opened his mouth, thou shalt find a piece of money: that take, and give unto them for me and thee.

33a ¶ And he came to Că·pĕr′·nă·ŭm:

111. DISCOURSE ON HUMILITY, SERVICE AND FORGIVENESS

CHAPTER 18

AT the same time came the disciples unto Jesus, saying, Who is the greatest in the kingdom of heaven?

33b and being in the house he asked them, What was it that ye disputed among yourselves by the way?

34 But they held their peace: for by the way they had disputed among themselves, who *should be* the greatest.

35 And he sat down, and called the twelve, and saith unto them, If any man desire to be first, *the same* shall be last of all, and servant of all.

---

46 ¶ Then there arose a reasoning among them, which of them should be greatest.

---

2 And Jesus called a little child unto him, and set him in the midst of them,

3 And said, Verily I say unto you, Except ye be converted, and become as little children, ye shall not enter into the kingdom of heaven.

4 Whosoever therefore shall humble himself as this little child, the same is greatest in the kingdom of heaven.

5 And whoso shall receive one such little child in my name receiveth me.

---

36 And he took a child, and set him in the midst of them: and when he had taken him in his arms, he said unto them,

---

47 And Jesus, perceiving the thought of their heart, took a child, and set him by him,

---

37 Whosoever shall receive one of such children in my name, receiveth me: and whosoever shall receive me, receiveth not me, but him that sent me.

---

48 And said unto them, Whosoever shall receive this child in my name receiveth me: and whosoever shall receive me receiveth him that sent me: for he that is least among you all, the same shall be great.

---

38 ¶ And John answered him, saying, Master, we saw one casting out devils in thy name, and he followeth not us: and we forbad him, because he followeth not us.

39 But Jesus said, Forbid him not: for there is no man which shall do a miracle in my name, that can lightly speak evil of me.

40 For he that is not against us is on our part.

41 For whosoever shall give you a cup of water to drink in my name, because ye belong to Christ, verily I say unto you, he shall not lose his reward.

---

49 ¶ And John answered and said, Master, we saw one casting out devils in thy name; and we forbad him, because he followeth not with us.

50 And Jesus said unto him, Forbid *him* not:

for he that is not against us is for us.

---

6 But whoso shall offend one of these little ones which believe in me, it were better for him that a millstone were hanged about his neck, and *that* he were drowned in the depth of the sea.

---

42 And whosoever shall offend one of *these* little ones that believe in me, it is better for him that a millstone were hanged about his neck, and he were cast into the sea.

MATTHEW – 18

7 ¶ Woe unto the world because of offences! for it must needs be that offences come; but woe to that man by whom the offence cometh!

8 Wherefore if thy hand or thy foot offend thee, cut them off, and cast *them* from thee: it is better for thee to enter into life halt or maimed, rather than having two hands or two feet to be cast into everlasting fire.

9 And if thine eye offend thee, pluck it out, and cast *it* from thee: it is better for thee to enter into life with one eye, rather than having two eyes to be cast into hell fire.

10 Take heed that ye despise not one of these little ones; for I say unto you, That in heaven their angels do always behold the face of my Father which is in heaven.

11 For the Son of man is come to save that which was lost.

12 How think ye? if a man have an hundred sheep, and one of them be gone astray, doth he not leave the ninety and nine, and goeth into the mountains, and seeketh that which is gone astray?

13 And if so be that he find it, verily I say unto you, he rejoiceth more of that *sheep*, than of the ninety and nine which went not astray.

14 Even so it is not the will of your Father which is in heaven, that one of these little ones should perish.

15 ¶ Moreover if thy brother shall trespass against thee, go and tell him his fault between thee and him alone: if he shall hear thee, thou hast gained thy brother.

16 But if he will not hear *thee*, *then* take with thee one or two more, that in the mouth of two or three witnesses every word may be established.

17 And if he shall neglect to hear them, tell *it* unto the church: but if he neglect to hear the church, let him be unto thee as an heathen man and a publican.

18 Verily I say unto you, Whatsoever ye shall bind on earth shall be bound in heaven: and whatsoever ye shall loose on earth shall be loosed in heaven.

MARK – 9

43 And if thy hand offend thee, cut it off: it is better for thee to enter into life maimed, than having two hands to go into hell, into the fire that never shall be quenched:

44 Where their worm dieth not, and the fire is not quenched.

45 And if thy foot offend thee, cut it off: it is better for thee to enter halt into life, than having two feet to be cast into hell, into the fire that never shall be quenched:

46 Where their worm dieth not, and the fire is not quenched.

47 And if thine eye offend thee, pluck it out: it is better for thee to enter into the kingdom of God with one eye, than having two eyes to be cast into hell fire:

48 Where their worm dieth not, and the fire is not quenched.

49 For every one shall be salted with fire, and every sacrifice shall be salted with salt.

50 Salt *is* good: but if the salt have lost his saltness, wherewith will ye season it? Have salt in yourselves, and have peace one with another.

19 Again I say unto you, That if two of you shall agree on earth as touching any thing that they shall ask, it shall be done for them of my Father which is in heaven.

20 For where two or three are gathered together in my name, there am I in the midst of them.

21 ¶ Then came Peter to him, and said, Lord, how oft shall my brother sin against me, and I forgive him? till seven times?

22 Jesus saith unto him, I say not unto thee, Until seven times: but, Until seventy times seven.

23 ¶ Therefore is the kingdom of heaven likened unto a certain king, which would take account of his servants.

24 And when he had begun to reckon, one was brought unto him, which owed him ten thousand talents.

25 But forasmuch as he had not to pay, his lord commanded him to be sold, and his wife, and children, and all that he had, and payment to be made.

26 The servant therefore fell down, and worshipped him, saying, Lord, have patience with me, and I will pay thee all.

27 Then the lord of that servant was moved with compassion, and loosed him, and forgave him the debt.

28 But the same servant went out, and found one of his fellowservants, which owed him an hundred pence: and he laid hands on him, and took *him* by the throat, saying, Pay me that thou owest.

29 And his fellowservant fell down at his feet, and besought him, saying, Have patience with me, and I will pay thee all.

30 And he would not: but went and cast him into prison, till he should pay the debt.

31 So when his fellowservants saw what was done, they were very sorry, and came and told unto their lord all that was done.

32 Then his lord, after that he had called him, said unto him, O thou wicked servant, I forgave thee all that debt, because thou desiredst me:

33 Shouldest not thou also have had compassion on thy fellowservant, even as I had pity on thee?

34 And his lord was wroth, and delivered him to the tormentors, till he should pay all that was due unto him.

35 So likewise shall my heavenly Father do also unto you, if ye from your hearts forgive not every one his brother their trespasses.

112. JESUS SENDS FORTH THE SEVENTY *

CHAPTER 10

AFTER these things the Lord appointed other seventy also, and sent them two and two before his face into every city and place, whither he himself would come.

*When and from where were the Seventy sent forth? See note 112.

LUKE – 10

2 Therefore said he unto them, The harvest truly *is* great, but the labourers *are* few: pray ye therefore the Lord of the harvest, that he would send forth labourers into his harvest.

3 Go your ways: behold, I send you forth as lambs among wolves.

4 Carry neither purse, nor scrip, nor shoes: and salute no man by the way.

5 And into whatsoever house ye enter, first say, Peace *be* to this house.

6 And if the son of peace be there, your peace shall rest upon it: if not, it shall turn to you again.

7 And in the same house remain, eating and drinking such things as they give: for the labourer is worthy of his hire. Go not from house to house.

8 And into whatsoever city ye enter, and they receive you, eat such things as are set before you:

9 And heal the sick that are therein, and say unto them, The kingdom of God is come nigh unto you.

10 But into whatsoever city ye enter, and they receive you not, go your ways out into the streets of the same, and say,

11 Even the very dust of your city, which cleaveth on us, we do wipe off against you: notwithstanding be ye sure of this, that the kingdom of God is come nigh unto you.

12 But I say unto you, that it shall be more tolerable in that day for Sodom, than for that city.

MATTHEW – 11

20 ¶ Then began he to upbraid the cities wherein most of his mighty works were done, because they repented not:

21 Woe unto thee, Chō·ra´·zĭn! woe unto thee, Bĕth·sā´·ĭ·dă! for if the mighty works, which were done in you, had been done in Tyre and Sī´·dŏn, they would have repented long ago in sackcloth and ashes.

22 But I say unto you, It shall be more tolerable for Tyre and Sī´·dŏn at the day of judgment, than for you.

23 And thou, Că·pĕr´·nă·ŭm, which art exalted unto heaven, shalt be brought down to hell: for if the mighty works, which have been done in thee, had been done in Sodom, it would have remained until this day.

24 But I say unto you, That it shall be more tolerable for the land of Sodom in the day of judgment, than for thee.

LUKE – 10

13 Woe unto thee, Chō·ra´·zĭn! woe unto thee, Bĕth·sā´·ĭ·dă! for if the mighty works had been done in Tyre and Sī´·dŏn, which have been done in you, they had a great while ago repented, sitting in sackcloth and ashes.

14 But it shall be more tolerable for Tyre and Sī´·dŏn at the judgment, than for you.

15 And thou, Că·pĕr´·nă·ŭm, which art exalted to heaven, shalt be thrust down to hell.

16 He that heareth you heareth me; and he that despiseth you despiseth me; and he that despiseth me despiseth him that sent me.

VI.   THE LATER JUDEAN MINISTRY

113. JESUS IS URGED TO ATTEND THE FEAST OF TABERNACLES *

2 Now the Jews' feast of tabernacles was at hand.

3 His brethren therefore said unto him, Depart hence, and go into Judæa, that thy disciples also may see the works that thou doest.

4 For *there is* no man *that* doeth any thing in secret, and he himself seeketh to be known openly. If thou do these things, shew thyself to the world.

5 For neither did his brethren believe in him.

6 Then Jesus said unto them, My time is not yet come: but your time is alway ready.

7 The world cannot hate you; but me it hateth, because I testify of it, that the works thereof are evil.

8 Go ye up unto this feast: I go not up yet unto this feast; for my time is not yet full come.

9 When he had said these words unto them, he abode *still* in Galilee.

114. JESUS GOES TO THE FEAST IN SECRET

51 ¶ And it came to pass, when the time was come that he should be received up, he stedfastly set his face to go to Jerusalem,

52 And sent messengers before his face: and they went, and entered into a village of the Să-măr´-ĭ-tăns, to make ready for him.

53 And they did not receive him, because his face was as though he would go to Jerusalem.

54 And when his disciples James and John saw *this*, they said, Lord, wilt thou that we command fire to come down from heaven, and consume them, even as Ē-lī´-ăs did?

55 But he turned, and rebuked them, and said, Ye know not what manner of spirit ye are of.

56 For the Son of man is not come to destroy men's lives, but to save *them*. And they went to another village.

10 ¶ But when his brethren were gone up, then went he also up unto the feast, not openly, but as it were in secret.

115. SACRIFICE REQUIRED TO FOLLOW JESUS

19 And a certain scribe came, and said unto him, Master, I will follow thee whithersoever thou goest.

20 And Jesus saith unto him, The foxes have holes, and the birds of the air *have* nests; but the Son of man hath not where to lay *his* head.

57 ¶ And it came to pass, that, as they went in the way, a certain *man* said unto him, Lord, I will follow thee whithersoever thou goest.

58 And Jesus said unto him, Foxes have holes, and birds of the air *have* nests; but the Son of man hath not where to lay *his* head.

*Feast of Tabernacles, see note 113.

MATTHEW – 8	MARK –	LUKE – 9	JOHN – 7
21 And another of his disciples said unto him, Lord, suffer me first to go and bury my father. 22 But Jesus said unto him, Follow me; and let the dead bury their dead.		59 And he said unto another, Follow me. But he said, Lord, suffer me first to go and bury my father. 60 Jesus said unto him. Let the dead bury their dead: but go thou and preach the kingdom of God. 61 And another also said, Lord, I will follow thee; but let me first go bid them fare-well, which are at home at my house. 62 And Jesus said unto him, No man, having put his hand to the plough, and looking back, is fit for the kingdom of God.	

116. CROWDS AT THE FEAST DISCUSSING JESUS

			11 Then the Jews sought him at the feast, and said, Where is he? 12 And there was much mur-muring among the people con-cerning him: for some said, He is a good man: others said, Nay; but he deceiveth the people. 13 Howbeit no man spake openly of him for fear of the Jews.

117. JESUS TEACHES AT THE TEMPLE *

			14 ¶ Now about the midst of the feast Jesus went up into the temple, and taught. 15 And the Jews marvelled, saying, How knoweth this man letters, having never learned? 16 Jesus answered them, and said, My doctrine is not mine, but his that sent me. 17 If any man will do his will, he shall know of the doctrine, whether it be of God, or *whether* I speak of myself. 18 He that speaketh of himself seeketh his own glory: but he that seeketh his glory that sent him, the same is true, and no unrighteousness is in him. 19 Did not Moses give you the law, and *yet* none of you keep-eth the law? Why go ye about to kill me? 20 The people answered and said, Thou hast a devil: who goeth about to kill thee? 21 Jesus answered and said unto them, I have done one work, and ye all marvel. 22 Moses therefore gave unto you circumcision; (not because it is of Moses, but of the fa-thers;) and ye on the sabbath day circumcise a man. 23 If a man on the sabbath day receive circumcision, that the law of Moses should not be broken; are ye angry at me, because I have made a man every whit whole on the sab-bath day? 24 Judge not according to the appearance, but judge righteous judgment. 25 Then said some of them of Jerusalem, Is not this he, whom they seek to kill? 26 But, lo, he speaketh boldly, and they say nothing unto him. Do the rulers know indeed that this is the very Christ?

*See note 117.

MATTHEW –	MARK –	LUKE –	JOHN – 7
			27 Howbeit we know this man whence he is: but when Christ cometh, no man knoweth whence he is.
			28 Then cried Jesus in the temple as he taught, saying, Ye both know me, and ye know whence I am: and I am not come of myself, but he that sent me is true, whom ye know not.
			29 But I know him: for I am from him, and he hath sent me.
			30 Then they sought to take him: but no man laid hands on him, because his hour was not yet come.
			31 And many of the people believed on him, and said, When Christ cometh, will he do more miracles than these which this *man* hath done?
			32 ¶ The Pharisees heard that the people murmured such things concerning him; and the Pharisees and the chief priests sent officers to take him.
			33 Then said Jesus unto them, Yet a little while am I with you, and *then* I go unto him that sent me.
			34 Ye shall seek me, and shall not find *me:* and where I am, *thither* ye cannot come.
			35 Then said the Jews among themselves, Whither will he go, that we shall not find him? will he go unto the dispersed among the Gentiles, and teach the Gentiles?
			36 What *manner of* saying is this that he said, Ye shall seek me, and shall not find *me:* and where I am, *thither* ye cannot come?

118. CONFUSED CROWDS DEBATING ABOUT JESUS

MATTHEW	MARK	LUKE	JOHN
			37 In the last day, that great *day* of the feast, Jesus stood and cried, saying, If any man thirst, let him come unto me, and drink.
			38 He that believeth on me, as the scripture hath said, out of his belly shall flow rivers of living water.
			39 (But this spake he of the Spirit, which they that believe on him should receive: for the Holy Ghost was not yet *given;* because that Jesus was not yet glorified.)
			40 ¶ Many of the people therefore, when they heard this saying, said, Of a truth this is the Prophet.
			41 Others said, This is the Christ. But some said, Shall Christ come out of Galilee?
			42 Hath not the scripture said, That Christ cometh of the seed of David, and out of the town of Bethlehem, where David was?
			43 So there was a division among the people because of him.
			44 And some of them would have taken him; but no man laid hands on him.
			45 ¶ Then came the officers to the chief priests and Pharisees; and they said unto them, Why have ye not brought him?
			46 The officers answered, Never man spake like this man.

MATTHEW –	MARK –	LUKE –	JOHN – 7,8
			47 Then answered them the Pharisees, Are ye also deceived?
			48 Have any of the rulers or of the Pharisees believed on him?
			49 But this people who knoweth not the law are cursed.
			50 Nĭc-ŏ-dē´-mŭs saith unto them, (he that came to Jesus by night, being one of them,)
			51 Doth our law judge *any* man, before it hear him, and know what he doeth?
			52 They answered and said unto him, Art thou also of Galilee? Search, and look: for out of Galilee ariseth no prophet.
			53 And every man went unto his own house.

119. WOMAN TAKEN IN ADULTERY

MATTHEW	MARK	LUKE	JOHN
			CHAPTER 8
			JESUS went unto the mount of Olives.
			2 And early in the morning he came again into the temple, and all the people came unto him; and he sat down, and taught them.
			3 And the scribes and Pharisees brought unto him a woman taken in adultery; and when they had set her in the midst,
			4 They say unto him, Master, this woman was taken in adultery, in the very act.
			5 Now Moses in the law commanded us, that such should be stoned: but what sayest thou?
			6 This they said, tempting him, that they might have to accuse him. But Jesus stooped down, and with *his* finger wrote on the ground, *as though he heard them not.*
			7 So when they continued asking him, he lifted up himself, and said unto them, He that is without sin among you, let him first cast a stone at her.
			8 And again he stooped down, and wrote on the ground.
			9 And they which heard *it*, being convicted by *their own* conscience, went out one by one, beginning at the eldest, *even* unto the last: and Jesus was left alone, and the woman standing in the midst.
			10 When Jesus had lifted up himself, and saw none but the woman, he said unto her, Woman, where are those thine accusers? hath no man condemned thee?
			11 She said, No man, Lord. And Jesus said unto her, Neither do I condemn thee: go, and sin no more.

120. JESUS TESTIFIES OF HIMSELF

MATTHEW	MARK	LUKE	JOHN
			12 ¶ Then spake Jesus again unto them, saying, I am the light of the world: he that followeth me shall not walk in darkness, but shall have the light of life.
			13 The Pharisees therefore said unto him, Thou bearest record of thyself; thy record is not true.

			14 Jesus answered and said unto them, Though I bear record of myself, *yet* my record is true: for I know whence I came, and whither I go; but ye cannot tell whence I come, and whither I go. 15 Ye judge after the flesh; I judge no man. 16 And yet if I judge, my judgment is true: for I am not alone, but I and the Father that sent me. 17 It is also written in your law, that the testimony of two men is true. 18 I am one that bear witness of myself, and the Father that sent me beareth witness of me. 19 Then said they unto him, Where is thy Father? Jesus answered, Ye neither know me, nor my Father: if ye had known me, ye should have known my Father also. 20 These words spake Jesus in the treasury, as he taught in the temple: and no man laid hands on him; for his hour was not yet come. 21 Then said Jesus again unto them, I go my way, and ye shall seek me, and shall die in your sins: whither I go, ye cannot come. 22 Then said the Jews, Will he kill himself? because he saith, Whither I go, ye cannot come. 23 And he said unto them, Ye are from beneath; I am from above: ye are of this world; I am not of this world. 24 I said therefore unto you, that ye shall die in your sins: for if ye believe not that I am *he*, ye shall die in your sins. 25 Then said they unto him, Who art thou? And Jesus saith unto them, Even *the same* that I said unto you from the beginning. 26 I have many things to say and to judge of you: but he that sent me is true; and I speak to the world those things which I have heard of him. 27 They understood not that he spake to them of the Father. 28 Then said Jesus unto them, When ye have lifted up the Son of man, then shall ye know that I am *he*, and *that* I do nothing of myself; but as my Father hath taught me, I speak these things. 29 And he that sent me is with me: the Father hath not left me alone; for I do always those things that please him. 30 As he spake these words, many believed on him.

121. WHO IS ABRAHAM'S SEED?

			31 Then said Jesus to those Jews which believed on him, If ye continue in my word, *then* are ye my disciples indeed; 32 And ye shall know the truth, and the truth shall make you free. 33 ¶ They answered him, We be Abraham's seed, and were never in bondage to any man: how sayest thou, Ye shall be made free?

34 Jesus answered them, Verily, verily, I say unto you, Whosoever committeth sin is the servant of sin.

35 And the servant abideth not in the house for ever: *but* the Son abideth ever.

36 If the Son therefore shall make you free, ye shall be free indeed.

37 I know that ye are Abraham's seed; but ye seek to kill me, because my word hath no place in you.

38 I speak that which I have seen with my Father: and ye do that which ye have seen with your father.

39 They answered and said unto him, Abraham is our father. Jesus saith unto them, If ye were Abraham's children, ye would do the works of Abraham.

40 But now ye seek to kill me, a man that hath told you the truth, which I have heard of God: this did not Abraham.

41 Ye do the deeds of your father. Then said they to him, We be not born of fornication; we have one Father, *even* God.

42 Jesus said unto them, If God were your Father, ye would love me: for I proceeded forth and came from God; neither came I of myself, but he sent me.

43 Why do ye not understand my speech? *even* because ye cannot hear my word.

44 Ye are of *your* father the devil, and the lusts of your father ye will do. He was a murderer from the beginning, and abode not in the truth, because there is no truth in him. When he speaketh a lie, he speaketh of his own: for he is a liar, and the father of it.

45 And because I tell *you* the truth, ye believe me not.

46 Which of you convinceth me of sin? And if I say the truth, why do ye not believe me?

47 He that is of God heareth God's words: ye therefore hear *them* not, because ye are not of God.

48 Then answered the Jews, and said unto him, Say we not well that thou art a Să·măr´·ĭ·tăn, and hast a devil?

49 Jesus answered, I have not a devil; but I honour my Father, and ye do dishonour me.

50 And I seek not mine own glory: there is one that seeketh and judgeth.

51 Verily, verily, I say unto you, If a man keep my saying, he shall never see death.

52 Then said the Jews unto him, Now we know that thou hast a devil. Abraham is dead, and the prophets; and thou sayest, If a man keep my saying, he shall never taste of death.

53 Art thou greater than our father Abraham, which is dead? and the prophets are dead: whom makest thou thyself?

54 Jesus answered, If I honour myself, my honour is nothing: it is my Father that honoureth me; of whom ye say, that he is your God:

MATTHEW –	MARK –	LUKE –	JOHN – 8,9
			55 Yet ye have not known him; but I know him: and if I should say, I know him not, I shall be a liar like unto you: but I know him, and keep his saying.
			56 Your father Abraham rejoiced to see my day: and he saw *it*, and was glad.
			57 Then said the Jews unto him, Thou art not yet fifty years old, and hast thou seen Abraham?
			58 Jesus said unto them, Verily, verily, I say unto you, Before Abraham was, I am.
			59 Then took they up stones to cast at him: but Jesus hid himself, and went out of the temple, going through the midst of them, and so passed by.

122. JESUS HEALS A MAN BORN BLIND

MATTHEW	MARK	LUKE	JOHN
			CHAPTER 9
AND as *Jesus* passed by, he saw a man which was blind from *his* birth.
			2 And his disciples asked him, saying, Master, who did sin, this man, or his parents, that he was born blind?
			3 Jesus answered, Neither hath this man sinned, nor his parents: but that the works of God should be made manifest in him.
			4 I must work the works of him that sent me, while it is day: the night cometh, when no man can work.
			5 As long as I am in the world, I am the light of the world.
			6 When he had thus spoken, he spat on the ground, and made clay of the spittle, and he anointed the eyes of the blind man with the clay,
			7 And said unto him, Go, wash in the pool of Sĭ·lō´·ăm, (which is by interpretation, Sent.) He went his way therefore, and washed, and came seeing.
			8 ¶ The neighbours therefore, and they which before had seen him that he was blind, said, Is not this he that sat and begged?
			9 Some said, This is he: others *said*, He is like him: *but* he said, I am *he*.
			10 Therefore said they unto him, How were thine eyes opened?
			11 He answered and said, A man that is called Jesus made clay, and anointed mine eyes, and said unto me, Go to the pool of Sĭ·lō´·ăm, and wash: and I went and washed, and I received sight.
			12 Then said they unto him, Where is he? He said, I know not.
			13 ¶ They brought to the Pharisees him that aforetime was blind.
			14 And it was the sabbath day when Jesus made the clay, and opened his eyes.
			15 Then again the Pharisees also asked him how he had received his sight. He said unto them, He put clay upon mine eyes, and I washed, and do see.

MATTHEW –	MARK –	LUKE –	JOHN – 9
			16 Therefore said some of the Pharisees, This man is not of God, because he keepeth not the sabbath day. Others said, How can a man that is a sinner do such miracles? And there was a division among them.
			17 They say unto the blind man again, What sayest thou of him, that he hath opened thine eyes? He said, He is a prophet.
			18 But the Jews did not believe concerning him, that he had been blind, and received his sight, until they called the parents of him that had received his sight.
			19 And they asked them, saying, Is this your son, who ye say was born blind? how then doth he now see?
			20 His parents answered them and said, We know that this is our son, and that he was born blind:
			21 But by what means he now seeth, we know not; or who hath opened his eyes, we know not: he is of age; ask him: he shall speak for himself.
			22 These *words* spake his parents, because they feared the Jews: for the Jews had agreed already, that if any man did confess that he was Christ, he should be put out of the synagogue.
			23 Therefore said his parents, He is of age; ask him.
			24 Then again called they the man that was blind, and said unto him, Give God the praise: we know that this man is a sinner.
			25 He answered and said, Whether he be a sinner *or no*, I know not: one thing I know, that, whereas I was blind, now I see.
			26 Then said they to him again, What did he to thee? how opened he thine eyes?
			27 He answered them, I have told you already, and ye did not hear: wherefore would ye hear *it* again? will ye also be his disciples?
			28 Then they reviled him, and said, Thou art his disciple; but we are Moses' disciples.
			29 We know that God spake unto Moses: *as for* this *fellow*, we know not from whence he is.
			30 The man answered and said unto them, Why herein is a marvellous thing, that ye know not from whence he is, and *yet* he hath opened mine eyes.
			31 Now we know that God heareth not sinners: but if any man be a worshipper of God, and doeth his will, him he heareth.
			32 Since the world began was it not heard that any man opened the eyes of one that was born blind.
			33 If this man were not of God, he could do nothing.
			34 They answered and said unto him, Thou wast altogether born in sins, and dost thou teach us? And they cast him out.
			35 Jesus heard that they had cast him out; and when he had found him, he said unto him, Dost thou believe on the Son of God?

79

36 He answered and said, Who is he, Lord, that I might believe on him?

37 And Jesus said unto him, Thou hast both seen him, and it is he that talketh with thee.

38 And he said, Lord, I believe. And he worshipped him.

39 ¶ And Jesus said, For judgment I am come into this world, that they which see not might see; and that they which see might be made blind.

40 And *some* of the Pharisees which were with him heard these words, and said unto him, Are we blind also?

41 Jesus said unto them, If ye were blind, ye should have no sin: but now ye say, We see; therefore your sin remaineth.

123. JESUS IS THE GOOD SHEPHERD

CHAPTER 10

VERILY, verily, I say unto you, He that entereth not by the door into the sheepfold, but climbeth up some other way, the same is a thief and a robber.

2 But he that entereth in by the door is the shepherd of the sheep.

3 To him the porter openeth; and the sheep hear his voice: and he calleth his own sheep by name, and leadeth them out.

4 And when he putteth forth his own sheep, he goeth before them, and the sheep follow him: for they know his voice.

5 And a stranger will they not follow, but will flee from him: for they know not the voice of strangers.

6 This parable spake Jesus unto them: but they understood not what things they were which he spake unto them.

7 Then said Jesus unto them again, Verily, verily, I say unto you, I am the door of the sheep.

8 All that ever came before me are thieves and robbers: but the sheep did not hear them.

9 I am the door: by me if any man enter in, he shall be saved, and shall go in and out, and find pasture.

10 The thief cometh not, but for to steal, and to kill, and to destroy: I am come that they might have life, and that they might have *it* more abundantly.

11 I am the good shepherd: the good shepherd giveth his life for the sheep.

12 But he that is an hireling, and not the shepherd, whose own the sheep are not, seeth the wolf coming, and leaveth the sheep, and fleeth: and the wolf catcheth them, and scattereth the sheep.

13 The hireling fleeth, because he is an hireling, and careth not for the sheep.

14 I am the good shepherd, and know my *sheep*, and am known of mine.

15 As the Father knoweth me, even so know I the Father: and I lay down my life for the sheep.

MATTHEW –	MARK –	LUKE – 10*	JOHN – 10
			16 And other sheep I have, which are not of this fold: them also I must bring, and they shall hear my voice; and there shall be one fold, *and* one shepherd.
			17 Therefore doth my Father love me, because I lay down my life, that I might take it again.
			18 No man taketh it from me, but I lay it down of myself. I have power to lay it down, and I have power to take it again. This commandment have I received of my Father.
			19 ¶ There was a division therefore again among the Jews for these sayings.
			20 And many of them said, He hath a devil, and is mad; why hear ye him?
			21 Others said, These are not the words of him that hath a devil. Can a devil open the eyes of the blind?

124. PARABLE OF THE GOOD SAMARITAN

LUKE

25 ¶ And, behold, a certain lawyer stood up, and tempted him, saying, Master, what shall I do to inherit eternal life?

26 He said unto him, What is written in the law? how readest thou?

27 And he answering said, Thou shalt love the Lord thy God with all thy heart, and with all thy soul, and with all thy strength, and with all thy mind; and thy neighbour as thyself.

28 And he said unto him, Thou hast answered right: this do, and thou shalt live.

29 But he, willing to justify himself, said unto Jesus, And who is my neighbour?

30 And Jesus answering said, A certain *man* went down from Jerusalem to Jericho, and fell among thieves, which stripped him of his raiment, and wounded *him*, and departed, leaving *him* half dead.

31 And by chance there came down a certain priest that way: and when he saw him, he passed by on the other side.

32 And likewise a Levite, when he was at the place, came and looked *on him*, and passed by on the other side.

33 But a certain Să-măr'-ĭ-tăn, as he journeyed, came where he was: and when he saw him, he had compassion *on him*,

34 And went to *him*, and bound up his wounds, pouring in oil and wine, and set him on his own beast, and brought him to an inn, and took care of him.

35 And on the morrow when he departed, he took out two pence, and gave *them* to the host, and said unto him, Take care of him; and whatsoever thou spendest more, when I come again, I will repay thee.

36 Which now of these three, thinkest thou, was neighbour unto him that fell among the thieves?

37 And he said, He that shewed mercy on him. Then said Jesus unto him, Go, and do thou likewise.

125. JESUS VISITS MARTHA AND MARY

38 ¶ Now it came to pass, as they went, that he entered into a certain village: and a certain woman named Martha received him into her house.

39 And she had a sister called Mary, which also sat at Jesus' feet, and heard his word.

40 But Martha was cumbered about much serving, and came to him, and said, Lord, dost thou not care that my sister hath left me to serve alone? bid her therefore that she help me.

41 And Jesus answered and said unto her, Martha, Martha, thou art careful and troubled about many things:

42 But one thing is needful: and Mary hath chosen that good part, which shall not be taken away from her.

126. DISCIPLES REQUEST, "TEACH US TO PRAY"

CHAPTER 11

AND it came to pass, that, as he was praying in a certain place, when he ceased, one of his disciples said unto him, Lord, teach us to pray, as John also taught his disciples.

2 And he said unto them, When ye pray, say, Our Father which art in heaven, Hallowed be thy name. Thy kingdom come. Thy will be done, as in heaven, so in earth.

3 Give us day by day our daily bread.

4 And forgive us our sins; for we also forgive every one that is indebted to us. And lead us not into temptation; but deliver us from evil.

5 And he said unto them, Which of you shall have a friend, and shall go unto him at midnight, and say unto him, Friend, lend me three loaves;

6 For a friend of mine in his journey is come to me, and I have nothing to set before him?

7 And he from within shall answer and say, Trouble me not: the door is now shut, and my children are with me in bed; I cannot rise and give thee.

8 I say unto you, Though he will not rise and give him, because he is his friend, yet because of his importunity he will rise and give him as many as he needeth.

9 And I say unto you, Ask, and it shall be given you; seek, and ye shall find; knock, and it shall be opened unto you.

10 For every one that asketh receiveth; and he that seeketh findeth; and to him that knocketh it shall be opened.

11 If a son shall ask bread of any of you that is a father, will he give him a stone? or if he ask a fish, will he for a fish give him a serpent?

12 Or if he shall ask an egg, will he offer him a scorpion?

13 If ye then, being evil, know how to give good gifts unto your children: how much more shall your heavenly Father give the Holy Spirit to them that ask him?

127. ACCUSED AGAIN OF CASTING OUT DEVILS BY BEELZEBUB

14 ¶ And he was casting out a devil, and it was dumb. And it came to pass, when the devil was gone out, the dumb spake; and the people wondered.

15 But some of them said, He casteth out devils through Bē-ĕl′-zĕ-bŭb the chief of the devils.

16 And others, tempting *him*, sought of him a sign from heaven.

17 But he, knowing their thoughts, said unto them, Every kingdom divided against itself is brought to desolation; and a house *divided* against a house falleth.

18 If Satan also be divided against himself, how shall his kingdom stand? because ye say that I cast out devils through Bē-ĕl′-zĕ-bŭb.

19 And if I by Bē-ĕl′-zĕ-bŭb cast out devils, by whom do your sons cast *them* out? therefore shall they be your judges.

20 But if I with the finger of God cast out devils, no doubt the kingdom of God is come upon you.

21 When a strong man armed keepeth his palace, his goods are in peace:

22 But when a stronger than he shall come upon him, and overcome him, he taketh from him all his armour wherein he trusted, and divideth his spoils.

23 He that is not with me is against me: and he that gathereth not with me scattereth.

24 When the unclean spirit is gone out of a man, he walketh through dry places, seeking rest; and finding none, he saith, I will return unto my house whence I came out.

25 And when he cometh, he findeth *it* swept and garnished.

26 Then goeth he, and taketh *to him* seven other spirits more wicked than himself; and they enter in, and dwell there: and the last *state* of that man is worse than the first.

27 ¶ And it came to pass, as he spake these things, a certain woman of the company lifted up her voice, and said unto him, Blessed *is* the womb that bare thee, and the paps which thou hast sucked.

28 But he said, Yea rather, blessed *are* they that hear the word of God, and keep it.

29 ¶ And when the people were gathered thick together, he began to say, This is an evil generation: they seek a sign; and there shall no sign be given it, but the sign of Jonas the prophet.

30 For as Jonas was a sign unto the Nĭn′-ĕ-vītes, so shall also the Son of man be to this generation.

31 The queen of the south shall rise up in the judgment with the men of this generation, and condemn them: for she came from the utmost parts of the earth to hear the wisdom of Solomon; and, behold, a greater than Solomon *is* here.

32 The men of Nĭn´-ĕ-vĕ shall rise up in the judgment with this generation, and shall condemn it: for they repented at the preaching of Jonas; and, behold, a greater than Jonas *is* here.

33 No man, when he hath lighted a candle, putteth *it* in a secret place, neither under a bushel, but on a candlestick, that they which come in may see the light.

34 The light of the body is the eye: therefore when thine eye is single, thy whole body also is full of light; but when *thine eye* is evil, thy body also *is* full of darkness.

35 Take heed therefore that the light which is in thee be not darkness.

36 If thy whole body therefore *be* full of light, having no part dark, the whole shall be full of light, as when the bright shining of a candle doth give thee light.

128. REBUKES PHARISEES, SCRIBES AND LAWYERS FOR HYPOCRISY

37 ¶ And as he spake, a certain Pharisee besought him to dine with him: and he went in, and sat down to meat.

38 And when the Pharisee saw *it*, he marvelled that he had not first washed before dinner.

39 And the Lord said unto him, Now do ye Pharisees make clean the outside of the cup and the platter; but your inward part is full of ravening and wickedness.

40 *Ye* fools, did not he that made that which is without make that which is within also?

41 But rather give alms of such things as ye have; and, behold, all things are clean unto you.

42 But woe unto you, Pharisees! for ye tithe mint and rue and all manner of herbs, and pass over judgment and the love of God: these ought ye to have done, and not to leave the other undone.

43 Woe unto you, Pharisees! for ye love the uppermost seats in the synagogues, and greetings in the markets.

44 Woe unto you, scribes and Pharisees, hypocrites! for ye are as graves which appear not, and the men that walk over *them* are not aware *of them.*

45 ¶ Then answered one of the lawyers, and said unto him, Master, thus saying thou reproachest us also.

46 And he said, Woe unto you also, *ye* lawyers! for ye lade men with burdens grievous to be borne, and ye yourselves touch not the burdens with one of your fingers.

47 Woe unto you! for ye build the sepulchres of the prophets, and your fathers killed them.

48 Truly ye bear witness that ye allow the deeds of your fathers: for they indeed killed them, and ye build their sepulchres.

| | | 49 Therefore also said the wisdom of God, I will send them prophets and apostles, and *some* of them they shall slay and persecute: | |

LUKE

49 Therefore also said the wisdom of God, I will send them prophets and apostles, and *some* of them they shall slay and persecute:

50 That the blood of all the prophets, which was shed from the foundation of the world, may be required of this generation;

51 From the blood of Abel unto the blood of Zăch·ă·rī´·ăs, which perished between the altar and the temple: verily I say unto you, It shall be required of this generation.

52 Woe unto you, lawyers! for ye have taken away the key of knowledge: ye entered not in yourselves, and them that were entering in ye hindered.

53 And as he said these things unto them, the scribes and the Pharisees began to urge *him* vehemently, and to provoke him to speak of many things:

54 Laying wait for him, and seeking to catch something out of his mouth, that they might accuse him.

129. TEACHES TO BEWARE OF THE PHARISEES

CHAPTER 12

IN the mean time, when there were gathered together an innumerable multitude of people, insomuch that they trode one upon another, he began to say unto his disciples first of all, Beware ye of the leaven of the Pharisees, which is hypocrisy.

2 For there is nothing covered, that shall not be revealed; neither hid, that shall not be known.

3 Therefore whatsoever ye have spoken in darkness shall be heard in the light; and that which ye have spoken in the ear in closets shall be proclaimed upon the housetops.

4 And I say unto you my friends, Be not afraid of them that kill the body, and after that have no more that they can do.

5 But I will forewarn you whom ye shall fear: Fear him, which after he hath killed hath power to cast into hell; yea, I say unto you, Fear him.

6 Are not five sparrows sold for two farthings, and not one of them is forgotten before God?

7 But even the very hairs of your head are all numbered. Fear not therefore: ye are of more value than many sparrows.

8 Also I say unto you, Whosoever shall confess me before men, him shall the Son of man also confess before the angels of God:

9 But he that denieth me before men shall be denied before the angels of God.

10 And whosoever shall speak a word against the Son of man, it shall be forgiven him: but unto him that blasphemeth against the Holy Ghost it shall not be forgiven.

11 And when they bring you unto the synagogues, and *unto* magistrates, and powers, take ye no thought how or what thing ye shall answer, or what ye shall say:

12 For the Holy Ghost shall teach you in the same hour what ye ought to say.

130. PARABLE OF THE RICH FOOL

13 ¶ And one of the company said unto him, Master, speak to my brother, that he divide the inheritance with me.

14 And he said unto him, Man, who made me a judge or a divider over you?

15 And he said unto them, Take heed, and beware of covetousness: for a man's life consisteth not in the abundance of the things which he possesseth.

16 And he spake a parable unto them, saying, The ground of a certain rich man brought forth plentifully:

17 And he thought within himself, saying, What shall I do, because I have no room where to bestow my fruits?

18 And he said, This will I do: I will pull down my barns, and build greater; and there will I bestow all my fruits and my goods.

19 And I will say to my soul, Soul, thou hast much goods laid up for many years; take thine ease, eat, drink, *and* be merry.

20 But God said unto him, *Thou* fool, this night thy soul shall be required of thee: then whose shall those things be, which thou hast provided?

21 So *is* he that layeth up treasure for himself, and is not rich toward God.

131. DISCIPLES TO SEEK THE KINGDOM OF GOD BEFORE EARTHLY TREASURES

22 ¶ :And he said unto his disciples, Therefore I say unto you, Take no thought for your life, what ye shall eat; neither for the body, what ye shall put on.

23 The life is more than meat, and the body *is more* than raiment.

24 Consider the ravens: for they neither sow nor reap; which neither have storehouse nor barn; and God feedeth them: how much more are ye better than the fowls?

25 And which of you with taking thought can add to his stature one cubit?

26 If ye then be not able to do that thing which is least, why take ye thought for the rest?

27 Consider the lilies how they grow: they toil not, they spin not; and yet I say unto you, that Solomon in all his glory was not arrayed like one of these.

28 If then God so clothe the grass, which is to day in the field, and to morrow is cast into the oven; how much more *will he clothe* you, O ye of little faith?

29 And seek not ye what ye shall eat, or what ye shall drink, neither be ye of doubtful mind.

30 For all these things do the nations of the world seek after: and your Father knoweth that ye have need of these things.

31 ¶ But rather seek ye the kingdom of God; and all these things shall be added unto you.

| | | 32 Fear not, little flock; for it is your Father's good pleasure to give you the kingdom.
33 Sell that ye have, and give alms; provide yourselves bags which wax not old, a treasure in the heavens that faileth not, where no thief approacheth, neither moth corrupteth.
34 For where your treasure is, there will your heart be also. | |

132. ALWAYS BE PREPARED FOR THE COMING OF THE LORD

35 Let your loins be girded about, and *your* lights burning;

36 And ye yourselves like unto men that wait for their lord, when he will return from the wedding; that when he cometh and knocketh, they may open unto him immediately.

37 Blessed *are* those servants, whom the lord when he cometh shall find watching: verily I say unto you, that he shall gird himself, and make them to sit down to meat, and will come forth and serve them.

38 And if he shall come in the second watch, or come in the third watch, and find *them* so, blessed are those servants.

39 And this know, that if the goodman of the house had known what hour the thief would come, he would have watched, and not have suffered his house to be broken through.

40 Be ye therefore ready also: for the Son of man cometh at an hour when ye think not.

41 ¶ Then Peter said unto him, Lord, speakest thou this parable unto us, or even to all?

42 And the Lord said, Who then is that faithful and wise steward, whom *his* lord shall make ruler over his household, to give *them their* portion of meat in due season?

43 Blessed *is* that servant, whom his lord when he cometh shall find so doing.

44 Of a truth I say unto you, that he will make him ruler over all that he hath.

45 But and if that servant say in his heart, My lord delayeth his coming; and shall begin to beat the menservants and maidens, and to eat and drink, and to be drunken;

46 The lord of that servant will come in a day when he looketh not for *him*, and at an hour when he is not aware, and will cut him in sunder, and will appoint him his portion with the unbelievers.

47 And that servant, which knew his lord's will, and prepared not *himself*, neither did according to his will, shall be beaten with many *stripes*.

48 But he that knew not, and did commit things worthy of stripes, shall be beaten with few *stripes*. For unto whomsoever much is given, of him shall be much required: and to whom men have committed much, of him they will ask the more.

49 ¶ I am come to send fire on the earth; and what will I, if it be already kindled?

MATTHEW –	MARK –	LUKE – 12,13	JOHN –

50 But I have a baptism to be baptized with; and how am I straitened till it be accomplished!

51 Suppose ye that I am come to give peace on earth? I tell you, Nay; but rather division:

52 For from henceforth there shall be five in one house divided, three against two, and two against three.

53 The father shall be divided against the son, and the son against the father; the mother against the daughter, and the daughter against the mother; the mother in law against her daughter in law, and the daughter in law against her mother in law.

54 ¶ And he said also to the people, When ye see a cloud rise out of the west, straightway ye say, There cometh a shower; and so it is.

55 And when ye *see* the south wind blow, ye say, There will be heat; and it cometh to pass.

56 *Ye* hypocrites, ye can discern the face of the sky and of the earth; but how is it that ye do not discern this time?

57 Yea, and why even of yourselves judge ye not what is right?

58 ¶ When thou goest with thine adversary to the magistrate, *as thou art* in the way, give diligence that thou mayest be delivered from him; lest he hale thee to the judge, and the judge deliver thee to the officer, and the officer cast thee into prison.

59 I tell thee, thou shalt not depart thence, till thou hast paid the very last mite.

133. REPENT OR PERISH

CHAPTER 13

THERE were present at that season some that told him of the Galilæans, whose blood Pilate had mingled with their sacrifices.

2 And Jesus answering said unto them, Suppose ye that these Galilæans were sinners above all the Galilæans, because they suffered such things?

3 I tell you, Nay: but, except ye repent, ye shall all likewise perish.

4 Or those eighteen, upon whom the tower in Sĭ-lō-ăm fell, and slew them, think ye that they were sinners above all men that dwelt in Jerusalem?

5 I tell you, Nay: but, except ye repent, ye shall all likewise perish.

134. PARABLE OF THE BARREN FIG TREE

6 ¶ He spake also this parable; A certain *man* had a fig tree planted in his vineyard; and he came and sought fruit thereon, and found none.

7 Then said he unto the dresser of his vineyard, Behold, these three years I come seeking fruit on this fig tree, and find none: cut it down; why cumbereth it the ground?

MATTHEW	MARK	LUKE	JOHN
		8 And he answering said unto him, Lord, let it alone this year also, till I shall dig about it, and dung *it:* 9 And if it bear fruit, *well:* and if not, *then* after that thou shalt cut it down.	

135. HEALS WOMAN ON THE SABBATH

MATTHEW	MARK	LUKE	JOHN
		10 And he was teaching in one of the synagogues on the sabbath. 11 ¶ And, behold, there was a woman which had a spirit of infirmity eighteen years, and was bowed together, and could in no wise lift up *herself.* 12 And when Jesus saw her, he called *her to him,* and said unto her, Woman, thou art loosed from thine infirmity. 13 And he laid *his* hands on her: and immediately she was made straight, and glorified God. 14 And the ruler of the synagogue answered with indignation, because that Jesus had healed on the sabbath day, and said unto the people, There are six days in which men ought to work: in them therefore come and be healed, and not on the sabbath day. 15 The Lord then answered him, and said, *Thou* hypocrite, doth not each one of you on the sabbath loose his ox or *his* ass from the stall, and lead *him* away to watering? 16 And ought not this woman, being a daughter of Abraham, whom Satan hath bound, lo, these eighteen years, be loosed from this bond on the sabbath day? 17 And when he had said these things, all his adversaries were ashamed: and all the people rejoiced for all the glorious things that were done by him.	

136. KINGDOM OF GOD LIKE UNTO MUSTARD SEED AND LEAVEN

MATTHEW	MARK	LUKE	JOHN
		18 ¶ Then said he, Unto what is the kingdom of God like? and whereunto shall I resemble it? 19 It is like a grain of mustard seed, which a man took, and cast into his garden; and it grew, and waxed a great tree; and the fowls of the air lodged in the branches of it. 20 And again he said, Whereunto shall I liken the kingdom of God? 21 It is like leaven, which a woman took and hid in three measures of meal, till the whole was leavened.	

137. RETURN OF THE SEVENTY

MATTHEW	MARK	LUKE	JOHN
		Ch. 10 17 ¶ And the seventy returned again with joy, saying, Lord, even the devils are subject unto us through thy name. 18 And he said unto them, I beheld Satan as lightning fall from heaven. 19 Behold, I give unto you power to tread on serpents and scorpions, and over all the power of the enemy: and nothing shall by any means hurt you.	

MATTHEW – 11	MARK –	LUKE – 10	JOHN – 10
		20 Notwithstanding in this rejoice not, that the spirits are subject unto you; but rather rejoice, because your names are written in heaven.	
25 ¶ At that time Jesus answered and said, I thank thee, O Father, Lord of heaven and earth, because thou hast hid these things from the wise and prudent, and hast revealed them unto babes.		21 ¶ In that hour Jesus rejoiced in spirit, and said, I thank thee, O Father, Lord of heaven and earth, that thou hast hid these things from the wise and prudent, and hast revealed them unto babes: even so, Father; for so it seemed good in thy sight.	
26 Even so, Father: for so it seemed good in thy sight.			
27 All things are delivered unto me of my Father: and no man knoweth the Son, but the Father; neither knoweth any man the Father, save the Son, and *he* to whomsoever the Son will reveal *him.*		22 All things are delivered to me of my Father: and no man knoweth who the Son is, but the Father; and who the Father is, but the Son, and *he* to whom the Son will reveal *him.*	
		23 ¶ And he turned him unto *his* disciples, and said privately, Blessed *are* the eyes which see the things that ye see:	
		24 For I tell you, that many prophets and kings have desired to see those things which ye see, and have not seen *them;* and to hear those things which ye hear, and have not heard *them.*	

138. CALL TO FOLLOW JESUS AND FIND REST

MATTHEW – 11	MARK –	LUKE – 10	JOHN – 10
28 ¶ Come unto me, all *ye* that labour and are heavy laden, and I will give you rest.			
29 Take my yoke upon you, and learn of me; for I am meek and lowly in heart: and ye shall find rest unto your souls.			
30 For my yoke *is* easy, and my burden is light.			

139. JESUS AT THE FEAST OF DEDICATION IN JERUSALEM *

MATTHEW – 11	MARK –	LUKE – 10	JOHN – 10
			22 ¶ And it was at Jerusalem the feast of the dedication, and it was winter.
			23 And Jesus walked in the temple in Solomon's porch.
			**24 Then came the Jews round about him, and said unto him, How long dost thou make us to doubt? If thou be the Christ, tell us plainly.
			25 Jesus answered them, I told you, and ye believed not: the works that I do in my Father's name, they bear witness of me.
			26 But ye believe not, because ye are not of my sheep, as I said unto you.
			27 My sheep hear my voice, and I know them, and they follow me:
			28 And I give unto them eternal life; and they shall never perish, neither shall any *man* pluck them out of my hand.
			29 My Father, which gave *them* me, is greater than all; and no *man* is able to pluck *them* out of my Father's hand.
			30 I and *my* Father are one.
			31 Then the Jews took up stones again to stone him.
			32 Jesus answered them, Many good works have I shewed you from my Father; for which of those works do ye stone me?
			33 The Jews answered him, saying, For a good work we stone thee not; but for blasphemy; and because that thou, being a man, makest thyself God.

*Feast of Dedication, see note 139.

**See note 117.

MATTHEW –	MARK –	LUKE – 13	JOHN – 10
			34 Jesus answered them, Is it not written in your law, I said, Ye are gods?
			35 If he called them gods, unto whom the word of God came, and the scripture cannot be broken;
			36 Say ye of him, whom the Father hath sanctified, and sent into the world, Thou blasphemest; because I said, I am the Son of God?
			37 If I do not the works of my Father, believe me not.
			38 But if I do, though ye believe not me, believe the works: that ye may know, and believe, that the Father *is* in me, and I in him.
			39a Therefore they sought again to take him:

140. JESUS ESCAPES FROM THE JEWS BY GOING ACROSS THE JORDAN

MATTHEW	MARK	LUKE	JOHN
			39b but he escaped out of their hand,
			40 And went away again beyond Jordan into the place where John at first baptized; and there he abode.
			41 And many resorted unto him, and said, John did no miracle: but all things that John spake of this man were true.
			42 And many believed on him there.

VII.   THE PEREAN MINISTRY

141. TEACHING AND TRAVELING WHILE AWAITING THE PASSOVER AT JERUSALEM

MATTHEW	MARK	LUKE	JOHN
		22 And he went through the cities and villages, teaching, and journeying toward Jerusalem.	

142. WHO SHALL BE SAVED?

MATTHEW	MARK	LUKE	JOHN
		23 Then said one unto him, Lord, are there few that be saved? And he said unto them,	
		24 ¶ Strive to enter in at the strait gate: for many, I say unto you, will seek to enter in, and shall not be able.	
		25 When once the master of the house is risen up, and hath shut to the door, and ye begin to stand without, and to knock at the door, saying, Lord, Lord, open unto us; and he shall answer and say unto you, I know you not whence ye are:	
		26 Then shall ye begin to say, We have eaten and drunk in thy presence, and thou hast taught in our streets.	
		27 But he shall say, I tell you, I know you not whence ye are; depart from me, all *ye* workers of iniquity.	
		28 There shall be weeping and gnashing of teeth, when ye shall see Abraham, and Isaac, and Jacob, and all the prophets, in the kingdom of God, and you *yourselves* thrust out.	
		29 And they shall come from the east, and *from* the west, and from the north, and *from* the south, and shall sit down in the kingdom of God.	
		30 And, behold, there are last which shall be first, and there are first which shall be last.	

143. LAMENTATION OVER JERUSALEM

31 ¶ The same day there came certain of the Pharisees, saying unto him, Get thee out, and depart hence: for Herod will kill thee.

32 And he said unto them, Go ye, and tell that fox, Behold, I cast out devils, and I do cures to day and to morrow, and the third *day* I shall be perfected.

33 Nevertheless I must walk to day, and to morrow, and the *day* following: for it cannot be that a prophet perish out of Jerusalem.

34 O Jerusalem, Jerusalem, which killest the prophets, and stonest them that are sent unto thee; how often would I have gathered thy children together, as a hen *doth gather* her brood under *her* wings, and ye would not!

35 Behold, your house is left unto you desolate: and verily I say unto you, Ye shall not see me, until *the time* come when ye shall say, Blessed *is* he that cometh in the name of the Lord.

144. HEALS A MAN WITH DROPSY ON THE SABBATH

CHAPTER 14

AND it came to pass, as he went into the house of one of the chief Pharisees to eat bread on the sabbath day, that they watched him.

2 And, behold, there was a certain man before him which had the dropsy.

3 And Jesus answering spake unto the lawyers and Pharisees, saying, Is it lawful to heal on the sabbath day?

4 And they held their peace. And he took *him*, and healed him, and let him go;

5 And answered them, saying, Which of you shall have an ass or an ox fallen into a pit, and will not straightway pull him out on the sabbath day?

6 And they could not answer him again to these things.

145. HUMILITY: PARABLE OF THE WEDDING FEAST

7 ¶ And he put forth a parable to those which were bidden, when he marked how they chose out the chief rooms; saying unto them,

8 When thou art bidden of any *man* to a wedding, sit not down in the highest room; lest a more honourable man than thou be bidden of him;

9 And he that bade thee and him come and say to thee, Give this man place; and thou begin with shame to take the lowest room.

10 But when thou art bidden, go and sit down in the lowest room; that when he that bade thee cometh, he may say unto thee, Friend, go up higher: then shalt thou have worship in the presence of them that sit at meat with thee.

| | | 11 For whosoever exalteth himself shall be abased; and he that humbleth himself shall be exalted. | |

146. PARABLE OF THE GREAT SUPPER

| | | 12 ¶ Then said he also to him that bade him, When thou makest a dinner or a supper, call not thy friends, nor thy brethren, neither thy kinsmen, nor *thy* rich neighbours; lest they also bid thee again, and a recompence be made thee.
13 But when thou makest a feast, call the poor, the maimed, the lame, the blind:
14 And thou shalt be blessed; for they cannot recompense thee: for thou shalt be recompensed at the resurrection of the just.
15 ¶ And when one of them that sat at meat with him heard these things, he said unto him, Blessed *is* he that shall eat bread in the kingdom of God.
16 Then said he unto him, A certain man made a great supper, and bade many:
17 And sent his servant at supper time to say to them that were bidden, Come; for all things are now ready.
18 And they all with one con-sent began to make excuse. The first said unto him, I have bought a piece of ground, and I must needs go and see it: I pray thee have me excused.
19 And another said, I have bought five yoke of oxen, and I go to prove them: I pray thee have me excused.
20 And another said, I have married a wife, and therefore I cannot come.
21 So that servant came, and shewed his lord these things. Then the master of the house being angry said to his servant, Go out quickly into the streets and lanes of the city, and bring in hither the poor, and the maimed, and the halt, and the blind.
22 And the servant said, Lord, it is done as thou hast commanded, and yet there is room.
23 And the lord said unto the servant, Go out into the highways and hedges, and compel *them* to come in, that my house may be filled.
24 For I say unto you, That none of those men which were bidden shall taste of my supper. | |

147. SACRIFICE REQUIRED TO FOLLOW JESUS

| | | 25 ¶ And there went great multitudes with him: and he turned, and said unto them,
26 If any *man* come to me, and hate not his father, and mother, and wife, and children, and brethren, and sisters, yea, and his own life also, he cannot be my disciple.
27 And whosoever doth not bear his cross, and come after me, cannot be my disciple.
28 For which of you, intending to build a tower, sitteth not down first, and counteth the cost, whether he have *sufficient* to finish *it?* | |

29 Lest haply, after he hath laid the foundation, and is not able to finish *it*, all that behold *it* begin to mock him,

30 Saying, This man began to build, and was not able to finish.

31 Or what king, going to make war against another king, sitteth not down first, and consulteth whether he be able with ten thousand to meet him that cometh against him with twenty thousand?

32 Or else, while the other is yet a great way off, he sendeth an ambassage, and desireth conditions of peace.

33 So likewise, whosoever he be of you that forsaketh not all that he hath, he cannot be my disciple.

34 ¶ Salt *is* good: but if the salt have lost his savour, wherewith shall it be seasoned?

35 It is neither fit for the land, nor yet for the dunghill; *but* men cast it out. He that hath ears to hear, let him hear.

148. PARABLE OF THE LOST SHEEP

CHAPTER 15

THEN drew near unto him all the publicans and sinners for to hear him.

2 And the Pharisees and scribes murmured, saying, This man receiveth sinners, and eateth with them.

3 ¶ And he spake this parable unto them, saying,

4 What man of you, having an hundred sheep, if he lose one of them, doth not leave the ninety and nine in the wilderness, and go after that which is lost, until he find it?

5 And when he hath found *it*, he layeth *it* on his shoulders, rejoicing.

6 And when he cometh home, he calleth together *his* friends and neighbours, saying unto them, Rejoice with me; for I have found my sheep which was lost.

7 I say unto you, that likewise joy shall be in heaven over one sinner that repenteth, more than over ninety and nine just persons, which need no repentance.

149. PARABLE OF THE LOST COIN

8 ¶ Either what woman having ten pieces of silver, if she lose one piece, doth not light a candle, and sweep the house, and seek diligently till she find *it*?

9 And when she hath found *it*, she calleth *her* friends and *her* neighbours together, saying, Rejoice with me; for I have found the piece which I had lost.

10 Likewise, I say unto you, there is joy in the presence of the angels of God over one sinner that repenteth.

150. PARABLE OF THE PRODIGAL SON

11 ¶ And he said, A certain man had two sons:

12 And the younger of them said to *his* father, Father, give me the portion of goods that falleth *to me*. And he divided unto them *his* living.

13 And not many days after the younger son gathered all together, and took his journey into a far country, and there wasted his substance with riotous living.

14 And when he had spent all, there arose a mighty famine in that land; and he began to be in want.

15 And he went and joined himself to a citizen of that country; and he sent him into his fields to feed swine.

16 And he would fain have filled his belly with the husks that the swine did eat: and no man gave unto him.

17 And when he came to himself, he said, How many hired servants of my father's have bread enough and to spare, and I perish with hunger!

18 I will arise and go to my father, and will say unto him, Father, I have sinned against heaven, and before thee,

19 And am no more worthy to be called thy son: make me as one of thy hired servants.

20 And he arose, and came to his father. But when he was yet a great way off, his father saw him, and had compassion, and ran, and fell on his neck, and kissed him.

21 And the son said unto him, Father, I have sinned against heaven, and in thy sight, and am no more worthy to be called thy son.

22 But the father said to his servants, Bring forth the best robe, and put *it* on him; and put a ring on his hand, and shoes on *his* feet:

23 And bring hither the fatted calf, and kill *it;* and let us eat, and be merry:

24 For this my son was dead, and is alive again; he was lost, and is found. And they began to be merry.

25 Now his elder son was in the field: and as he came and drew nigh to the house, he heard musick and dancing.

26 And he called one of the servants, and asked what these things meant.

27 And he said unto him, Thy brother is come; and thy father hath killed the fatted calf, because he hath received him safe and sound.

28 And he was angry, and would not go in: therefore came his father out, and intreated him.

29 And he answering said to *his* father, Lo, these many years do I serve thee, neither transgressed I at any time thy commandment: and yet thou never gavest me a kid, that I might make merry with my friends:

30 But as soon as this thy son was come, which hath devoured thy living with harlots, thou hast killed for him the fatted calf.

31 And he said unto him, Son, thou art ever with me, and all that I have is thine.

32 It was meet that we should make merry, and be glad: for this thy brother was dead, and is alive again; and was lost, and is found.

151. PARABLE OF THE UNJUST STEWARD

CHAPTER 16

AND he said also unto his disciples, There was a certain rich man, which had a steward; and the same was accused unto him that he had wasted his goods.

2 And he called him, and said unto him, How is it that I hear this of thee? give an account of thy stewardship; for thou mayest be no longer steward.

3 Then the steward said within himself, What shall I do? for my lord taketh away from me the stewardship: I cannot dig; to beg I am ashamed.

4 I am resolved what to do, that, when I am put out of the stewardship, they may receive me into their houses.

5 So he called every one of his lord's debtors *unto him*, and said unto the first, How much owest thou unto my lord?

6 And he said, An hundred measures of oil. And he said unto him, Take thy bill, and sit down quickly, and write fifty.

7 Then said he to another, And how much owest thou? And he said, An hundred measures of wheat. And he said unto him, Take thy bill, and write fourscore.

8 And the lord commended the unjust steward, because he had done wisely: for the children of this world are in their generation wiser than the children of light.

9 And I say unto you, Make to yourselves friends of the mammon of unrighteousness; that, when ye fail, they may receive you into everlasting habitations.

10 He that is faithful in that which is least is faithful also in much: and he that is unjust in the least is unjust also in much.

11 If therefore ye have not been faithful in the unrighteous mammon, who will commit to your trust the true *riches*?

12 And if ye have not been faithful in that which is another man's, who shall give you that which is your own?

13 ¶ No servant can serve two masters: for either he will hate the one, and love the other; or else he will hold to the one, and despise the other. Ye cannot serve God and mammon.

152. HYPOCRISY OF THE PHARISEES

14 And the Pharisees also, who were covetous, heard all these things: and they derided him.

15 And he said unto them, Ye are they which justify yourselves before men; but God knoweth your hearts: for that which is highly esteemed among men is abomination in the sight of God.

16 The law and the prophets *were* until John: since that time the kingdom of God is preached, and every man presseth into it.

17 And it is easier for heaven and earth to pass, than one tittle of the law to fail.

18 Whosoever putteth away his wife, and marrieth another, committeth adultery: and whosoever marrieth her that is put away from *her* husband committeth adultery.

153. PARABLE OF THE RICH MAN AND LAZARUS

19 ¶ There was a certain rich man, which was clothed in purple and fine linen, and fared sumptuously every day:

20 And there was a certain beggar named Lăz'-ă-rŭs, which was laid at his gate, full of sores,

21 And desiring to be fed with the crumbs which fell from the rich man's table: moreover the dogs came and licked his sores.

22 And it came to pass, that the beggar died, and was carried by the angels into Abraham's bosom: the rich man also died, and was buried;

23 And in hell he lift up his eyes, being in torments, and seeth Abraham afar off, and Lăz'-ă-rŭs in his bosom.

24 And he cried and said, Father Abraham, have mercy on me, and send Lăz'-ă-rŭs, that he may dip the tip of his finger in water, and cool my tongue; for I am tormented in this flame.

25 But Abraham said, Son, remember that thou in thy lifetime receivedst thy good things, and likewise Lăz'-ă-rŭs evil things: but now he is comforted, and thou art tormented.

26 And beside all this, between us and you there is a great gulf fixed: so that they which would pass from hence to you cannot; neither can they pass to us, that *would come* from thence.

27 Then he said, I pray thee therefore, father, that thou wouldest send him to my father's house:

28 For I have five brethren; that he may testify unto them, lest they also come into this place of torment.

29 Abraham saith unto him, They have Moses and the prophets; let them hear them.

30 And he said, Nay, father Abraham: but if one went unto them from the dead, they will repent.

31 And he said unto him, If they hear not Moses and the prophets, neither will they be persuaded, though one rose from the dead.

154. SAYINGS ON SIN, FORGIVENESS, FAITH AND DUTY

CHAPTER 17

THEN said he unto the disciples, It is impossible but that offences will come: but woe *unto him*, through whom they come!

2 It were better for him that a millstone were hanged about his neck, and he cast into the sea, than that he should offend one of these little ones.

3 ¶ Take heed to yourselves: If thy brother trespass against thee, rebuke him; and if he repent, forgive him.

4 And if he trespass against thee seven times in a day, and seven times in a day turn again to thee, saying, I repent; thou shalt forgive him.

5 And the apostles said unto the Lord, Increase our faith.

6 And the Lord said, If ye had faith as a grain of mustard seed, ye might say unto this sycamine tree, Be thou plucked up by the root, and be thou planted in the sea; and it should obey you.

7 But which of you, having a servant plowing or feeding cattle, will say unto him by and by, when he is come from the field, Go and sit down to meat?

8 And will not rather say unto him, Make ready wherewith I may sup, and gird thyself, and serve me, till I have eaten and drunken; and afterward thou shalt eat and drink?

9 Doth he thank that servant because he did the things that were commanded him? I trow not.

10 So likewise ye, when ye shall have done all those things which are commanded you, say, We are unprofitable servants: we have done that which was our duty to do.

155. JESUS RAISES LAZARUS FROM THE DEAD

CHAPTER 11

NOW a certain *man* was sick, *named* Lăz´-ȧ-rŭs, of Bethany, the town of Mary and her sister Martha.

2 (It was *that* Mary which anointed the Lord with ointment, and wiped his feet with her hair, whose brother Lăz´-ȧ-rŭs was sick.)

3 Therefore his sisters sent unto him, saying, Lord, behold, he whom thou lovest is sick.

4 When Jesus heard *that*, he said, This sickness is not unto death, but for the glory of God, that the Son of God might be glorified thereby.

5 Now Jesus loved Martha, and her sister, and Lăz´-ȧ-rŭs.

6 When he had heard therefore that he was sick, he abode two days still in the same place where he was.

7 Then after that saith he to *his* disciples, Let us go into Judæa again.

8 *His* disciples say unto him, Master, the Jews of late sought to stone thee; and goest thou thither again?

9 Jesus answered, Are there not twelve hours in the day? If any man walk in the day, he stumbleth not, because he seeth the light of this world.

10 But if a man walk in the night, he stumbleth, because there is no light in him.

11 These things said he: and after that he saith unto them, Our friend Lăz´-ȧ-rŭs sleepeth; but I go, that I may awake him out of sleep.

12 Then said his disciples, Lord, if he sleep, he shall do well.

13 Howbeit Jesus spake of his death: but they thought that he had spoken of taking of rest in sleep.

14 Then said Jesus unto them plainly, Lăz´-ȧ-rŭs is dead.

15 And I am glad for your sakes that I was not there, to the intent ye may believe; nevertheless let us go unto him.

16 Then said Thomas, which is called Dĭd´-ў-mŭs, unto his fellowdisciples, Let us also go, that we may die with him.

17 Then when Jesus came, he found that he had *lain* in the grave four days already.

18 Now Bethany was nigh unto Jerusalem, about fifteen furlongs off:

19 And many of the Jews came to Martha and Mary, to comfort them concerning their brother.

20 Then Martha, as soon as she heard that Jesus was coming, went and met him: but Mary sat *still* in the house.

21 Then said Martha unto Jesus, Lord, if thou hadst been here, my brother had not died.

22 But I know, that even now, whatsoever thou wilt ask of God, God will give *it* thee.

23 Jesus saith unto her, Thy brother shall rise again.

24 Martha saith unto him, I know that he shall rise again in the resurrection at the last day.

25 Jesus said unto her, I am the resurrection, and the life: he that believeth in me, though he were dead, yet shall he live:

26 And whosoever liveth and believeth in me shall never die. Believest thou this?

27 She saith unto him, Yea, Lord: I believe that thou art the Christ, the Son of God, which should come into the world.

28 And when she had so said, she went her way, and called Mary her sister secretly, saying, The Master is come, and calleth for thee.

29 As soon as she heard *that*, she arose quickly, and came unto him.

30 Now Jesus was not yet come into the town, but was in that place where Martha met him.

31 The Jews then which were with her in the house, and comforted her, when they saw Mary, that she rose up hastily and went out, followed her, saying, She goeth unto the grave to weep there.

32 Then when Mary was come where Jesus was, and saw him, she fell down at his feet, saying unto him, Lord, if thou hadst been here, my brother had not died.

MATTHEW –	MARK –	LUKE –	JOHN – 11
			33 When Jesus therefore saw her weeping, and the Jews also weeping which came with her, he groaned in the spirit, and was troubled,
			34 And said, Where have ye laid him? They said unto him, Lord, come and see.
			35 Jesus wept.
			36 Then said the Jews, Behold how he loved him!
			37 And some of them said, Could not this man, which opened the eyes of the blind, have caused that even this man should not have died?
			38 Jesus therefore again groaning in himself cometh to the grave. It was a cave, and a stone lay upon it.
			39 Jesus said, Take ye away the stone. Martha, the sister of him that was dead, saith unto him, Lord, by this time he stinketh: for he hath been *dead* four days.
			40 Jesus saith unto her, Said I not unto thee, that, if thou wouldest believe, thou shouldest see the glory of God?
			41 Then they took away the stone *from the place* where the dead was laid. And Jesus lifted up *his* eyes, and said, Father, I thank thee that thou hast heard me.
			42 And I knew that thou hearest me always: but because of the people which stand by I said *it*, that they may believe that thou hast sent me.
			43 And when he thus had spoken, he cried with a loud voice, Lăz′-à-rŭs, come forth.
			44 And he that was dead came forth, bound hand and foot with graveclothes: and his face was bound about with a napkin. Jesus saith unto them, Loose him, and let him go.
			45 Then many of the Jews which came to Mary, and had seen the things which Jesus did, believed on him.
			46 But some of them went their ways to the Pharisees, and told them what things Jesus had done.

156. CHIEF PRIESTS AND PHARISEES COUNSEL TO KILL JESUS

MATTHEW	MARK	LUKE	JOHN
			47 ¶ Then gathered the chief priests and the Pharisees a council, and said, What do we? for this man doeth many miracles.
			48 If we let him thus alone, all *men* will believe on him: and the Romans shall come and take away both our place and nation.
			49 And one of them, *named* Cāi′-à-phăs, being the high priest that same year, said unto them, Ye know nothing at all,
			50 Nor consider that it is expedient for us, that one man should die for the people, and that the whole nation perish not.
			51 And this spake he not of himself: but being high priest that year, he prophesied that Jesus should die for that nation;

MATTHEW –	MARK –	LUKE – 17	JOHN – 11
			52 And not for that nation only, but that also he should gather together in one the children of God that were scattered abroad. **53** Then from that day forth they took counsel together for to put him to death.

157. JESUS SEEKS REFUGE IN EPHRAIM

MATTHEW	MARK	LUKE	JOHN
			54 Jesus therefore walked no more openly among the Jews; but went thence unto a country near to the wilderness, into a city called Ē·phrā·ĭm, and there continued with his disciples.

158. NORTH INTO SAMARIA AND GALILEE *

MATTHEW	MARK	LUKE	JOHN
		11 ¶ And it came to pass, as he went to Jerusalem, that he passed through the midst of Sä·mär´·ĭ·ä and Galilee.	

159. JESUS CLEANSES TEN LEPERS

MATTHEW	MARK	LUKE	JOHN
		12 And as he entered into a certain village, there met him ten men that were lepers, which stood afar off: **13** And they lifted up *their* voices, and said, Jesus, Master, have mercy on us. **14** And when he saw *them*, he said unto them, Go shew yourselves unto the priests. And it came to pass, that, as they went, they were cleansed. **15** And one of them, when he saw that he was healed, turned back, and with a loud voice glorified God, **16** And fell down on *his* face at his feet, giving him thanks: and he was a Sä·mär´·ĭ·tăn. **17** And Jesus answering said, Were there not ten cleansed? but where *are* the nine? **18** There are not found that returned to give glory to God, save this stranger. **19** And he said unto him, Arise, go thy way: thy faith hath made thee whole.	

160. SIGNS AND TIMES OF THE KINGDOM OF GOD

MATTHEW	MARK	LUKE	JOHN
		20 ¶ And when he was demanded of the Pharisees, when the kingdom of God should come, he answered them and said, The kingdom of God cometh not with observation: **21** Neither shall they say, Lo here! or, lo there! for, behold, the kingdom of God is within you. **22** And he said unto the disciples, The days will come, when ye shall desire to see one of the days of the Son of man, and ye shall not see *it*. **23** And they shall say to you, See here; or, see there: go not after *them*, nor follow *them*. **24** For as the lightning, that lighteneth out of the one *part* under heaven, shineth unto the other *part* under heaven; so shall also the Son of man be in his day.	

*Where did Jesus go after retiring to Ephraim? See note 158.

25 But first must he suffer many things, and be rejected of this generation.

26 And as it was in the days of Nō'-ē, so shall it be also in the days of the Son of man.

27 They did eat, they drank, they married wives, they were given in marriage, until the day that Nō'-ē entered into the ark, and the flood came, and destroyed them all.

28 Likewise also as it was in the days of Lot; they did eat, they drank, they bought, they sold, they planted, they builded;

29 But the same day that Lot went out of Sodom it rained fire and brimstone from heaven, and destroyed *them* all.

30 Even thus shall it be in the day when the Son of man is revealed.

31 In that day, he which shall be upon the housetop, and his stuff in the house, let him not come down to take it away: and he that is in the field, let him likewise not return back.

32 Remember Lot's wife.

33 Whosoever shall seek to save his life shall lose it; and whosoever shall lose his life shall preserve it.

34 I tell you, in that night there shall be two *men* in one bed; the one shall be taken, and the other shall be left.

35 Two *women* shall be grinding together; the one shall be taken, and the other left.

36 Two *men* shall be in the field; the one shall be taken, and the other left.

37 And they answered and said unto him, Where, Lord? And he said unto them, Wheresoever the body *is*, thither will the eagles be gathered together.

161. PARABLE ON PRAYER

CHAPTER 18

AND he spake a parable unto them *to this end,* that men ought always to pray, and not to faint;

2 Saying, There was in a city a judge, which feared not God, neither regarded man:

3 And there was a widow in that city; and she came unto him, saying, Avenge me of mine adversary.

4 And he would not for a while: but afterward he said within himself, Though I fear not God, nor regard man;

5 Yet because this widow troubleth me, I will avenge her, lest by her continual coming she weary me.

6 And the Lord said, Hear what the unjust judge saith.

7 And shall not God avenge his own elect, which cry day and night unto him, though he bear long with them?

8 I tell you that he will avenge them speedily. Nevertheless when the Son of man cometh, shall he find faith on the earth?

162. PARABLE ON HUMILITY

9 And he spake this parable unto certain which trusted in themselves that they were righteous, and despised others:

10 Two men went up into the temple to pray; the one a Pharisee, and the other a publican.

11 The Pharisee stood and prayed thus with himself, God, I thank thee, that I am not as other men *are*, extortioners, unjust, adulterers, or even as this publican.

12 I fast twice in the week, I give tithes of all that I possess.

13 And the publican, standing afar off, would not lift up so much as *his* eyes unto heaven, but smote upon his breast, saying, God be merciful to me a sinner.

14 I tell you, this man went down to his house justified *rather* than the other: for every one that exalteth himself shall be abased; and he that humbleth himself shall be exalted.

163. JESUS TRAVELS FROM GALILEE TO JUDEA

CHAPTER 19

AND it came to pass, *that* when Jesus had finished these sayings, he departed from Galilee, and came into the coasts of Judæa beyond Jordan;

2 And great multitudes followed him; and he healed them there.

CHAPTER 10

AND he arose from thence, and cometh into the coasts of Judæa by the farther side of Jordan: and the people resort unto him again; and, as he was wont, he taught them again.

164. TEACHES ABOUT MARRIAGE AND DIVORCE

3 ¶ The Pharisees also came unto him, tempting him, and saying unto him, Is it lawful for a man to put away his wife for every cause?

2 ¶ And the Pharisees came to him, and asked him, Is it lawful for a man to put away *his* wife? tempting him.

3 And he answered and said unto them, What did Moses command you?

4 And they said, Moses suffered to write a bill of divorcement, and to put *her* away.

4 And he answered and said unto them, Have ye not read, that he which made *them* at the beginning made them male and female,

5 And said, For this cause shall a man leave father and mother, and shall cleave to his wife: and they twain shall be one flesh?

6 Wherefore they are no more twain, but one flesh. What therefore God hath joined together, let not man put asunder.

7 They say unto him, Why did Moses then command to give a writing of divorcement, and to put her away?

8 He saith unto them, Moses because of the hardness of your hearts suffered you to put away your wives: but from the beginning it was not so.

6 But from the beginning of the creation God made them male and female.

7 For this cause shall a man leave his father and mother, and cleave to his wife;

8 And they twain shall be one flesh: so then they are no more twain, but one flesh.

9 What therefore God hath joined together, let not man put asunder.

5 And Jesus answered and said unto them, For the hardness of your heart he wrote you this precept.

10 And in the house his disciples asked him again of the same *matter*.

MATTHEW – 19	MARK – 10	LUKE – 18	JOHN –
9 And I say unto you, Whosoever shall put away his wife, except *it be* for fornication, and shall marry another, committeth adultery: and whoso marrieth her which is put away doth commit adultery. 10 ¶ His disciples say unto him, If the case of the man be so with *his* wife, it is not good to marry. 11 But he said unto them, All *men* cannot receive this saying, save *they* to whom it is given. 12 For there are some eunuchs, which were so born from *their* mother's womb: and there are some eunuchs, which were made eunuchs of men: and there be eunuchs, which have made themselves eunuchs for the kingdom of heaven's sake. He that is able to receive *it*, let him receive *it*.	11 And he saith unto them, Whosoever shall put away his wife, and marry another, committeth adultery against her. 12 And if a woman shall put away her husband, and be married to another, she committeth adultery.		

165. BLESSES LITTLE CHILDREN

MATTHEW – 19	MARK – 10	LUKE – 18	JOHN –
13 ¶ Then were there brought unto him little children, that he should put *his* hands on them, and pray: and the disciples rebuked them. 14 But Jesus said, Suffer little children, and forbid them not, to come unto me: for of such is the kingdom of heaven. 15 And he laid *his* hands on them, and departed thence.	13 ¶ And they brought young children to him, that he should touch them: and *his* disciples rebuked those that brought *them*. 14 But when Jesus saw *it*, he was much displeased, and said unto them, Suffer the little children to come unto me, and forbid them not: for of such is the kingdom of God. 15 Verily I say unto you, Whosoever shall not receive the kingdom of God as a little child, he shall not enter therein. 16 And he took them up in his arms, put *his* hands upon them, and blessed them.	15 And they brought unto him also infants, that he would touch them: but when *his* disciples saw *it*, they rebuked them. 16 But Jesus called them *unto him*, and said, Suffer little children to come unto me, and forbid them not: for of such is the kingdom of God. 17 Verily I say unto you, Whosoever shall not receive the kingdom of God as a little child shall in no wise enter therein.	

166. TEACHES A RICH YOUNG RULER

MATTHEW – 19	MARK – 10	LUKE – 18	JOHN –
16 ¶ And, behold, one came and said unto him, Good Master, what good thing shall I do, that I may have eternal life? 17 And he said unto him, Why callest thou me good? *there is* none good but one, *that is*, God: but if thou wilt enter into life, keep the commandments. 18 He saith unto him, Which? Jesus said, Thou shalt do no murder, Thou shalt not commit adultery, Thou shalt not steal, Thou shalt not bear false witness, 19 Honour thy father and *thy* mother: and, Thou shalt love thy neighbour as thyself. 20 The young man saith unto him, All these things have I kept from my youth up: what lack I yet? 21 Jesus said unto him, If thou wilt be perfect, go *and* sell that thou hast, and give to the poor, and thou shalt have treasure in heaven: and come *and* follow me. 22 But when the young man heard that saying, he went away sorrowful: for he had great possessions.	17 ¶ And when he was gone forth into the way, there came one running, and kneeled to him, and asked him, Good Master, what shall I do that I may inherit eternal life? 18 And Jesus said unto him, Why callest thou me good? *there is* none good but one, *that is*, God. 19 Thou knowest the commandments, Do not commit adultery, Do not kill, Do not steal, Do not bear false witness, Defraud not, Honour thy father and mother. 20 And he answered and said unto him, Master, all these have I observed from my youth. 21 Then Jesus beholding him loved him, and said unto him, One thing thou lackest: go thy way, sell whatsoever thou hast, and give to the poor, and thou shalt have treasure in heaven: and come, take up the cross, and follow me. 22 And he was sad at that saying, and went away grieved: for he had great possessions.	18 And a certain ruler asked him, saying, Good Master, what shall I do to inherit eternal life? 19 And Jesus said unto him, Why callest thou me good? none *is* good, save one, *that is*, God. 20 Thou knowest the commandments, Do not commit adultery, Do not kill, Do not steal, Do not bear false witness, Honour thy father and thy mother. 21 And he said, All these have I kept from my youth up. 22 Now when Jesus heard these things, he said unto him, Yet lackest thou one thing: sell all that thou hast, and distribute unto the poor, and thou shalt have treasure in heaven: and come, follow me. 23 And when he heard this, he was very sorrowful: for he was very rich.	

MATTHEW – 19,20	MARK – 10	LUKE – 18	JOHN –
23 ¶ Then said Jesus unto his disciples, Verily I say unto you, That a rich man shall hardly enter into the kingdom of heaven.	23 ¶ And Jesus looked round about, and saith unto his disciples, How hardly shall they that have riches enter into the kingdom of God! 24 And the disciples were astonished at his words. But Jesus answereth again, and saith unto them, Children, how hard is it for them that trust in riches to enter into the kingdom of God!	24 And when Jesus saw that he was very sorrowful, he said, How hardly shall they that have riches enter into the kingdom of God!	
24 And again I say unto you, It is easier for a camel to go through the eye of a needle, than for a rich man to enter into the kingdom of God. 25 When his disciples heard *it*, they were exceedingly amazed, saying, Who then can be saved?	25 It is easier for a camel to go through the eye of a needle, than for a rich man to enter into the kingdom of God. 26 And they were astonished out of measure, saying among themselves, Who then can be saved?	25 For it is easier for a camel to go through a needle's eye, than for a rich man to enter into the kingdom of God. 26 And they that heard *it* said, Who then can be saved?	
26 But Jesus beheld *them*, and said unto them, With men this is impossible; but with God all things are possible.	27 And Jesus looking upon them saith, With men *it is* impossible, but not with God: for with God all things are possible.	27 And he said, The things which are impossible with men are possible with God.	

167. RESULTS OF FOLLOWING JESUS

MATTHEW	MARK	LUKE	JOHN
27 ¶ Then answered Peter and said unto him, Behold, we have forsaken all, and followed thee; what shall we have therefore? 28 And Jesus said unto them, Verily I say unto you, That ye which have followed me, in the regeneration when the Son of man shall sit in the throne of his glory, ye also shall sit upon twelve thrones, judging the twelve tribes of Israel.	28 ¶ Then Peter began to say unto him, Lo, we have left all, and have followed thee.	28 Then Peter said, Lo, we have left all, and followed thee.	
29 And every one that hath forsaken houses, or brethren, or sisters, or father, or mother, or wife, or children, or lands, for my name's sake, shall receive an hundredfold, and shall inherit everlasting life.	29 And Jesus answered and said, Verily I say unto you, There is no man that hath left house, or brethren, or sisters, or father, or mother, or wife, or children, or lands, for my sake, and the gospel's, 30 But he shall receive an hundredfold now in this time, houses, and brethren, and sisters, and mothers, and children, and lands, with persecutions; and in the world to come eternal life.	29 And he said unto them, Verily I say unto you, There is no man that hath left house, or parents, or brethren, or wife, or children, for the kingdom of God's sake, 30 Who shall not receive manifold more in this present time, and in the world to come life everlasting.	
30 But many *that are* first shall be last; and the last *shall be* first.	31 But many *that are* first shall be last; and the last first.		

168. PARABLE OF LABORERS IN THE VINEYARD

MATTHEW	MARK	LUKE	JOHN
CHAPTER 20 FOR the kingdom of heaven is like unto a man *that is* an householder, which went out early in the morning to hire labourers into his vineyard. 2 And when he had agreed with the labourers for a penny a day, he sent them into his vineyard. 3 And he went out about the third hour, and saw others standing idle in the marketplace, 4 And said unto them; Go ye also into the vineyard, and whatsoever is right I will give you. And they went their way. 5 Again he went out about the sixth and ninth hour, and did likewise. 6 And about the eleventh hour he went out, and found others standing idle, and saith unto them, Why stand ye here all the day idle?			

MATTHEW – 20	MARK – 10	LUKE – 18	JOHN –
7 They say unto him, Because no man hath hired us. He saith unto them, Go ye also into the vineyard; and whatsoever is right, *that* shall ye receive. 8 So when even was come, the lord of the vineyard saith unto his steward, Call the labourers, and give them *their* hire, beginning from the last unto the first. 9 And when they came that *were hired* about the eleventh hour, they received every man a penny. 10 But when the first came, they supposed that they should have received more; and they likewise received every man a penny. 11 And when they had received *it*, they murmured against the goodman of the house, 12 Saying, These last have wrought *but* one hour, and thou hast made them equal unto us, which have borne the burden and heat of the day. 13 But he answered one of them, and said, Friend, I do thee no wrong: didst not thou agree with me for a penny? 14 Take *that* thine *is*, and go thy way: I will give unto this last, even as unto thee. 15 Is it not lawful for me to do what I will with mine own? Is thine eye evil, because I am good? 16 So the last shall be first, and the first last: for many be called, but few chosen.			

169. JESUS FORETELLS HIS DEATH AND RESURRECTION IN JERUSALEM

MATTHEW – 20	MARK – 10	LUKE – 18	JOHN –
17 ¶ And Jesus going up to Jerusalem took the twelve disciples apart in the way, and said unto them, 18 Behold, we go up to Jerusalem; and the Son of man shall be betrayed unto the chief priests and unto the scribes, and they shall condemn him to death, 19 And shall deliver him to the Gentiles to mock, and to scourge, and to crucify *him*: and the third day he shall rise again.	32 ¶ And they were in the way going up to Jerusalem; and Jesus went before them: and they were amazed; and as they followed, they were afraid. And he took again the twelve, and began to tell them what things should happen unto him, 33 *Saying*, Behold, we go up to Jerusalem; and the Son of man shall be delivered unto the chief priests, and unto the scribes; and they shall condemn him to death, and shall deliver him to the Gentiles: 34 And they shall mock him, and shall scourge him, and shall spit upon him, and shall kill him: and the third day he shall rise again.	31 ¶ Then he took *unto him* the twelve, and said unto them, Behold, we go up to Jerusalem, and all things that are written by the prophets concerning the Son of man shall be accomplished. 32 For he shall be delivered unto the Gentiles, and shall be mocked, and spitefully entreated, and spitted on: 33 And they shall scourge *him*, and put him to death: and the third day he shall rise again. 34 And they understood none of these things: and this saying was hid from them, neither knew they the things which were spoken.	

170. SEEKING GREATNESS IN THE KINGDOM

MATTHEW – 20	MARK – 10	LUKE – 18	JOHN –
20 ¶ Then came to him the mother of Zĕb´-ĕ-dĕe's children with her sons, worshipping *him*, and desiring a certain thing of him.	35 ¶ And James and John, the sons of Zĕb´-ĕ-dĕe, come unto him, saying, Master, we would that thou shouldest do for us whatsoever we shall desire.		

MATTHEW – 20

21 And he said unto her, What wilt thou? She saith unto him, Grant that these my two sons may sit, the one on thy right hand, and the other on the left, in thy kingdom.

22 But Jesus answered and said, Ye know not what ye ask. Are ye able to drink of the cup that I shall drink of, and to be baptized with the baptism that I am baptized with? They say unto him, We are able.

23 And he saith unto them, Ye shall drink indeed of my cup, and be baptized with the baptism that I am baptized with: but to sit on my right hand, and on my left, is not mine to give, but *it shall be given to them* for whom it is prepared of my Father.

24 And when the ten heard *it,* they were moved with indignation against the two brethren.

25 But Jesus called them *unto him,* and said, Ye know that the princes of the Gentiles exercise dominion over them, and they that are great exercise authority upon them.

26 But it shall not be so among you: but whosoever will be great among you, let him be your minister;

27 And whosoever will be chief among you, let him be your servant:

28 Even as the Son of man came not to be ministered unto, but to minister, and to give his life a ransom for many.

MARK – 10

36 And he said unto them, What would ye that I should do for you?

37 They said unto him, Grant unto us that we may sit, one on thy right hand, and the other on thy left hand, in thy glory.

38 But Jesus said unto them, Ye know not what ye ask: can ye drink of the cup that I drink of? and be baptized with the baptism that I am baptized with?

39 And they said unto him, We can. And Jesus said unto them, Ye shall indeed drink of the cup that I drink of; and with the baptism that I am baptized withal shall ye be baptized:

40 But to sit on my right hand and on my left hand is not mine to give; but *it shall be given to them* for whom it is prepared.

41 And when the ten heard *it,* they began to be much displeased with James and John.

42 But Jesus called them *to him,* and saith unto them, Ye know that they which are accounted to rule over the Gentiles exercise lordship over them; and their great ones exercise authority upon them.

43 But so shall it not be among you: but whosoever will be great among you, shall be your minister:

44 And whosoever of you will be the chiefest, shall be servant of all.

45 For even the Son of man came not to be ministered unto, but to minister, and to give his life a ransom for many.

171. BLIND BARTIMAEUS AND ANOTHER HEALED NEAR JERICHO

MATTHEW – 20

29 And as they departed from Jericho, a great multitude followed him.

30 ¶ And, behold, two blind men sitting by the way side,

when they heard that Jesus passed by, cried out, saying, Have mercy on us, O Lord, *thou* Son of David.

31 And the multitude rebuked them, because they should hold their peace: but they cried the more, saying, Have mercy on us, O Lord, *thou* Son of David.

32 And Jesus stood still, and called them, and said, What will ye that I shall do unto you?

33 They say unto him, Lord, that our eyes may be opened.

34 So Jesus had compassion *on them,* and touched their eyes: and immediately their eyes received sight, and they followed him.

MARK – 10

46 ¶ And they came to Jericho: and as he went out of Jericho with his disciples and a great number of people, blind Bär-tĭ-mæ´-ŭs, the son of Tĭ-mæ´-ŭs, sat by the highway side begging.

47 And when he heard that it was Jesus of Nazareth, he began to cry out, and say, Jesus, *thou* Son of David, have mercy on me.

48 And many charged him that he should hold his peace: but he cried the more a great deal, *Thou* Son of David, have mercy on me.

49 And Jesus stood still, and commanded him to be called. And they call the blind man, saying unto him, Be of good comfort, rise; he calleth thee.

50 And he, casting away his garment, rose, and came to Jesus.

51 And Jesus answered and said unto him, What wilt thou that I should do unto thee? The blind man said unto him, Lord, that I might receive my sight.

52 And Jesus said unto him, Go thy way; thy faith hath made thee whole. And immediately he received his sight, and followed Jesus in the way.

LUKE – 18

35 ¶ And it came to pass, that as he was come nigh unto Jericho, a certain blind man sat by the way side begging:

36 And hearing the multitude pass by, he asked what it meant.

37 And they told him, that Jesus of Nazareth passeth by.

38 And he cried, saying, Jesus, *thou* Son of David, have mercy on me.

39 And they which went before rebuked him, that he should hold his peace: but he cried so much the more, *Thou* Son of David, have mercy on me.

40 And Jesus stood, and commanded him to be brought unto him: and when he was come near, he asked him,

41 Saying, What wilt thou that I shall do unto thee? And he said, Lord, that I may receive my sight.

42 And Jesus said unto him, Receive thy sight: thy faith hath saved thee.

43 And immediately he received his sight, and followed him, glorifying God: and all the people, when they saw *it,* gave praise unto God.

172. ZACCHAEUS THE SINNER IS SAVED

CHAPTER 19

AND *Jesus* entered and passed through Jericho.

2 And, behold, *there was* a man named Zăc-chæ′-ŭs, which was the chief among the publicans, and he was rich.

3 And he sought to see Jesus who he was; and could not for the press, because he was little of stature.

4 And he ran before, and climbed up into a sycomore tree to see him: for he was to pass that *way*.

5 And when Jesus came to the place, he looked up, and saw him, and said unto him, Zăc-chæ′-ŭs, make haste, and come down; for to day I must abide at thy house.

6 And he made haste, and came down, and received him joyfully.

7 And when they saw *it*, they all murmured, saying, That he was gone to be guest with a man that is a sinner.

8 And Zăc-chæ′-ŭs stood, and said unto the Lord; Behold, Lord, the half of my goods I give to the poor; and if I have taken any thing from any man by false accusation, I restore *him* fourfold.

9 And Jesus said unto him, This day is salvation come to this house, forsomuch as he also is a son of Abraham.

10 For the Son of man is come to seek and to save that which was lost.

173. PARABLE SHOWING THE KINGDOM OF GOD NOT TO APPEAR IMMEDIATELY

11 And as they heard these things, he added and spake a parable, because he was nigh to Jerusalem, and because they thought that the kingdom of God should immediately appear.

12 He said therefore, A certain nobleman went into a far country to receive for himself a kingdom, and to return.

13 And he called his ten servants, and delivered them ten pounds, and said unto them, Occupy till I come.

14 But his citizens hated him, and sent a message after him, saying, We will not have this *man* to reign over us.

15 And it came to pass, that when he was returned, having received the kingdom, then he commanded these servants to be called unto him, to whom he had given the money, that he might know how much every man had gained by trading.

16 Then came the first, saying, Lord, thy pound hath gained ten pounds.

17 And he said unto him, Well, thou good servant: because thou hast been faithful in a very little, have thou authority over ten cities.

18 And the second came, saying, Lord, thy pound hath gained five pounds.

19 And he said likewise to him, Be thou also over five cities.

MATTHEW – 26	MARK – 14	LUKE – 19	JOHN – 11,12
		20 And another came, saying, Lord, behold, *here is* thy pound, which I have kept laid up in a napkin: 21 For I feared thee, because thou art an austere man: thou takest up that thou layedst not down, and reapest that thou didst not sow. 22 And he saith unto him, Out of thine own mouth will I judge thee, *thou* wicked servant. Thou knewest that I was an austere man, taking up that I laid not down, and reaping that I did not sow: 23 Wherefore then gavest not thou my money into the bank, that at my coming I might have required mine own with usury? 24 And he said unto them that stood by, Take from him the pound, and give *it* to him that hath ten pounds. 25 (And they said unto him, Lord, he hath ten pounds.) 26 For I say unto you, That unto every one which hath shall be given; and from him that hath not, even that he hath shall be taken away from him. 27 But those mine enemies, which would not that I should reign over them, bring hither, and slay *them* before me.	

174. JESUS APPROACHES JERUSALEM FOR THE PASSOVER

| | | 28 ¶ And when he had thus spoken, he went before, ascending up to Jerusalem. | |

175. MANY SEEK JESUS AT THE PASSOVER

| | | | 55 ¶ And the Jews' passover was nigh at hand: and many went out of the country up to Jerusalem before the passover, to purify themselves. 56 Then sought they for Jesus, and spake among themselves, as they stood in the temple, What think ye, that he will not come to the feast? 57 Now both the chief priests and the Pharisees had given a commandment, that, if any man knew where he were, he should shew *it*, that they might take him. |

176. MARY ANOINTS JESUS AT THE HOME OF SIMON THE LEPER *

MATTHEW – 26	MARK – 14	LUKE – 19	JOHN – 11,12
6 ¶ Now when Jesus was in Bethany, in the house of Simon the leper, 7 There came unto him a woman having an alabaster box of very precious ointment, and poured it on his head, as he sat *at meat.*	3 ¶ And being in Bethany in the house of Simon the leper, as he sat at meat, there came a woman having an alabaster box of ointment of spikenard very precious; and she brake the box, and poured *it* on his head.		**CHAPTER 12** THEN Jesus six days before the passover came to Bethany, where Lăz′-ă-rŭs was which had been dead, whom he raised from the dead. 2 There they made him a supper; and Martha served: but Lăz′-ă-rŭs was one of them that sat at the table with him. 3 Then took Mary a pound of ointment of spikenard, very costly, and anointed the feet of Jesus, and wiped his feet with her hair: and the house was filled with the odour of the ointment.

*Matthew and Mark place the anointing two days before the Passover while John states it was six days.

109

MATTHEW – 26	MARK – 14	LUKE –	JOHN – 12
8 But when his disciples saw *it*, they had indignation, saying, To what purpose *is* this waste?	4 And there were some that had indignation within themselves, and said, Why was this waste of the ointment made?		
9 For this ointment might have been sold for much, and given to the poor.	5 For it might have been sold for more than three hundred pence, and have been given to the poor.		4 Then saith one of his disciples, Judas Iscariot, Simon's *son*, which should betray him, 5 Why was not this ointment sold for three hundred pence, and given to the poor? 6 This he said, not that he cared for the poor; but because he was a thief, and had the bag, and bare what was put therein.
10 When Jesus understood *it*, he said unto them, Why trouble ye the woman? for she hath wrought a good work upon me. 11 For ye have the poor always with you; but me ye have not always.	And they murmured against her. 6 And Jesus said, Let her alone; why trouble ye her? she hath wrought a good work on me. 7 For ye have the poor with you always, and whensoever ye will ye may do them good: but me ye have not always.		7 Then said Jesus, Let her alone: against the day of my burying hath she kept this. 8 For the poor always ye have with you; but me ye have not always.
12 For in that she hath poured this ointment on my body, she did *it* for my burial. 13 Verily I say unto you, Wheresoever this gospel shall be preached in the whole world, *there* shall also this, that this woman hath done, be told for a memorial of her.	8 She hath done what she could: she is come aforehand to anoint my body to the burying. 9 Verily I say unto you, Wheresoever this gospel shall be preached throughout the whole world, *this* also that she hath done shall be spoken of for a memorial of her.		

177. MANY SEE LAZARUS AT BETHANY AND BELIEVE

			9 Much people of the Jews therefore knew that he was there: and they came not for Jesus' sake only, but that they might see Lăz´-ă-rŭs also, whom he had raised from the dead. 10 ¶ But the chief priests consulted that they might put Lăz´-ă-rŭs also to death; 11 Because that by reason of him many of the Jews went away, and believed on Jesus.

VIII. THE WEEK OF ATONEMENT

Sunday

178. THE TRIUMPHAL ENTRY INTO JERUSALEM AND RETURN TO BETHANY

CHAPTER 21

AND when they drew nigh unto Jerusalem, and were come to Bĕth´-phă-ġē, unto the mount of Olives, then sent Jesus two disciples,

2 Saying unto them, Go into the village over against you, and straightway ye shall find an ass tied, and a colt with her: loose *them*, and bring *them* unto me.

3 And if any *man* say ought unto you, ye shall say, The Lord hath need of them; and straightway he will send them.

6 And the disciples went, and did as Jesus commanded them,

7 And brought the ass, and the colt, and put on them their clothes, and they set *him* thereon.

4 All this was done, that it might be fulfilled which was spoken by the prophet, saying,

5 Tell ye the daughter of Sĭ´-on, Behold, thy King cometh unto thee, meek, and sitting upon an ass, and a colt the foal of an ass.

8 And a very great multitude spread their garments in the way; others cut down branches from the trees, and strawed *them* in the way.

CHAPTER 11

AND when they came nigh to Jerusalem, unto Bĕth´-phă-ġē and Bethany, at the mount of Olives, he sendeth forth two of his disciples,

2 And saith unto them, Go your way into the village over against you: and as soon as ye be entered into it, ye shall find a colt tied, whereon never man sat; loose him, and bring *him*.

3 And if any man say unto you, Why do ye this? say ye that the Lord hath need of him; and straightway he will send him hither.

4 And they went their way, and found the colt tied by the door without in a place where two ways met; and they loose him.

5 And certain of them that stood there said unto them, What do ye, loosing the colt?

6 And they said unto them even as Jesus had commanded: and they let them go.

7 And they brought the colt to Jesus, and cast their garments on him; and he sat upon him.

8 And many spread their garments in the way: and others cut down branches off the trees, and strawed *them* in the way.

29 And it came to pass, when he was come nigh to Bĕth´-phă-ġē and Bethany, at the mount called *the mount* of Olives, he sent two of his disciples,

30 Saying, Go ye into the village over against *you;* in the which at your entering ye shall find a colt tied, whereon yet never man sat: loose him, and bring *him hither*.

31 And if any man ask you, Why do ye loose *him?* thus shall ye say unto him, Because the Lord hath need of him.

32 And they that were sent went their way, and found even as he had said unto them.

33 And as they were loosing the colt, the owners thereof said unto them, Why loose ye the colt?

34 And they said, The Lord hath need of him.

35 And they brought him to Jesus: and they cast their garments upon the colt, and they set Jesus thereon.

36 And as he went, they spread their clothes in the way.

37 And when he was come nigh, even now at the descent of the mount of Olives, the whole multitude of the disciples began to rejoice and praise God with a loud voice for all the mighty works that they had seen;

12 ¶ On the next day much people that were come to the feast, when they heard that Jesus was coming to Jerusalem,

13 Took branches of palm trees, and went forth to meet him, and cried, Hō-săn´-nă: Blessed *is* the King of Israel that cometh in the name of the Lord.

14 And Jesus, when he had found a young ass, sat thereon; as it is written,

15 Fear not, daughter of Sĭ´-on: behold, thy King cometh, sitting on an ass's colt.

16 These things understood not his disciples at the first: but when Jesus was glorified, then remembered they that these things were written of him, and *that* they had done these things unto him.

17 The people therefore that was with him when he called Lăz´-ă-rŭs out of his grave, and raised him from the dead, bare record.

18 For this cause the people also met him, for that they heard that he had done this miracle.

111

MATTHEW – 21	MARK – 11	LUKE – 19	JOHN – 12
9 And the multitudes that went before, and that followed, cried, saying, Hō-săn´-nă to the Son of David: Blessed is he that cometh in the name of the Lord; Hō-săn´-nă in the highest.	9 And they that went before, and they that followed, cried, saying, Hō-săn´-nă; Blessed is he that cometh in the name of the Lord: 10 Blessed be the kingdom of our father David, that cometh in the name of the Lord: Hō-săn´-nă in the highest.	38 Saying, Blessed be the King that cometh in the name of the Lord: peace in heaven, and glory in the highest. 39 And some of the Pharisees from among the multitude said unto him, Master, rebuke thy disciples. 40 And he answered and said unto them, I tell you that, if these should hold their peace, the stones would immediately cry out.	19 The Pharisees therefore said among themselves, Perceive ye how ye prevail nothing? behold, the world is gone after him.
		41 ¶ And when he was come near, he beheld the city, and wept over it, 42 Saying, If thou hadst known, even thou, at least in this thy day, the things which belong unto thy peace! but now they are hid from thine eyes. 43 For the days shall come upon thee, that thine enemies shall cast a trench about thee, and compass thee round, and keep thee in on every side, 44 And shall lay thee even with the ground, and thy children within thee; and they shall not leave in thee one stone upon another; because thou knewest not the time of thy visitation.	
10 And when he was come into Jerusalem, all the city was moved, saying, Who is this? 11 And the multitude said, This is Jesus the prophet of Nazareth of Galilee.	11 And Jesus entered into Jerusalem, and into the temple: and when he had looked round about upon all things, and now the eventide was come, he went out unto Bethany with the twelve.		

Monday

179. JESUS CURSES A FIG TREE

18 Now in the morning as he returned into the city, he hungered. 19 And when he saw a fig tree in the way, he came to it, and found nothing thereon, but leaves only, and said unto it, Let no fruit grow on thee henceforward for ever. And presently the fig tree withered away.	12 ¶ And on the morrow, when they were come from Bethany, he was hungry: 13 And seeing a fig tree afar off having leaves, he came, if haply he might find any thing thereon: and when he came to it, he found nothing but leaves; for the time of figs was not yet. 14 And Jesus answered and said unto it, No man eat fruit of thee hereafter for ever. And his disciples heard it.		

180. SECOND CLEANSING OF THE TEMPLE

12 ¶ And Jesus went into the temple of God, and cast out all them that sold and bought in the temple, and overthrew the tables of the moneychangers, and the seats of them that sold doves,	15 ¶ And they come to Jerusalem: and Jesus went into the temple, and began to cast out them that sold and bought in the temple, and overthrew the tables of the moneychangers, and the seats of them that sold doves;	45 And he went into the temple, and began to cast out them that sold therein, and them that bought;	

112

MATTHEW – 21	MARK – 11	LUKE – 19,21	JOHN –
	16 And would not suffer that any man should carry *any* vessel through the temple. 17 And he taught, saying unto them, Is it not written, My house shall be called of all nations the house of prayer? but ye have made it a den of thieves.		
13 And said unto them, It is written, My house shall be called the house of prayer; but ye have made it a den of thieves. 14 And the blind and the lame came to him in the temple; and he healed them. 15 And when the chief priests and scribes saw the wonderful things that he did, and the children crying in the temple, and saying, Hō-săn'-nă to the Son of David; they were sore displeased, 16 And said unto him, Hearest thou what these say? And Jesus saith unto them, Yea; have ye never read, Out of the mouth of babes and sucklings thou hast perfected praise?		46 Saying unto them, It is written, My house is the house of prayer: but ye have made it a den of thieves.	
		47 And he taught daily in the temple. But the chief priests and the scribes and the chief of the people sought to destroy him, 48 And could not find what they might do: for all the people were very attentive to hear him.	
	18 And the scribes and chief priests heard *it*, and sought how they might destroy him: for they feared him, because all the people was astonished at his doctrine.		

181. RETURN TO BETHANY

MATTHEW	MARK	LUKE	JOHN
17 ¶ And he left them, and went out of the city into Bethany; and he lodged there.	19 And when even was come, he went out of the city.	Ch. 21 37 And in the day time he was teaching in the temple; and at night he went out, and abode in the mount that is called *the mount* of Olives.	

Tuesday

182. SEEING WITHERED FIG TREE, TEACHES ON FAITH, PRAYER AND FORGIVENESS

MATTHEW	MARK	LUKE	JOHN
	20 ¶ And in the morning, as they passed by, they saw the fig tree dried up from the roots. 21 And Peter calling to remembrance saith unto him, Master, behold, the fig tree which thou cursedst is withered away. 22 And Jesus answering saith unto them, Have faith in God.		
20 And when the disciples saw *it*, they marvelled, saying, How soon is the fig tree withered away! 21 Jesus answered and said unto them, Verily I say unto you, If ye have faith, and doubt not, ye shall not only do this *which is done* to the fig tree, but also if ye shall say unto this mountain, Be thou removed, and be thou cast into the sea; it shall be done.	23 For verily I say unto you, That whosoever shall say unto this mountain, Be thou removed, and be thou cast into the sea; and shall not doubt in his heart, but shall believe that those things which he saith shall come to pass; he shall have whatsoever he saith. 24 Therefore I say unto you, What things soever ye desire, when ye pray, believe that ye receive *them*, and ye shall have *them*.		
22 And all things, whatsoever ye shall ask in prayer, believing, ye shall receive.	25 And when ye stand praying, forgive, if ye have ought against any: that your Father also which is in heaven may forgive you your trespasses. 26 But if ye do not forgive, neither will your Father which is in heaven forgive your trespasses.		

183. JESUS ASKED BY WHAT AUTHORITY HE ACTS

38 And all the people came early in the morning to him in the temple, for to hear him.

CHAPTER 20

AND it came to pass, *that* on one of those days, as he taught the people in the temple, and preached the gospel, the chief priests and the scribes came upon *him* with the elders,

23 ¶ And when he was come into the temple, the chief priests and the elders of the people came unto him as he was teaching, and said, By what authority doest thou these things? and who gave thee this authority?

27 ¶ And they come again to Jerusalem: and as he was walking in the temple, there come to him the chief priests, and the scribes, and the elders,

28 And say unto him, By what authority doest thou these things? and who gave thee this authority to do these things?

2 And spake unto him, saying, Tell us, by what authority doest thou these things? or who is he that gave thee this authority?

24 And Jesus answered and said unto them, I also will ask you one thing, which if ye tell me, I in like wise will tell you by what authority I do these things.

29 And Jesus answered and said unto them, I will also ask of you one question, and answer me, and I will tell you by what authority I do these things.

3 And he answered and said unto them, I will also ask you one thing; and answer me:

25 The baptism of John, whence was it? from heaven, or of men?

30 The baptism of John, was *it* from heaven, or of men? answer me.

4 The baptism of John, was it from heaven, or of men?

And they reasoned with themselves, saying, If we shall say, From heaven; he will say unto us, Why did ye not then believe him?

31 And they reasoned with themselves, saying, If we shall say, From heaven; he will say, Why then did ye not believe him?

5 And they reasoned with themselves, saying, If we shall say, From heaven; he will say, Why then believed ye him not?

26 But if we shall say, Of men; we fear the people; for all hold John as a prophet.

32 But if we shall say, Of men; they feared the people: for all *men* counted John, that he was a prophet indeed.

6 But and if we say, Of men; all the people will stone us: for they be persuaded that John was a prophet.

27 And they answered Jesus, and said, We cannot tell. And he said unto them, Neither tell I you by what authority I do these things.

33 And they answered and said unto Jesus, We cannot tell. And Jesus answering saith unto them, Neither do I tell you by what authority I do these things.

7 And they answered, that they could not tell whence *it was.*

8 And Jesus said unto them, Neither tell I you by what authority I do these things.

184. PARABLE OF THE TWO SONS

28 ¶ But what think ye? A *certain* man had two sons; and he came to the first, and said, Son, go work to day in my vineyard.

29 He answered and said, I will not: but afterward he repented, and went.

30 And he came to the second, and said likewise. And he answered and said, I *go,* sir: and went not.

31 Whether of them twain did the will of *his* father? They say unto him, The first. Jesus saith unto them, Verily I say unto you, That the publicans and the harlots go into the kingdom of God before you.

32 For John came unto you in the way of righteousness, and ye believed him not: but the publicans and the harlots believed him: and ye, when ye had seen *it,* repented not afterward, that ye might believe him.

185. PARABLE OF THE WICKED HUSBANDMEN

CHAPTER 12

33 ¶ Hear another parable: There was a certain householder, which planted a vineyard, and hedged it round about, and digged a winepress in it, and built a tower, and let it out to husbandmen, and went into a far country:

AND he began to speak unto them by parables. A *certain* man planted a vineyard, and set an hedge about *it,* and digged *a place for* the winefat, and built a tower, and let it out to husbandmen, and went into a far country.

9 Then began he to speak to the people this parable; A certain man planted a vineyard, and let it forth to husbandmen, and went into a far country for a long time.

MATTHEW – 21,22	MARK – 12	LUKE – 20	JOHN –
34 And when the time of the fruit drew near, he sent his servants to the husbandmen, that they might receive the fruits of it. 35 And the husbandmen took his servants, and beat one, and killed another, and stoned another. 36 Again, he sent other servants more than the first: and they did unto them likewise.	2 And at the season he sent to the husbandmen a servant, that he might receive from the husbandmen of the fruit of the vineyard. 3 And they caught *him*, and beat him, and sent *him* away empty. 4 And again he sent unto them another servant; and at him they cast stones, and wounded *him* in the head, and sent *him* away shamefully handled. 5 And again he sent another; and him they killed, and many others; beating some, and killing some.	10 And at the season he sent a servant to the husbandmen, that they should give him of the fruit of the vineyard: but the husbandmen beat him, and sent *him* away empty. 11 And again he sent another servant: and they beat him also, and entreated *him* shamefully, and sent *him* away empty. 12 And again he sent a third: and they wounded him also, and cast *him* out.	
37 But last of all he sent unto them his son, saying, They will reverence my son. 38 But when the husbandmen saw the son, they said among themselves, This is the heir; come, let us kill him, and let us seize on his inheritance. 39 And they caught him, and cast *him* out of the vineyard, and slew *him*. 40 When the lord therefore of the vineyard cometh, what will he do unto those husbandmen?	6 Having yet therefore one son, his wellbeloved, he sent him also last unto them, saying, They will reverence my son. 7 But those husbandmen said among themselves, This is the heir; come, let us kill him, and the inheritance shall be ours. 8 And they took him, and killed *him*, and cast *him* out of the vineyard.	13 Then said the lord of the vineyard, What shall I do? I will send my beloved son: it may be they will reverence *him* when they see him. 14 But when the husbandmen saw him, they reasoned among themselves, saying, This is the heir: come, let us kill him, that the inheritance may be ours. 15 So they cast him out of the vineyard, and killed *him*. What therefore shall the lord of the vineyard do unto them?	
41 They say unto him, He will miserably destroy those wicked men, and will let out *his* vineyard unto other husbandmen, which shall render him the fruits in their seasons.	9 What shall therefore the lord of the vineyard do? he will come and destroy the husbandmen, and will give the vineyard unto others.	16 He shall come and destroy these husbandmen, and shall give the vineyard to others. And when they heard *it*, they said, God forbid.	
42 Jesus saith unto them, Did ye never read in the scriptures, The stone which the builders rejected, the same is become the head of the corner: this is the Lord's doing, and it is marvellous in our eyes? 43 Therefore say I unto you, The kingdom of God shall be taken from you, and given to a nation bringing forth the fruits thereof.	10 And have ye not read this scripture; The stone which the builders rejected is become the head of the corner: 11 This was the Lord's doing, and it is marvellous in our eyes?	17 And he beheld them, and said, What is this then that is written, The stone which the builders rejected, the same is become the head of the corner?	
44 And whosoever shall fall on this stone shall be broken: but on whomsoever it shall fall, it will grind him to powder. 45 And when the chief priests and Pharisees had heard his parables, they perceived that he spake of them. 46 But when they sought to lay hands on him, they feared the multitude, because they took him for a prophet.	12 And they sought to lay hold on him, but feared the people: for they knew that he had spoken the parable against them: and they left him, and went their way.	18 Whosoever shall fall upon that stone shall be broken; but on whomsoever it shall fall, it will grind him to powder. 19 ¶ And the chief priests and the scribes the same hour sought to lay hands on him; and they feared the people: for they perceived that he had spoken this parable against them.	

186. PARABLE OF THE MARRIAGE OF THE KING'S SON

CHAPTER 22

AND Jesus answered and spake unto them again by parables, and said,

2 The kingdom of heaven is like unto a certain king, which made a marriage for his son,

3 And sent forth his servants to call them that were bidden to the wedding: and they would not come.

4 Again, he sent forth other servants, saying, Tell them which are bidden, Behold, I have prepared my dinner: my oxen and *my* fatlings *are* killed, and all things *are* ready: come unto the marriage.

5 But they made light of *it*, and went their ways, one to his farm, another to his merchandise:

6 And the remnant took his servants, and entreated *them* spitefully, and slew *them*.

7 But when the king heard *thereof*, he was wroth: and he sent forth his armies, and destroyed those murderers, and burned up their city.

8 Then saith he to his servants, The wedding is ready, but they which were bidden were not worthy.

9 Go ye therefore into the highways, and as many as ye shall find, bid to the marriage.

10 So those servants went out into the highways, and gathered together all as many as they found, both bad and good: and the wedding was furnished with guests.

11 ¶ And when the king came in to see the guests, he saw there a man which had not on a wedding garment:

12 And he saith unto him, Friend, how camest thou in hither not having a wedding garment? And he was speechless.

13 Then said the king to the servants, Bind him hand and foot, and take him away, and cast *him* into outer darkness; there shall be weeping and gnashing of teeth.

14 For many are called, but few *are* chosen.

187. QUESTIONED ABOUT PAYING TRIBUTE TO CAESAR

15 ¶ Then went the Pharisees, and took counsel how they might entangle him in *his* talk.

16 And they sent out unto him their disciples with the Hĕ-rō'-di-ăns, saying, Master, we know that thou art true, and teachest the way of God in truth, neither carest thou for any *man*: for thou regardest not the person of men.

17 Tell us therefore, What thinkest thou? Is it lawful to give tribute unto Cæsar, or not?

18 But Jesus perceived their wickedness, and said, Why tempt ye me, *ye* hypocrites?

19 Shew me the tribute money. And they brought unto him a penny.

20 And he saith unto them, Whose *is* this image and superscription?

21 They say unto him, Cæsar's. Then saith he unto them, Render therefore unto Cæsar the things which are Cæsar's; and unto God the things that are God's.

22 When they had heard *these words*, they marvelled, and left him, and went their way.

13 ¶ And they send unto him certain of the Pharisees and of the Hĕ-rō'-di-ăns, to catch him in *his* words.

14 And when they were come, they say unto him, Master, we know that thou art true, and carest for no man: for thou regardest not the person of men, but teachest the way of God in truth: Is it lawful to give tribute to Cæsar, or not?

15 Shall we give, or shall we not give? But he, knowing their hypocrisy, said unto them, Why tempt ye me? bring me a penny, that I may see *it*.

16 And they brought *it*. And he saith unto them, Whose *is* this image and superscription? And they said unto him, Cæsar's.

17 And Jesus answering said unto them, Render to Cæsar the things that are Cæsar's, and to God the things that are God's.

And they marvelled at him.

20 And they watched *him*, and sent forth spies, which should feign themselves just men, that they might take hold of his words, that so they might deliver him unto the power and authority of the governor.

21 And they asked him, saying, Master, we know that thou sayest and teachest rightly, neither acceptest thou the person *of any*, but teachest the way of God truly:

22 Is it lawful for us to give tribute unto Cæsar, or no?

23 But he perceived their craftiness, and said unto them, Why tempt ye me?

24 Shew me a penny. Whose image and superscription hath it? They answered and said, Cæsar's.

25 And he said unto them, Render therefore unto Cæsar the things which be Cæsar's, and unto God the things which be God's.

26 And they could not take hold of his words before the people: and they marvelled at his answer, and held their peace.

188. QUESTIONED ABOUT MARRIAGE AND THE RESURRECTION

MATTHEW – 22

23 ¶ The same day came to him the Săd´-dū-çĕeṡ, which say that there is no resurrection, and asked him,

24 Saying, Master, Moses said, If a man die, having no children, his brother shall marry his wife, and raise up seed unto his brother.

25 Now there were with us seven brethren: and the first, when he had married a wife, deceased, and, having no issue, left his wife unto his brother:

26 Likewise the second also, and the third, unto the seventh.

27 And last of all the woman died also.

28 Therefore in the resurrection whose wife shall she be of the seven? for they all had her.

29 Jesus answered and said unto them, Ye do err, not knowing the scriptures, nor the power of God.

30 For in the resurrection they neither marry, nor are given in marriage, but are as the angels of God in heaven.

31 But as touching the resurrection of the dead, have ye not read that which was spoken unto you by God, saying,

32 I am the God of Abraham, and the God of Isaac, and the God of Jacob? God is not the God of the dead, but of the living.

33 And when the multitude heard *this*, they were astonished at his doctrine.

MARK – 12

18 ¶ Then come unto him the Săd´-dū-çĕeṡ, which say there is no resurrection; and they asked him, saying,

19 Master, Moses wrote unto us, If a man's brother die, and leave *his* wife *behind him*, and leave no children, that his brother should take his wife, and raise up seed unto his brother.

20 Now there were seven brethren: and the first took a wife, and dying left no seed.

21 And the second took her, and died, neither left he any seed: and the third likewise.

22 And the seven had her, and left no seed: last of all the woman died also.

23 In the resurrection therefore, when they shall rise, whose wife shall she be of them? for the seven had her to wife.

24 And Jesus answering said unto them, Do ye not therefore err, because ye know not the scriptures, neither the power of God?

25 For when they shall rise from the dead, they neither marry, nor are given in marriage; but are as the angels which are in heaven.

26 And as touching the dead, that they rise: have ye not read in the book of Moses, how in the bush God spake unto him, saying, I *am* the God of Abraham, and the God of Isaac, and the God of Jacob?

27 He is not the God of the dead, but the God of the living: ye therefore do greatly err.

LUKE – 20

27 ¶ Then came to *him* certain of the Săd´-dū-çĕeṡ, which deny that there is any resurrection; and they asked him,

28 Saying, Master, Moses wrote unto us, If any man's brother die, having a wife, and he die without children, that his brother should take his wife, and raise up seed unto his brother.

29 There were therefore seven brethren: and the first took a wife, and died without children.

30 And the second took her to wife, and he died childless.

31 And the third took her; and in like manner the seven also: and they left no children, and died.

32 Last of all the woman died also.

33 Therefore in the resurrection whose wife of them is she? for seven had her to wife.

34 And Jesus answering said unto them, The children of this world marry, and are given in marriage:

35 But they which shall be accounted worthy to obtain that world, and the resurrection from the dead, neither marry, nor are given in marriage:

36 Neither can they die any more: for they are equal unto the angels; and are the children of God, being the children of the resurrection.

37 Now that the dead are raised, even Moses shewed at the bush, when he calleth the Lord the God of Abraham, and the God of Isaac, and the God of Jacob.

38 For he is not a God of the dead, but of the living: for all live unto him.

39 ¶ Then certain of the scribes answering said, Master, thou hast well said.

189. "WHICH IS THE GREAT COMMANDMENT IN THE LAW?"

MATTHEW – 22

34 ¶ But when the Pharisees had heard that he had put the Săd´-dū-çĕeṡ to silence, they were gathered together.

35 Then one of them, *which was* a lawyer, asked *him a question*, tempting him, and saying,

36 Master, which *is* the great commandment in the law?

37 Jesus said unto him,

Thou shalt love the Lord thy God with all thy heart, and with all thy soul, and with all thy mind.

38 This is the first and great commandment.

39 And the second *is* like unto it, Thou shalt love thy neighbour as thyself.

MARK – 12

28 ¶ And one of the scribes came, and having heard them reasoning together, and perceiving that he had answered them well, asked him, Which is the first commandment of all?

29 And Jesus answered him, The first of all the commandments *is*, Hear, O Israel; The Lord our God is one Lord:

30 And thou shalt love the Lord thy God with all thy heart, and with all thy soul, and with all thy mind, and with all thy strength: this *is* the first commandment.

31 And the second *is* like, *namely* this, Thou shalt love thy neighbour as thyself. There is none other commandment greater than these.

MATTHEW – 22,23	MARK – 12	LUKE – 20	JOHN –
40 On these two commandments hang all the law and the prophets.	32 And the scribe said unto him, Well, Master, thou hast said the truth: for there is one God; and there is none other but he: 33 And to love him with all the heart, and with all the understanding, and with all the soul, and with all the strength, and to love *his* neighbour as himself, is more than all whole burnt offerings and sacrifices. 34 And when Jesus saw that he answered discreetly, he said unto him, Thou art not far from the kingdom of God. And no man after that durst ask him *any question.*	40 And after that they durst not ask him any *question at all.*	

190. "WHAT THINK YE OF CHRIST? WHOSE SON IS HE?"

MATTHEW	MARK	LUKE	JOHN
41 ¶ While the Pharisees were gathered together, Jesus asked them, 42 Saying, What think ye of Christ? whose son is he? They say unto him, *The Son* of David. 43 He saith unto them, How then doth David in spirit call him Lord, saying, 44 The LORD said unto my Lord, Sit thou on my right hand, till I make thine enemies thy footstool? 45 If David then call him Lord, how is he his son? 46 And no man was able to answer him a word, neither durst any *man* from that day forth ask him any more *questions.*	35 ¶ And Jesus answered and said, while he taught in the temple, How say the scribes that Christ is the Son of David? 36 For David himself said by the Holy Ghost, The LORD said to my Lord, Sit thou on my right hand, till I make thine enemies thy footstool. 37 David therefore himself calleth him Lord; and whence is he *then* his son? And the common people heard him gladly.	41 And he said unto them, How say they that Christ is David's son? 42 And David himself saith in the book of Psalms, The LORD said unto my Lord, Sit thou on my right hand, 43 Till I make thine enemies thy footstool. 44 David therefore calleth him Lord, how is he then his son?	

191. JESUS WARNS AGAINST AND CONDEMNS THE SCRIBES AND PHARISEES

MATTHEW	MARK	LUKE	JOHN
CHAPTER 23 THEN spake Jesus to the multitude, and to his disciples, 2 Saying, The scribes and the Pharisees sit in Moses' seat: 3 All therefore whatsoever they bid you observe, *that* observe and do; but do not ye after their works: for they say, and do not. 4 For they bind heavy burdens and grievous to be borne, and lay *them* on men's shoulders; but they *themselves* will not move them with one of their fingers. 5 But all their works they do for to be seen of men: they make broad their phylacteries, and enlarge the borders of their garments, 6 And love the uppermost rooms at feasts, and the chief seats in the synagogues, 7 And greetings in the markets, and to be called of men, Rabbi, Rabbi. 8 But be not ye called Rabbi: for one is your Master, *even* Christ; and all ye are brethren. 9 And call no *man* your father upon the earth: for one is your Father, which is in heaven.	38 ¶ And he said unto them in his doctrine, Beware of the scribes, which love to go in long clothing, and *love* salutations in the marketplaces, 39 And the chief seats in the synagogues, and the uppermost rooms at feasts:	45 ¶ Then in the audience of all the people he said unto his disciples, 46 Beware of the scribes, which desire to walk in long robes, and love greetings in the markets, and the highest seats in the synagogues, and the chief rooms at feasts;	

10 Neither be ye called masters: for one is your Master, *even* Christ.

11 But he that is greatest among you shall be your servant.

12 And whosoever shall exalt himself shall be abased; and he that shall humble himself shall be exalted.

13 ¶ But woe unto you, scribes and Pharisees, hypocrites! for ye shut up the kingdom of heaven against men: for ye neither go in *yourselves*, neither suffer ye them that are entering to go in.

14 Woe unto you, scribes and Pharisees, hypocrites! for ye devour widows' houses, and for a pretence make long prayer: therefore ye shall receive the greater damnation.

15 Woe unto you, scribes and Pharisees, hypocrites! for ye compass sea and land to make one proselyte, and when he is made, ye make him twofold more the child of hell than yourselves.

16 Woe unto you, *ye* blind guides, which say, Whosoever shall swear by the temple, it is nothing; but whosoever shall swear by the gold of the temple, he is a debtor!

17 *Ye* fools and blind: for whether is greater, the gold, or the temple that sanctifieth the gold?

18 And, Whosoever shall swear by the altar, it is nothing; but whosoever sweareth by the gift that is upon it, he is guilty.

19 *Ye* fools and blind: for whether *is* greater, the gift, or the altar that sanctifieth the gift?

20 Whoso therefore shall swear by the altar, sweareth by it, and by all things thereon.

21 And whoso shall swear by the temple, sweareth by it, and by him that dwelleth therein.

22 And he that shall swear by heaven, sweareth by the throne of God, and by him that sitteth thereon.

23 Woe unto you, scribes and Pharisees, hypocrites! for ye pay tithe of mint and anise and cummin, and have omitted the weightier *matters* of the law, judgment, mercy, and faith: these ought ye to have done, and not to leave the other undone.

24 *Ye* blind guides, which strain at a gnat, and swallow a camel.

25 Woe unto you, scribes and Pharisees, hypocrites! for ye make clean the outside of the cup and of the platter. but within they are full of extortion and excess.

26 *Thou* blind Pharisee, cleanse first that *which is* within the cup and platter, that the outside of them may be clean also.

27 Woe unto you, scribes and Pharisees, hypocrites! for ye are like unto whited sepulchres, which indeed appear beautiful outward, but are within full of dead *men's* bones, and of all uncleanness.

28 Even so ye also outwardly appear righteous unto men, but within ye are full of hypocrisy and iniquity.

MARK

40 Which devour widows' houses, and for a pretence make long prayers: these shall receive greater damnation.

LUKE

47 Which devour widows' houses, and for a shew make long prayers: the same shall receive greater damnation.

MATTHEW – 23	MARK – 12	LUKE – 21	JOHN – 12
29 Woe unto you, scribes and Pharisees, hypocrites! because ye build the tombs of the prophets, and garnish the sepulchres of the righteous, 30 And say, If we had been in the days of our fathers, we would not have been partakers with them in the blood of the prophets. 31 Wherefore ye be witnesses unto yourselves, that ye are the children of them which killed the prophets. 32 Fill ye up then the measure of your fathers. 33 *Ye* serpents, *ye* generation of vipers, how can ye escape the damnation of hell? 34 ¶ Wherefore, behold, I send unto you prophets, and wise men, and scribes: and *some* of them ye shall kill and crucify; and *some* of them shall ye scourge in your synagogues, and persecute *them* from city to city: 35 That upon you may come all the righteous blood shed upon the earth, from the blood of righteous Abel unto the blood of Zăch·ȧ·rī´·ȧs son of Băr·ȧ·chī´·ȧs, whom ye slew between the temple and the altar. 36 Verily I say unto you, All these things shall come upon this generation. 37 O Jerusalem, Jerusalem, *thou* that killest the prophets, and stonest them which are sent unto thee, how often would I have gathered thy children together, even as a hen gathereth her chickens under *her* wings, and ye would not! 38 Behold, your house is left unto you desolate. 39 For I say unto you, Ye shall not see me henceforth, till ye shall say, Blessed *is* he that cometh in the name of the Lord.			

192. THE WIDOW'S MITE

MATTHEW – 23	MARK – 12	LUKE – 21	JOHN – 12
	41 ¶ And Jesus sat over against the treasury, and beheld how the people cast money into the treasury: and many that were rich cast in much. 42 And there came a certain poor widow, and she threw in two mites, which make a farthing. 43 And he called *unto him* his disciples, and saith unto them, Verily I say unto you, That this poor widow hath cast more in, than all they which have cast into the treasury: 44 For all *they* did cast in of their abundance; but she of her want did cast in all that she had, *even* all her living.	CHAPTER 21 AND he looked up, and saw the rich men casting their gifts into the treasury. 2 And he saw also a certain poor widow casting in thither two mites. 3 And he said, Of a truth I say unto you, that this poor widow hath cast in more than they all: 4 For all these have of their abundance cast in unto the offerings of God: but she of her penury hath cast in all the living that she had.	

193. JESUS TESTIFIES OF HIS DEATH

MATTHEW – 23	MARK – 12	LUKE – 21	JOHN – 12
			20 ¶ And there were certain Greeks among them that came up to worship at the feast: 21 The same came therefore to Philip, which was of Bĕth·sā´·ĭ·dä of Galilee, and desired him, saying, Sir, we would see Jesus.

MATTHEW –	MARK –	LUKE –	JOHN – 12
			22 Philip cometh and telleth Andrew: and again Andrew and Philip tell Jesus.
			23 ¶ And Jesus answered them, saying, The hour is come, that the Son of man should be glorified.
			24 Verily, verily, I say unto you, Except a corn of wheat fall into the ground and die, it abideth alone: but if it die, it bringeth forth much fruit.
			25 He that loveth his life shall lose it; and he that hateth his life in this world shall keep it unto life eternal.
			26 If any man serve me, let him follow me; and where I am, there shall also my servant be: if any man serve me, him will *my* Father honour.
			27 Now is my soul troubled; and what shall I say? Father, save me from this hour: but for this cause came I unto this hour.
			28 Father, glorify thy name. Then came there a voice from heaven, *saying*, I have both glorified *it*, and will glorify *it* again.
			29 The people therefore, that stood by, and heard *it*, said that it thundered: others said, An angel spake to him.
			30 Jesus answered and said, This voice came not because of me, but for your sakes.
			31 Now is the judgment of this world: now shall the prince of this world be cast out.
			32 And I, if I be lifted up from the earth, will draw all *men* unto me.
			33 This he said, signifying what death he should die.
			34 The people answered him, We have heard out of the law that Christ abideth for ever: and how sayest thou, The Son of man must be lifted up? who is this Son of man?
			35 Then Jesus said unto them, Yet a little while is the light with you. Walk while ye have the light, lest darkness come upon you: for he that walketh in darkness knoweth not whither he goeth.
			36a While ye have light, believe in the light, that ye may be the children of light.

194. JESUS' RELATIONSHIP TO HIS FATHER

MATTHEW	MARK	LUKE	JOHN
			44 ¶ Jesus cried and said, He that believeth on me, believeth not on me, but on him that sent me.
			45 And he that seeth me seeth him that sent me.
			46 I am come a light into the world, that whosoever believeth on me should not abide in darkness.
			47 And if any man hear my words, and believe not, I judge him not: for I came not to judge the world, but to save the world.
			48 He that rejecteth me, and receiveth not my words, hath one that judgeth him: the word that I have spoken, the same shall judge him in the last day.

MATTHEW – 24	MARK – 13	LUKE – 21	JOHN – 12
			49 For I have not spoken of myself; but the Father which sent me, he gave me a commandment, what I should say, and what I should speak. 50 And I know that his commandment is life everlasting: whatsoever I speak therefore, even as the Father said unto me, so I speak.

195. JESUS DEPARTS FROM CROWDS AT THE TEMPLE

MATTHEW – 24	MARK – 13	LUKE – 21	JOHN – 12
			36b These things spake Jesus, and departed, and did hide himself from them.

196. REACTION OF PEOPLE TO JESUS' TEACHINGS

MATTHEW – 24	MARK – 13	LUKE – 21	JOHN – 12
			37 ¶ But though he had done so many miracles before them, yet they believed not on him: 38 That the saying of Ē·śāī'·ăs the prophet might be fulfilled, which he spake, Lord, who hath believed our report? and to whom hath the arm of the Lord been revealed? 39 Therefore they could not believe, because that Ē·śāī'·ăs said again, 40 He hath blinded their eyes, and hardened their heart; that they should not see with *their* eyes, nor understand with *their* heart, and be converted, and I should heal them. 41 These things said Ē·śāī'·ăs, when he saw his glory, and spake of him. 42 ¶ Nevertheless among the chief rulers also many believed on him; but because of the Pharisees they did not confess *him*, lest they should be put out of the synagogue: 43 For they loved the praise of men more than the praise of God.

197. SIGNS OF THE DESTRUCTION OF THE TEMPLE AND OF JESUS' SECOND COMING

MATTHEW – 24	MARK – 13	LUKE – 21	JOHN – 12
CHAPTER 24 AND Jesus went out, and departed from the temple: and his disciples came to *him* for to shew him the buildings of the temple. 2 And Jesus said unto them, See ye not all these things? verily I say unto you, There shall not be left here one stone upon another, that shall not be thrown down. 3 ¶ And as he sat upon the mount of Olives, the disciples came unto him privately, saying, Tell us, when shall these things be? and what *shall be* the sign of thy coming, and of the end of the world? 4 And Jesus answered and said unto them, Take heed that no man deceive you. 5 For many shall come in my name, saying, I am Christ; and shall deceive many.	**CHAPTER 13** AND as he went out of the temple, one of his disciples saith unto him, Master, see what manner of stones and what buildings *are here!* 2 And Jesus answering said unto him, Seest thou these great buildings? there shall not be left one stone upon another, that shall not be thrown down. 3 And as he sat upon the mount of Olives over against the temple, Peter and James and John and Andrew asked him privately, 4 Tell us, when shall these things be? and what *shall be* the sign when all these things shall be fulfilled? 5 And Jesus answering them began to say, Take heed lest any *man* deceive you: 6 For many shall come in my name, saying, I am *Christ;* and shall deceive many. 9 ¶ But take heed to yourselves: for they shall deliver you up to councils; and in the synagogues ye shall be beaten: and ye shall be brought before rulers and kings for my sake, for a testimony against them.	5 ¶ And as some spake of the temple, how it was adorned with goodly stones and gifts, he said, 6 *As for* these things which ye behold, the days will come, in the which there shall not be left one stone upon another, that shall not be thrown down. 7 And they asked him, saying, Master, but when shall these things be? and what sign *will there be* when these things shall come to pass? 8 And he said, Take heed that ye be not deceived: for many shall come in my name, saying, I am *Christ;* and the time draweth near: go ye not therefore after them. 12 But before all these, they shall lay their hands on you, and persecute *you*, delivering *you* up to the synagogues, and into prisons, being brought before kings and rulers for my name's sake. 13 And it shall turn to you for a testimony.	

MATTHEW – 24	MARK – 13	LUKE – 21	JOHN –
	11 But when they shall lead *you*, and deliver you up, take no thought beforehand what ye shall speak, neither do ye premeditate: but whatsoever shall be given you in that hour, that speak ye: for it is not ye that speak, but the Holy Ghost.	14 Settle *it* therefore in your hearts, not to meditate before what ye shall answer:	
	12 Now the brother shall betray the brother to death, and the father the son; and children shall rise up against *their* parents, and shall cause them to be put to death.	15 For I will give you a mouth and wisdom, which all your adversaries shall not be able to gainsay nor resist.	
9 Then shall they deliver you up to be afflicted, and shall kill you: and ye shall be hated of all nations for my name's sake.	13 And ye shall be hated of all *men* for my name's sake:	16 And ye shall be betrayed both by parents, and brethren, and kinsfolks, and friends; and *some* of you shall they cause to be put to death. 17 And ye shall be hated of all *men* for my name's sake. 18 But there shall not an hair of your head perish. 19 In your patience possess ye your souls.	
10 And then shall many be offended, and shall betray one another, and shall hate one another. 11 And many false prophets shall rise, and shall deceive many. 12 And because iniquity shall abound, the love of many shall wax cold. 13 But he that shall endure unto the end, the same shall be saved. 15 When ye therefore shall see the abomination of desolation, spoken of by Daniel the prophet, stand in the holy place, (whoso readeth, let him understand:) 16 Then let them which be in Judæa flee into the mountains: 17 Let him which is on the housetop not come down to take any thing out of his house: 18 Neither let him which is in the field return back to take his clothes. 19 And woe unto them that are with child, and to them that give suck in those days! 20 But pray ye that your flight be not in the winter, neither on the sabbath day:	but he that shall endure unto the end, the same shall be saved. 14 ¶ But when ye shall see the abomination of desolation, spoken of by Daniel the prophet, standing where it ought not, (let him that readeth understand,) then let them that be in Judæa flee to the mountains: 15 And let him that is on the housetop not go down into the house, neither enter *therein*, to take any thing out of his house: 16 And let him that is in the field not turn back again for to take up his garment. 17 But woe to them that are with child, and to them that give suck in those days! 18 And pray ye that your flight be not in the winter.	20 And when ye shall see Jerusalem compassed with armies, then know that the desolation thereof is nigh. 21 Then let them which are in Judæa flee to the mountains; and let them which are in the midst of it depart out; and let not them that are in the countries enter thereinto. 22 For these be the days of vengeance, that all things which are written may be fulfilled. 23 But woe unto them that are with child, and to them that give suck, in those days!	
21 For then shall be great tribulation, such as was not since the beginning of the world to this time, no, nor ever shall be.	19 For *in* those days shall be affliction, such as was not from the beginning of the creation which God created unto this time, neither shall be.	for there shall be great distress in the land, and wrath upon this people.	
		24 And they shall fall by the edge of the sword, and shall be led away captive into all nations: and Jerusalem shall be trodden down of the Gentiles, until the times of the Gentiles be fulfilled.	
8 All these *are* the beginning of sorrows. 22 And except those days should be shortened, there should no flesh be saved: but for the elect's sake those days shall be shortened. 23 Then if any man shall say unto you, Lo, here *is* Christ, or there; believe *it* not. 24 For there shall arise false Christs, and false prophets, and shall shew great signs and wonders; insomuch that, if *it were* possible, they shall deceive the very elect.	20 And except that the Lord had shortened those days, no flesh should be saved: but for the elect's sake, whom he hath chosen, he hath shortened the days. 21 And then if any man shall say to you, Lo, here *is* Christ; or, lo, *he is* there; believe *him* not: 22 For false Christs and false prophets shall rise, and shall shew signs and wonders, to seduce, if *it were* possible, even the elect.		

MATTHEW – 24	MARK – 13	LUKE – 21	JOHN –
6 And ye shall hear of wars and rumours of wars: see that ye be not troubled: for all *these things* must come to pass, but the end is not yet. 25 Behold, I have told you before. 26 Wherefore if they shall say unto you, Behold, he is in the desert; go not forth: behold, *he is* in the secret chambers; believe *it* not. 27 For as the lightning cometh out of the east, and shineth even unto the west; so shall also the coming of the Son of man be. 28 For wheresoever the carcase is, there will the eagles be gathered together.	7 And when ye shall hear of wars and rumours of wars, be ye not troubled: for *such things* must needs be; but the end *shall* not *be* yet. 23 But take ye heed: behold, I have foretold you all things.	9 But when ye shall hear of wars and commotions, be not terrified: for these things must first come to pass; but the end *is* not by and by.	
7 For nation shall rise against nation, and kingdom against kingdom: and there shall be famines, and pestilences, and earthquakes, in divers places. 14 And this gospel of the kingdom shall be preached in all the world for a witness unto all nations; and then shall the end come. 29 ¶ Immediately after the tribulation of those days shall the sun be darkened, and the moon shall not give her light, and the stars shall fall from heaven,	8 For nation shall rise against nation, and kingdom against kingdom: and there shall be earthquakes in divers places, and there shall be famines and troubles: these *are* the beginnings of sorrows. 10 And the gospel must first be published among all nations. 24 ¶ But in those days, after that tribulation, the sun shall be darkened, and the moon shall not give her light, 25 And the stars of heaven shall fall,	10 Then said he unto them, Nation shall rise against nation, and kingdom against kingdom: 11 And great earthquakes shall be in divers places, and famines, and pestilences; and fearful sights and great signs shall there be from heaven.	
and the powers of the heavens shall be shaken: 34 Verily I say unto you, This generation shall not pass, till all these things be fulfilled. 35 Heaven and earth shall pass away, but my words shall not pass away.	and the powers that are in heaven shall be shaken. 30 Verily I say unto you, that this generation shall not pass, till all these things be done. 31 Heaven and earth shall pass away: but my words shall not pass away.	25 ¶ And there shall be signs in the sun, and in the moon, and in the stars; and upon the earth distress of nations, with perplexity; the sea and the waves roaring; 26 Men's hearts failing them for fear, and for looking after those things which are coming on the earth: for the powers of heaven shall be shaken. 32 Verily I say unto you, This generation shall not pass away, till all be fulfilled. 33 Heaven and earth shall pass away: but my words shall not pass away. 28 And when these things begin to come to pass, then look up, and lift up your heads; for your redemption draweth nigh.	
30 And then shall appear the sign of the Son of man in heaven: and then shall all the tribes of the earth mourn, and they shall see the Son of man coming in the clouds of heaven with power and great glory. 31 And he shall send his angels with a great sound of a trumpet, and they shall gather together his elect from the four winds, from one end of heaven to the other.	26 And then shall they see the Son of man coming in the clouds with great power and glory. 27 And then shall he send his angels, and shall gather together his elect from the four winds, from the uttermost part of the earth to the uttermost part of heaven.	27 And then shall they see the Son of man coming in a cloud with power and great glory.	

198. PARABLE OF THE FIG TREE

MATTHEW – 24	MARK – 13	LUKE – 21	JOHN –
		29 And he spake to them a parable; Behold the fig tree, and all the trees;	
32 Now learn a parable of the fig tree; When his branch is yet tender, and putteth forth leaves, ye know that summer *is* nigh: 33 So likewise ye, when ye shall see all these things, know that it is near, *even* at the doors.	28 Now learn a parable of the fig tree; When her branch is yet tender, and putteth forth leaves, ye know that summer is near: 29 So ye in like manner, when ye shall see these things come to pass, know that it is nigh, *even* at the doors.	30 When they now shoot forth, ye see and know of your own selves that summer is now nigh at hand. 31 So likewise ye, when ye see these things come to pass, know ye that the kingdom of God is nigh at hand.	
36 ¶ But of that day and hour knoweth no *man*, no, not the angels of heaven, but my Father only.	32 ¶ But of that day and *that* hour knoweth no man, no, not the angels which are in heaven, neither the Son, but the Father.		

199. SECOND COMING LIKENED TO THE DAYS OF NOAH

MATTHEW – 24

37 But as the days of Nō´-ē *were*, so shall also the coming of the Son of man be.

38 For as in the days that were before the flood they were eating and drinking, marrying and giving in marriage, until the day that Nō´-ē entered into the ark,

39 And knew not until the flood came, and took them all away; so shall also the coming of the Son of man be.

40 Then shall two be in the field; the one shall be taken, and the other left.

41 Two *women shall be* grinding at the mill; the one shall be taken, and the other left.

42 ¶ Watch therefore: for ye know not what hour your Lord doth come.

MARK – 13

33 Take ye heed, watch and pray: for ye know not when the time is.

LUKE – 21

34 ¶ And take heed to yourselves, lest at any time your hearts be overcharged with surfeiting, and drunkenness, and cares of this life, and so that day come upon you unawares.

35 For as a snare shall it come on all them that dwell on the face of the whole earth.

36 Watch ye therefore, and pray always, that ye may be accounted worthy to escape all these things that shall come to pass, and to stand before the Son of man.

200. PARABLE OF A MAN TAKING A FAR JOURNEY

MARK – 13

34 *For the Son of man is* as a man taking a far journey, who left his house, and gave authority to his servants, and to every man his work, and commanded the porter to watch.

35 Watch ye therefore: for ye know not when the master of the house cometh, at even, or at midnight, or at the cockcrowing, or in the morning:

36 Lest coming suddenly he find you sleeping.

37 And what I say unto you I say unto all, Watch.

201. SON OF MAN TO COME AS A THIEF IN THE NIGHT

MATTHEW – 24

43 But know this, that if the goodman of the house had known in what watch the thief would come, he would have watched, and would not have suffered his house to be broken up.

44 Therefore be ye also ready: for in such an hour as ye think not the Son of man cometh.

202. THE FAITHFUL AND EVIL SERVANTS

MATTHEW – 24

45 Who then is a faithful and wise servant, whom his lord hath made ruler over his household, to give them meat in due season?

46 Blessed *is* that servant, whom his lord when he cometh shall find so doing.

47 Verily I say unto you, That he shall make him ruler over all his goods.

48 But and if that evil servant shall say in his heart, My lord delayeth his coming;

MATTHEW – 24,25	MARK –	LUKE –	JOHN –

49 And shall begin to smite *his* fellowservants, and to eat and drink with the drunken;

50 The lord of that servant shall come in a day when he looketh not for *him*, and in an hour that he is not aware of,

51 And shall cut him asunder, and appoint *him* his portion with the hypocrites: there shall be weeping and gnashing of teeth.

203. PARABLE OF THE TEN VIRGINS

CHAPTER 25

THEN shall the kingdom of heaven be likened unto ten virgins, which took their lamps, and went forth to meet the bridegroom.

2 And five of them were wise, and five *were* foolish.

3 They that *were* foolish took their lamps, and took no oil with them:

4 But the wise took oil in their vessels with their lamps.

5 While the bridegroom tarried, they all slumbered and slept.

6 And at midnight there was a cry made, Behold, the bridegroom cometh; go ye out to meet him.

7 Then all those virgins arose, and trimmed their lamps.

8 And the foolish said unto the wise, Give us of your oil; for our lamps are gone out.

9 But the wise answered, saying, *Not so;* lest there be not enough for us and you: but go ye rather to them that sell, and buy for yourselves.

10 And while they went to buy, the bridegroom came; and they that were ready went in with him to the marriage: and the door was shut.

11 Afterward came also the other virgins, saying, Lord, Lord, open to us.

12 But he answered and said, Verily I say unto you, I know you not.

13 Watch therefore, for ye know neither the day nor the hour wherein the Son of man cometh.

204. PARABLE OF THE TALENTS

14 ¶ For *the kingdom of heaven is* as a man travelling into a far country, *who* called his own servants, and delivered unto them his goods.

15 And unto one he gave five talents, to another two, and to another one; to every man according to his several ability; and straightway took his journey.

16 Then he that had received the five talents went and traded with the same, and made *them* other five talents.

17 And likewise he that *had received* two, he also gained other two.

18 But he that had received one went and digged in the earth, and hid his lord's money.

19 After a long time the lord of those servants cometh, and reckoneth with them.

20 And so he that had received five talents came and brought other five talents, saying, Lord, thou deliveredst unto me five talents: behold, I have gained beside them five talents more.

21 His lord said unto him, Well done, *thou* good and faithful servant: thou hast been faithful over a few things, I will make thee ruler over many things: enter thou into the joy of thy lord.

22 He also that had received two talents came and said, Lord, thou deliveredst unto me two talents: behold, I have gained two other talents beside them.

23 His lord said unto him, Well done, good and faithful servant; thou hast been faithful over a few things, I will make thee ruler over many things: enter thou into the joy of thy lord.

24 Then he which had received the one talent came and said, Lord, I knew thee that thou art an hard man, reaping where thou hast not sown, and gathering where thou hast not strawed:

25 And I was afraid, and went and hid thy talent in the earth: lo, *there* thou hast *that is* thine.

26 His lord answered and said unto him, *Thou* wicked and slothful servant, thou knewest that I reap where I sowed not, and gather where I have not strawed:

27 Thou oughtest therefore to have put my money to the exchangers, and *then* at my coming I should have received mine own with usury.

28 Take therefore the talent from him, and give *it* unto him which hath ten talents.

29 For unto every one that hath shall be given, and he shall have abundance: but from him that hath not shall be taken away even that which he hath.

30 And cast ye the unprofitable servant into outer darkness: there shall be weeping and gnashing of teeth.

205. JESUS TO JUDGE THE WORLD

31 ¶ When the Son of man shall come in his glory, and all the holy angels with him, then shall he sit upon the throne of his glory:

32 And before him shall be gathered all nations: and he shall separate them one from another, as a shepherd divideth *his* sheep from the goats:

33 And he shall set the sheep on his right hand, but the goats on the left.

34 Then shall the King say unto them on his right hand, Come, ye blessed of my Father, inherit the kingdom prepared for you from the foundation of the world:

35 For I was an hungred, and ye gave me meat: I was thirsty, and ye gave me drink: I was a stranger, and ye took me in:

36 Naked, and ye clothed me: I was sick, and ye visited me: I was in prison, and ye came unto me.

37 Then shall the righteous answer him, saying, Lord, when saw we thee an hungred, and fed *thee?* or thirsty, and gave *thee* drink?

38 When saw we thee a stranger, and took *thee* in? or naked, and clothed *thee?*

39 Or when saw we thee sick, or in prison, and came unto thee?

40 And the King shall answer and say unto them, Verily I say unto you, Inasmuch as ye have done *it* unto one of the least of these my brethren, ye have done *it* unto me.

41 Then shall he say also unto them on the left hand, Depart from me, ye cursed, into everlasting fire, prepared for the devil and his angels:

42 For I was an hungred, and ye gave me no meat: I was thirsty, and ye gave me no drink:

43 I was a stranger, and ye took me not in: naked, and ye clothed me not: sick, and in prison, and ye visited me not.

44 Then shall they also answer him, saying, Lord, when saw we thee an hungred, or athirst, or a stranger, or naked, or sick, or in prison, and did not minister unto thee?

45 Then shall he answer them, saying, Verily I say unto you, Inasmuch as ye did *it* not to one of the least of these, ye did *it* not to me.

46 And these shall go away into everlasting punishment: but the righteous into life eternal.

206. JESUS FORETELLS HIS BETRAYAL AND CRUCIFIXION

CHAPTER 26

AND it came to pass, when Jesus had finished all these sayings, he said unto his disciples,

2 Ye know that after two days is *the feast of* the passover, and the Son of man is betrayed to be crucified.

1a **CHAPTER 14**

AFTER two days was *the feast of* the passover, and of unleavened bread:

CHAPTER 22

NOW the feast of unleavened bread drew nigh, which is called the Passover.

207. RULERS CONSULT HOW THEY CAN KILL JESUS

3 Then assembled together the chief priests, and the scribes, and the elders of the people, unto the palace of the high priest, who was called Cāi-ă-phăs,

4 And consulted that they might take Jesus by subtilty, and kill *him*.

5 But they said, Not on the feast *day*, lest there be an uproar among the people.

1b and the chief priests and the scribes sought how they might take him by craft, and put *him* to death.

2 But they said, Not on the feast *day*, lest there be an uproar of the people.

2 And the chief priests and scribes sought how they might kill him; for they feared the people.

208. JUDAS ISCARIOT PROMISES TO BETRAY JESUS

14 ¶ Then one of the twelve, called Judas Iscariot, went unto the chief priests,

15 And said *unto them*, What will ye give me, and I will deliver him unto you? And they covenanted with him for thirty pieces of silver.

16 And from that time he sought opportunity to betray him.

10 ¶ And Judas Iscariot, one of the twelve, went unto the chief priests, to betray him unto them.

11 And when they heard *it*, they were glad, and promised to give him money. And he sought how he might conveniently betray him.

3 ¶ Then entered Satan into Judas surnamed Iscariot, being of the number of the twelve.

4 And he went his way, and communed with the chief priests and captains, how he might betray him unto them.

5 And they were glad, and covenanted to give him money.

6 And he promised, and sought opportunity to betray him unto them in the absence of the multitude.

Wednesday–No Record

Thursday

209. PREPARATION FOR THE PASSOVER

17 ¶ Now the first *day* of the *feast of* unleavened bread the disciples came to Jesus, saying unto him, Where wilt thou that we prepare for thee to eat the passover?

12 ¶ And the first day of unleavened bread, when they killed the passover, his disciples said unto him, Where wilt thou that we go and prepare that thou mayest eat the passover?

13 And he sendeth forth two of his disciples, and saith unto them, Go ye into the city, and there shall meet you a man bearing a pitcher of water: follow him.

7 ¶ Then came the day of unleavened bread, when the passover must be killed.

8 And he sent Peter and John, saying, Go and prepare us the passover, that we may eat.

9 And they said unto him, Where wilt thou that we prepare?

10 And he said unto them, Behold, when ye are entered into the city, there shall a man meet you, bearing a pitcher of water; follow him into the house where he entereth in.

18 And he said, Go into the city to such a man, and say unto him, The Master saith, My time is at hand; I will keep the passover at thy house with my disciples.

14 And wheresoever he shall go in, say ye to the goodman of the house, The Master saith, Where is the guestchamber, where I shall eat the passover with my disciples?

15 And he will shew you a large upper room furnished *and* prepared: there make ready for us.

11 And ye shall say unto the goodman of the house, The Master saith unto thee, Where is the guestchamber, where I shall eat the passover with my disciples?

12 And he shall shew you a large upper room furnished: there make ready.

19 And the disciples did as Jesus had appointed them; and they made ready the passover.

16 And his disciples went forth, and came into the city, and found as he had said unto them: and they made ready the passover.

13 And they went, and found as he had said unto them: and they made ready the passover.

210. JESUS AND THE APOSTLES BEGIN LAST SUPPER

20 Now when the even was come, he sat down with the twelve.

17 And in the evening he cometh with the twelve.

14 And when the hour was come, he sat down, and the twelve apostles with him.

15 And he said unto them, With desire I have desired to eat this passover with you before I suffer:

16 For I say unto you, I will not any more eat thereof, until it be fulfilled in the kingdom of God.

17 And he took the cup, and gave thanks, and said, Take this, and divide *it* among yourselves:

18 For I say unto you, I will not drink of the fruit of the vine, until the kingdom of God shall come.

211. STRIFE AMONG THE APOSTLES OVER GREATNESS

24 ¶ And there was also a strife among them, which of them should be accounted the greatest.

25 And he said unto them, The kings of the Gentiles exercise lordship over them; and they that exercise authority upon them are called benefactors.

26 But ye *shall* not *be* so: but he that is greatest among you, let him be as the younger; and he that is chief, as he that doth serve.

27 For whether *is* greater, he that sitteth at meat, or he that serveth? *is* not he that sitteth at meat? but I am among you as he that serveth.

| | | 28 Ye are they which have continued with me in my temptations.
29 And I appoint unto you a kingdom, as my Father hath appointed unto me;
30 That ye may eat and drink at my table in my kingdom, and sit on thrones judging the twelve tribes of Israel. | |

212. JESUS WASHES THE APOSTLES' FEET

CHAPTER 13

NOW before the feast of the passover, when Jesus knew that his hour was come that he should depart out of this world unto the Father, having loved his own which were in the world, he loved them unto the end.

2 And supper being ended, * the devil having now put into the heart of Judas Iscariot, Simon's *son*, to betray him;

3 Jesus knowing that the Father had given all things into his hands, and that he was come from God, and went to God;

4 He riseth from supper, and laid aside his garments; and took a towel, and girded himself.

5 After that he poureth water into a bason, and began to wash the disciples' feet, and to wipe *them* with the towel wherewith he was girded.

6 Then cometh he to Simon Peter: and Peter saith unto him, Lord, dost thou wash my feet?

7 Jesus answered and said unto him, What I do thou knowest not now; but thou shalt know hereafter.

8 Peter saith unto him, Thou shalt never wash my feet. Jesus answered him, If I wash thee not, thou hast no part with me.

9 Simon Peter saith unto him, Lord, not my feet only, but also *my* hands and *my* head.

10 Jesus saith to him, He that is washed needeth not save to wash *his* feet, but is clean every whit: and ye are clean, but not all.

11 For he knew who should betray him; therefore said he, Ye are not all clean.

12 So after he had washed their feet, and had taken his garments, and was set down again, he said unto them, Know ye what I have done to you?

13 Ye call me Master and Lord: and ye say well; for *so* I am.

14 If I then, *your* Lord and Master, have washed your feet; ye also ought to wash one another's feet.

15 For I have given you an example, that ye should do as I have done to you.

16 Verily, verily, I say unto you, The servant is not greater than his lord; neither he that is sent greater than he that sent him.

17 If ye know these things, happy are ye if ye do them.

20 Verily, verily, I say unto you, He that receiveth whomsoever I send receiveth me; and he that receiveth me receiveth him that sent me.

*John 13:2 — "And supper being ended" reads "and during supper" in the Revised Standard Version.

130

213. ANNOUNCES HIS BETRAYAL

MATTHEW – 26	MARK – 14	LUKE – 22	JOHN – 13
21 And as they did eat, he said, Verily I say unto you, that one of you shall betray me.	18 And as they sat and did eat, Jesus said, Verily I say unto you, One of you which eateth with me shall betray me.	21 ¶ But, behold, the hand of him that betrayeth me *is* with me on the table.	21 When Jesus had thus said, he was troubled in spirit, and testified, and said, Verily, verily, I say unto you, that one of you shall betray me. 22 Then the disciples looked one on another, doubting of whom he spake. 18 ¶ I speak not of you all: I know whom I have chosen: but that the scripture may be fulfilled, He that eateth bread with me hath lifted up his heel against me. 19 Now I tell you before it come, that, when it is come to pass, ye may believe that I am *he*.
		23 And they began to inquire among themselves, which of them it was that should do this thing.	
22 And they were exceeding sorrowful, and began every one of them to say unto him, Lord, is it I? 23 And he answered and said, He that dippeth *his* hand with me in the dish, the same shall betray me. 24 The Son of man goeth as it is written of him: but woe unto that man by whom the Son of man is betrayed! it had been good for that man if he had not been born. 25 Then Judas, which betrayed him, answered and said, Master, is it I? He said unto him, Thou hast said.	19 And they began to be sorrowful, and to say unto him one by one, *Is* it I? and another said, *Is* it I? 20 And he answered and said unto them, *It is* one of the twelve, that dippeth with me in the dish. 21 The Son of man indeed goeth, as it is written of him: but woe to that man by whom the Son of man is betrayed! good were it for that man if he had never been born.	22 And truly the Son of man goeth, as it was determined: but woe unto that man by whom he is betrayed!	

214. JUDAS, ALONE, LEAVES THE UPPER ROOM

MATTHEW – 26	MARK – 14	LUKE – 22	JOHN – 13
			23 Now there was leaning on Jesus' bosom one of his disciples, whom Jesus loved. 24 Simon Peter therefore beckoned to him, that he should ask who it should be of whom he spake. 25 He then lying on Jesus' breast saith unto him, Lord, who is it? 26 Jesus answered, He it is, to whom I shall give a sop, when I have dipped *it*. And when he had dipped the sop, he gave *it* to Judas Iscariot, *the son* of Simon. 27 And after the sop Satan entered into him. Then said Jesus unto him, That thou doest, do quickly. 28 Now no man at the table knew for what intent he spake this unto him. 29 For some *of them* thought, because Judas had the bag, that Jesus had said unto him, Buy *those things* that we have need of against the feast; or, that he should give something to the poor. 30 He then having received the sop went immediately out: and it was night.

215. THE COMMANDMENT TO LOVE ONE ANOTHER

MATTHEW – 26	MARK – 14	LUKE – 22	JOHN – 13
			31 ¶ Therefore, when he was gone out, Jesus said, Now is the Son of man glorified, and God is glorified in him. 32 If God be glorified in him, God shall also glorify him in himself, and shall straightway glorify him.

131

MATTHEW – 26	MARK – 14	LUKE – 22	JOHN – 13
			33 Little children, yet a little while I am with you. Ye shall seek me: and as I said unto the Jews, Whither I go, ye cannot come; so now I say to you. 34 A new commandment I give unto you, That ye love one another; as I have loved you, that ye also love one another. 35 By this shall all *men* know that ye are my disciples, if ye have love one to another.

216. THE SACRAMENT

MATTHEW – 26	MARK – 14	LUKE – 22	JOHN – 13
26 ¶ And as they were eating, Jesus took bread, and blessed *it*, and brake *it*, and gave *it* to the disciples, and said, Take, eat; this is my body. 27 And he took the cup, and gave thanks, and gave *it* to them, saying, Drink ye all of it; 28 For this is my blood of the new testament, which is shed for many for the remission of sins. 29 But I say unto you, I will not drink henceforth of this fruit of the vine, until that day when I drink it new with you in my Father's kingdom.	22 ¶ And as they did eat, Jesus took bread, and blessed, and brake *it*, and gave to them, and said, Take, eat: this is my body. 23 And he took the cup, and when he had given thanks, he gave *it* to them: and they all drank of it. 24 And he said unto them, This is my blood of the new testament, which is shed for many. 25 Verily I say unto you, I will drink no more of the fruit of the vine, until that day that I drink it new in the kingdom of God.	19 ¶ And he took bread, and gave thanks, and brake *it*, and gave unto them, saying, This is my body which is given for you: this do in remembrance of me. 20 Likewise also the cup after supper, saying, This cup *is* the new testament in my blood, which is shed for you.	

217. JESUS PROPHESIES THE APOSTLES' REACTION TO HIS ARREST

MATTHEW – 26	MARK – 14	LUKE – 22	JOHN – 13
31 Then saith Jesus unto them, All ye shall be offended because of me this night: for it is written, I will smite the shepherd, and the sheep of the flock shall be scattered abroad. 32 But after I am risen again, I will go before you into Galilee. 33 Peter answered and said unto him, Though all *men* shall be offended because of thee, *yet* will I never be offended.	27 And Jesus saith unto them, All ye shall be offended because of me this night: for it is written, I will smite the shepherd, and the sheep shall be scattered. 28 But after that I am risen, I will go before you into Galilee. 29 But Peter said unto him, Although all shall be offended, yet *will* not I.	31 ¶ And the Lord said, Simon, Simon, behold, Satan hath desired *to have* you, that he may sift *you* as wheat: 32 But I have prayed for thee, that thy faith fail not: and when thou art converted, strengthen thy brethren.	

218. PETER'S DENIAL PROPHESIED THOUGH ALL THE APOSTLES PROFESS LOYALTY

MATTHEW – 26	MARK – 14	LUKE – 22	JOHN – 13
34 Jesus said unto him, Verily I say unto thee, That this night, before the cock crow, thou shalt deny me thrice. 35 Peter said unto him, Though I should die with thee, yet will I not deny thee. Likewise also said all the disciples.	30 And Jesus saith unto him, Verily I say unto thee, That this day, *even* in this night, before the cock crow twice, thou shalt deny me thrice. 31 But he spake the more vehemently, If I should die with thee, I will not deny thee in any wise. Likewise also said they all.	33 And he said unto him, Lord, I am ready to go with thee, both into prison, and to death. 34 And he said, I tell thee, Peter, the cock shall not crow this day, before that thou shalt thrice deny that thou knowest me. 35 And he said unto them, When I sent you without purse, and scrip, and shoes, lacked ye any thing? And they said, Nothing.	36 ¶ Simon Peter said unto him, Lord, whither goest thou? Jesus answered him, Whither I go, thou canst not follow me now; but thou shalt follow me afterwards. 37 Peter said unto him, Lord, why cannot I follow thee now? I will lay down my life for thy sake. 38 Jesus answered him, Wilt thou lay down thy life for my sake? Verily, verily, I say unto thee, The cock shall not crow, till thou hast denied me thrice.

MATTHEW –	MARK –	LUKE – 22	JOHN – 14

36 Then said he unto them, But now, he that hath a purse, let him take *it*, and likewise *his* scrip: and he that hath no sword, let him sell his garment, and buy one.

37 For I say unto you, that this that is written must yet be accomplished in me, And he was reckoned among the transgressors: for the things concerning me have an end.

38 And they said, Lord, behold, here *are* two swords. And he said unto them, It is enough.

219. DISCOURSE ON PEACE THROUGH KNOWING GOD

CHAPTER 14

LET not your heart be troubled: ye believe in God, believe also in me.

2 In my Father's house are many mansions: if *it were* not *so,* I would have told you. I go to prepare a place for you.

3 And if I go and prepare a place for you, I will come again, and receive you unto myself; that where I am, *there* ye may be also.

4 And whither I go ye know, and the way ye know.

5 Thomas saith unto him, Lord, we know not whither thou goest; and how can we know the way?

6 Jesus saith unto him, I am the way, the truth, and the life: no man cometh unto the Father, but by me.

7 If ye had known me, ye should have known my Father also: and from henceforth ye know him, and have seen him.

8 Philip saith unto him, Lord, shew us the Father, and it sufficeth us.

9 Jesus saith unto him, Have I been so long time with you, and yet hast thou not known me, Philip? he that hath seen me hath seen the Father; and how sayest thou *then,* Shew us the Father?

10 Believest thou not that I am in the Father, and the Father in me? the words that I speak unto you I speak not of myself: but the Father that dwelleth in me, he doeth the works.

11 Believe me that I *am* in the Father, and the Father in me: or else believe me for the very works' sake.

12 Verily, verily, I say unto you, He that believeth on me, the works that I do shall he do also; and greater *works* than these shall he do; because I go unto my Father.

13 And whatsoever ye shall ask in my name, that will I do, that the Father may be glorified in the Son.

14 If ye shall ask any thing in my name, I will do *it.*

15 ¶ If ye love me, keep my commandments.

16 And I will pray the Father, and he shall give you another Comforter, that he may abide with you for ever;

MATTHEW – 26	MARK – 14	LUKE – 22	JOHN – 14
			17 *Even* the Spirit of truth; whom the world cannot receive, because it seeth him not, neither knoweth him: but ye know him; for he dwelleth with you, and shall be in you.
			18 I will not leave you comfortless: I will come to you.
			19 Yet a little while, and the world seeth me no more; but ye see me: because I live, ye shall live also.
			20 At that day ye shall know that I *am* in my Father, and ye in me, and I in you.
			21 He that hath my commandments, and keepeth them, he it is that loveth me: and he that loveth me shall be loved of my Father, and I will love him, and will manifest myself to him.
			22 Judas saith unto him, not Iscariot, Lord, how is it that thou wilt manifest thyself unto us, and not unto the world?
			23 Jesus answered and said unto him, If a man love me, he will keep my words: and my Father will love him, and we will come unto him, and make our abode with him.
			24 He that loveth me not keepeth not my sayings: and the word which ye hear is not mine, but the Father's which sent me.
			25 These things have I spoken unto you, being *yet* present with you.
			26 But the Comforter, *which is* the Holy Ghost, whom the Father will send in my name, he shall teach you all things, and bring all things to your remembrance, whatsoever I have said unto you.
			27 Peace I leave with you, my peace I give unto you: not as the world giveth, give I unto you. Let not your heart be troubled, neither let it be afraid.
			28 Ye have heard how I said unto you, I go away, and come *again* unto you. If ye loved me, ye would rejoice, because I said, I go unto the Father: for my Father is greater than I.
			29 And now I have told you before it come to pass, that, when it is come to pass, ye might believe.
			30 Hereafter I will not talk much with you: for the prince of this world cometh, and hath nothing in me.
			31 But that the world may know that I love the Father; and as the Father gave me commandment, even so I do. Arise, let us go hence.

220. AFTER A SONG, DEPART TO MOUNT OF OLIVES

MATTHEW – 26	MARK – 14	LUKE – 22	JOHN – 14
30 And when they had sung an hymn, they went out into the mount of Olives.	26 ¶ And when they had sung an hymn, they went out into the mount of Olives.	39 ¶ And he came out, and went, as he was wont, to the mount of Olives; and his disciples also followed him.	

221. JESUS IS THE TRUE VINE

MATTHEW – 26	MARK – 14	LUKE – 22	JOHN – 14
			CHAPTER 15
			I AM the true vine, and my Father is the husbandman.
			2 Every branch in me that beareth not fruit he taketh away: and every *branch* that beareth fruit, he purgeth it, that it may bring forth more fruit.

MATTHEW –	MARK –	LUKE –	JOHN – 15
			3 Now ye are clean through the word which I have spoken unto you.
			4 Abide in me, and I in you. As the branch cannot bear fruit of itself, except it abide in the vine; no more can ye, except ye abide in me.
			5 I am the vine, ye *are* the branches: He that abideth in me, and I in him, the same bringeth forth much fruit: for without me ye can do nothing.
			6 If a man abide not in me, he is cast forth as a branch, and is withered; and men gather them, and cast *them* into the fire, and they are burned.
			7 If ye abide in me, and my words abide in you, ye shall ask what ye will, and it shall be done unto you.
			8 Herein is my Father glorified, that ye bear much fruit; so shall ye be my disciples.
			9 As the Father hath loved me, so have I loved you: continue ye in my love.
			10 If ye keep my commandments, ye shall abide in my love; even as I have kept my Father's commandments, and abide in his love.
			11 These things have I spoken unto you, that my joy might remain in you, and *that* your joy might be full.

222. APOSTLES FURTHER COMMANDED TO LOVE ONE ANOTHER

MATTHEW	MARK	LUKE	JOHN
			12 This is my commandment, That ye love one another, as I have loved you.
			13 Greater love hath no man than this, that a man lay down his life for his friends.
			14 Ye are my friends, if ye do whatsoever I command you.
			15 Henceforth I call you not servants; for the servant knoweth not what his lord doeth: but I have called you friends; for all things that I have heard of my Father I have made known unto you.
			16 Ye have not chosen me, but I have chosen you, and ordained you, that ye should go and bring forth fruit, and *that* your fruit should remain: that whatsoever ye shall ask of the Father in my name, he may give it you.
			17 These things I command you, that ye love one another.

223. THE WORLD TO HATE THE APOSTLES

MATTHEW	MARK	LUKE	JOHN
			18 If the world hate you, ye know that it hated me before *it hated* you.
			19 If ye were of the world, the world would love his own: but because ye are not of the world, but I have chosen you out of the world, therefore the world hateth you.
			20 Remember the word that I said unto you, The servant is not greater than his lord. If they have persecuted me, they will also persecute you; if they have kept my saying, they will keep yours also.
			21 But all these things will they do unto you for my name's sake, because they know not him that sent me.

MATTHEW –	MARK –	LUKE –	JOHN – 15,16
			22 If I had not come and spoken unto them, they had not had sin: but now they have no cloke for their sin.
			23 He that hateth me hateth my Father also.
			24 If I had not done among them the works which none other man did, they had not had sin: but now have they both seen and hated both me and my Father.
			25 But *this cometh to pass*, that the word might be fulfilled that is written in their law, They hated me without a cause.
			26 But when the Comforter is come, whom I will send unto you from the Father, *even* the Spirit of truth, which proceedeth from the Father, he shall testify of me:
			27 And ye also shall bear witness, because ye have been with me from the beginning.
			CHAPTER 16
			THESE things have I spoken unto you, that ye should not be offended.
			2 They shall put you out of the synagogues: yea, the time cometh, that whosoever killeth you will think that he doeth God service.
			3 And these things will they do unto you, because they have not known the Father, nor me.

224. FURTHER EXPLAINS HIS DEATH

MATTHEW –	MARK –	LUKE –	JOHN – 15,16
			4 But these things have I told you, that when the time shall come, ye may remember that I told you of them. And these things I said not unto you at the beginning, because I was with you.
			5 But now I go my way to him that sent me; and none of you asketh me, Whither goest thou?
			6 But because I have said these things unto you, sorrow hath filled your heart.
			7 Nevertheless I tell you the truth; It is expedient for you that I go away: for if I go not away, the Comforter will not come unto you; but if I depart, I will send him unto you.
			8 And when he is come, he will reprove the world of sin, and of righteousness, and of judgment:
			9 Of sin, because they believe not on me;
			10 Of righteousness, because I go to my Father, and ye see me no more;
			11 Of judgment, because the prince of this world is judged.
			12 I have yet many things to say unto you, but ye cannot bear them now.
			13 Howbeit when he, the Spirit of truth, is come, he will guide you into all truth: for he shall not speak of himself; but whatsoever he shall hear, *that* shall he speak: and he will shew you things to come.
			14 He shall glorify me: for he shall receive of mine, and shall shew *it* unto you.
			15 All things that the Father hath are mine: therefore said I, that he shall take of mine, and shall shew *it* unto you.

MATTHEW –	MARK –	LUKE –	JOHN – 16
			16 A little while, and ye shall not see me: and again, a little while, and ye shall see me, because I go to the Father.
			17 Then said *some* of his disciples among themselves, What is this that he saith unto us, A little while, and ye shall not see me: and again, a little while, and ye shall see me: and, Because I go to the Father?
			18 They said therefore, What is this that he saith, A little while? we cannot tell what he saith.
			19 Now Jesus knew that they were desirous to ask him, and said unto them, Do ye inquire among yourselves of that I said, A little while, and ye shall not see me: and again, a little while, and ye shall see me?
			20 Verily, verily, I say unto you, That ye shall weep and lament, but the world shall rejoice: and ye shall be sorrowful, but your sorrow shall be turned into joy.
			21 A woman when she is in travail hath sorrow, because her hour is come: but as soon as she is delivered of the child, she remembereth no more the anguish, for joy that a man is born into the world.
			22 And ye now therefore have sorrow: but I will see you again, and your heart shall rejoice, and your joy no man taketh from you.
			23 And in that day ye shall ask me nothing. Verily, verily, I say, unto you, Whatsoever ye shall ask the Father in my name, he will give *it* you.
			24 Hitherto have ye asked nothing in my name: ask, and ye shall receive, that your joy may be full.
			25 These things have I spoken unto you in proverbs: but the time cometh, when I shall no more speak unto you in proverbs, but I shall shew you plainly of the Father.
			26 At that day ye shall ask in my name: and I say not unto you, that I will pray the Father for you:
			27 For the Father himself loveth you, because ye have loved me, and have believed that I came out from God.
			28 I came forth from the Father, and am come into the world: again, I leave the world, and go to the Father.
			29 His disciples said unto him, Lo, now speakest thou plainly, and speakest no proverb.
			30 Now are we sure that thou knowest all things, and needest not that any man should ask thee: by this we believe that thou camest forth from God.
			31 Jesus answered them, Do ye now believe?
			32 Behold, the hour cometh, yea, is now come, that ye shall be scattered, every man to his own, and shall leave me alone: and yet I am not alone, because the Father is with me.
			33 These things I have spoken unto you, that in me ye might have peace. In the world ye shall have tribulation: but be of good cheer; I have overcome the world.

225. JESUS PRAYS FOR HIS DISCIPLES

CHAPTER 17

THESE words spake Jesus, and lifted up his eyes to heaven, and said, Father, the hour is come; glorify thy Son, that thy Son also may glorify thee:

2 As thou hast given him power over all flesh, that he should give eternal life to as many as thou hast given him.

3 And this is life eternal, that they might know thee the only true God, and Jesus Christ, whom thou hast sent.

4 I have glorified thee on the earth: I have finished the work which thou gavest me to do.

5 And now, O Father, glorify thou me with thine own self with the glory which I had with thee before the world was.

6 I have manifested thy name unto the men which thou gavest me out of the world: thine they were, and thou gavest them me; and they have kept thy word.

7 Now they have known that all things whatsoever thou hast given me are of thee.

8 For I have given unto them the words which thou gavest me; and they have received them, and have known surely that I came out from thee, and they have believed that thou didst send me.

9 I pray for them: I pray not for the world, but for them which thou hast given me; for they are thine.

10 And all mine are thine, and thine are mine; and I am glorified in them.

11 And now I am no more in the world, but these are in the world, and I come to thee. Holy Father, keep through thine own name those whom thou hast given me, that they may be one, as we are.

12 While I was with them in the world, I kept them in thy name: those that thou gavest me I have kept, and none of them is lost, but the son of perdition; that the scripture might be fulfilled.

13 And now come I to thee; and these things I speak in the world, that they might have my joy fulfilled in themselves.

14 I have given them thy word; and the world hath hated them, because they are not of the world, even as I am not of the world.

15 I pray not that thou shouldest take them out of the world, but that thou shouldest keep them from the evil.

16 They are not of the world, even as I am not of the world.

17 Sanctify them through thy truth: thy word is truth.

18 As thou hast sent me into the world, even so have I also sent them into the world.

19 And for their sakes I sanctify myself, that they also might be sanctified through the truth.

20 Neither pray I for these alone, but for them also which shall believe on me through their word;

| | | | 21 That they all may be one; as thou, Father, *art* in me, and I in thee, that they also may be one in us: that the world may believe that thou hast sent me. |

JOHN – 17,18 (continued):

21 That they all may be one; as thou, Father, *art* in me, and I in thee, that they also may be one in us: that the world may believe that thou hast sent me.

22 And the glory which thou gavest me I have given them; that they may be one, even as we are one:

23 I in them, and thou in me, that they may be made perfect in one; and that the world may know that thou hast sent me, and hast loved them, as thou hast loved me.

24 Father, I will that they also, whom thou hast given me, be with me where I am; that they may behold my glory, which thou hast given me: for thou lovedst me before the foundation of the world.

25 O righteous Father, the world hath not known thee: but I have known thee, and these have known that thou hast sent me.

26 And I have declared unto them thy name, and will declare *it:* that the love wherewith thou hast loved me may be in them, and I in them.

226. PRAYER AND AGONY OF GETHSEMANE

JOHN – CHAPTER 18

WHEN Jesus had spoken these words, he went forth with his disciples over the brook Çe̅′-dro̅n, where was a garden, into the which he entered, and his disciples.

MATTHEW – 26:

36 ¶ Then cometh Jesus with them unto a place called Gĕth-sĕm′-ă-ne̅, and saith unto the disciples, Sit ye here, while I go and pray yonder.

37 And he took with him Peter and the two sons of Zĕb′-ĕ-de̅e̅, and began to be sorrowful and very heavy.

38 Then saith he unto them, My soul is exceeding sorrowful, even unto death: tarry ye here, and watch with me.

39 And he went a little further, and fell on his face, and prayed,

saying, O my Father, if it be possible, let this cup pass from me: nevertheless not as I will, but as thou *wilt.*

40 And he cometh unto the disciples, and findeth them asleep, and saith unto Peter, What, could ye not watch with me one hour?

41 Watch and pray, that ye enter not into temptation: the spirit indeed *is* willing, but the flesh *is* weak.

42 He went away again the second time, and prayed, saying,

O my Father, if this cup may not pass away from me, except I drink it, thy will be done.

MARK – 14:

32 And they came to a place which was named Gĕth-sĕm′-ă-ne̅: and he saith to his disciples, Sit ye here, while I shall pray.

33 And he taketh with him Peter and James and John, and began to be sore amazed, and to be very heavy;

34 And saith unto them, My soul is exceeding sorrowful unto death: tarry ye here, and watch.

35 And he went forward a little, and fell on the ground, and prayed that, if it were possible, the hour might pass from him.

36 And he said, Abba, Father, all things *are* possible unto thee; take away this cup from me: nevertheless not what I will, but what thou wilt.

37 And he cometh, and findeth them sleeping, and saith unto Peter, Simon, sleepest thou? couldest not thou watch one hour?

38 Watch ye and pray, lest ye enter into temptation. The spirit truly *is* ready, but the flesh *is* weak.

39 And again he went away, and prayed, and spake the same words.

LUKE – 22:

40 And when he was at the place, he said unto them, Pray that ye enter not into temptation.

41 And he was withdrawn from them about a stone's cast, and kneeled down, and prayed,

42 Saying, Father, if thou be willing, remove this cup from me: nevertheless not my will, but thine, be done.

43 And there appeared an angel unto him from heaven, strengthening him.

44 And being in an agony he prayed more earnestly: and his sweat was as it were great drops of blood falling down to the ground.

45 And when he rose up from prayer, and was come to his disciples, he found them sleeping for sorrow,

46 And said unto them, Why sleep ye? rise and pray, lest ye enter into temptation.

MATTHEW – 26	MARK – 14	LUKE – 22	JOHN – 18
43 And he came and found them asleep again: for their eyes were heavy.	40 And when he returned, he found them asleep again, (for their eyes were heavy,) neither wist they what to answer him.		
44 And he left them, and went away again, and prayed the third time, saying the same words.			
45 Then cometh he to his disciples, and saith unto them, Sleep on now, and take *your* rest: behold, the hour is at hand, and the Son of man is betrayed into the hands of sinners.	41 And he cometh the third time, and saith unto them, Sleep on now, and take *your* rest: it is enough, the hour is come; behold, the Son of man is betrayed into the hands of sinners.		
46 Rise, let us be going: behold, he is at hand that doth betray me.	42 Rise up, let us go; lo, he that betrayeth me is at hand.		

Friday

227. THE BETRAYAL BY JUDAS

MATTHEW – 26	MARK – 14	LUKE – 22	JOHN – 18
			2 And Judas also, which betrayed him, knew the place: for Jesus ofttimes resorted thither with his disciples.
47 ¶ And while he yet spake, lo, Judas, one of the twelve, came, and with him a great multitude with swords and staves, from the chief priests and elders of the people.	43 ¶ And immediately, while he yet spake, cometh Judas, one of the twelve, and with him a great multitude with swords and staves, from the chief priests and the scribes and the elders.	47 ¶ And while he yet spake, behold a multitude, and he that was called Judas, one of the twelve, went before them, and drew near unto Jesus to kiss him.	3 Judas then, having received a band *of men* and officers from the chief priests and Pharisees, cometh thither with lanterns and torches and weapons.
48 Now he that betrayed him gave them a sign, saying, Whomsoever I shall kiss, that same is he: hold him fast.	44 And he that betrayed him had given them a token, saying, Whomsoever I shall kiss, that same is he; take him, and lead *him* away safely.		
49 And forthwith he came to Jesus, and said, Hail, master; and kissed him.	45 And as soon as he was come, he goeth straightway to him, and saith, Master, master; and kissed him.		
50a And Jesus said unto him, Friend, wherefore art thou come?		48 But Jesus said unto him, Judas, betrayest thou the Son of man with a kiss?	
			4 Jesus therefore, knowing all things that should come upon him, went forth, and said unto them, Whom seek ye?
			5 They answered him, Jesus of Nazareth. Jesus saith unto them, I am *he*. And Judas also, which betrayed him, stood with them.
			6 As soon then as he had said unto them, I am *he*, they went backward, and fell to the ground.
			7 Then asked he them again, Whom seek ye? And they said, Jesus of Nazareth.
			8 Jesus answered, I have told you that I am *he*: if therefore ye seek me, let these go their way:
			9 That the saying might be fulfilled, which he spake, Of them which thou gavest me have I lost none.

228. PETER REBUKED FOR TRYING TO STOP THE ARREST

MATTHEW – 26	MARK – 14	LUKE – 22	JOHN – 18
		49 When they which were about him saw what would follow, they said unto him, Lord, shall we smite with the sword?	
51 And, behold, one of them which were with Jesus stretched out *his* hand, and drew his sword, and struck a servant of the high priest's, and smote off his ear.	47 And one of them that stood by drew a sword, and smote a servant of the high priest, and cut off his ear.	50 And one of them smote the servant of the high priest, and cut off his right ear.	10 Then Simon Peter having a sword drew it, and smote the high priest's servant, and cut off his right ear. The servant's name was Mǎl'-chŭs.

140

MATTHEW – 26	MARK – 14	LUKE – 22	JOHN – 18
		51 And Jesus answered and said, Suffer ye thus far. And he touched his ear, and healed him.	
52 Then said Jesus unto him, Put up again thy sword into his place: for all they that take the sword shall perish with the sword. 53 Thinkest thou that I cannot now pray to my Father, and he shall presently give me more than twelve legions of angels? 54 But how then shall the scriptures be fulfilled, that thus it must be?			11 Then said Jesus unto Peter, Put up thy sword into the sheath: the cup which my Father hath given me, shall I not drink it ?
55 In that same hour said Jesus to the multitudes, Are ye come out as against a thief with swords and staves for to take me ? I sat daily with you teaching in the temple, and ye laid no hold on me.	48 And Jesus answered and said unto them, Are ye come out, as against a thief, with swords and *with* staves to take me ? 49 I was daily with you in the temple teaching, and ye took me not: but the scriptures must be fulfilled.	52 Then Jesus said unto the chief priests, and captains of the temple, and the elders, which were come to him, Be ye come out, as against a thief, with swords and staves ? 53 When I was daily with you in the temple, ye stretched forth no hands against me: but this is your hour, and the power of darkness.	

229. THE ARREST, APOSTLES FLEE

MATTHEW – 26	MARK – 14	LUKE – 22	JOHN – 18
50b Then came they, and laid hands on Jesus, and took him. 56 But all this was done, that the scriptures of the prophets might be fulfilled. Then all the disciples forsook him, and fled.	46 ¶ And they laid their hands on him, and took him. 50 And they all forsook him, and fled. 51 And there followed him a certain young man, having a linen cloth cast about *his* naked *body;* and the young men laid hold on him: 52 And he left the linen cloth, and fled from them naked.		12 Then the band and the captain and officers of the Jews took Jesus, and bound him,

230. TAKEN TO THE PALACE OF ANNAS AND CAIAPHAS FOLLOWED BY PETER AND ANOTHER *

MATTHEW – 26	MARK – 14	LUKE – 22	JOHN – 18
57 ¶ And they that had laid hold on Jesus led *him* away to Cāī′-ă-phăs the high priest, where the scribes and the elders were assembled.	53 ¶ And they led Jesus away to the high priest: and with him were assembled all the chief priests and the elders and the scribes.	54 ¶ Then took they him, and led *him,* and brought him into the high priest's house.	13 And led him away to Annas first; for he was father in law to Cāī′-ă-phăs, which was the high priest that same year. 14 Now Cāī′-ă-phăs was he, which gave counsel to the Jews, that it was expedient that one man should die for the people. 15 ¶ And Simon Peter followed Jesus, and *so did* another disciple: that disciple was known unto the high priest, and went in with Jesus into the palace of the high priest.
58 But Peter followed him afar off unto the high priest's palace,	54 And Peter followed him afar off, even into the palace of the high priest:	And Peter followed afar off.	16 But Peter stood at the door without. Then went out that other disciple, which was known unto the high priest, and spake unto her that kept the door, and brought in Peter.
and went in, and sat with the servants, to see the end.	and he sat with the servants, and warmed himself at the fire.	55 And when they had kindled a fire in the midst of the hall, and were set down together, Peter sat down among them.	18 And the servants and officers stood there, who had made a fire of coals; for it was cold: and they warmed themselves: and Peter stood with them, and warmed himself.

231. QUESTIONED FIRST BY ANNAS

MATTHEW – 26	MARK – 14	LUKE – 22	JOHN – 18
			19 ¶ The high priest then asked Jesus of his disciples, and of his doctrine. 20 Jesus answered him, I spake openly to the world; I ever taught in the synagogue, and in the temple, whither the Jews always resort; and in secret have I said nothing.

*For an explanation of the many conflicts between the arrest of Jesus and His presentation before Pilate, see note 230.

MATTHEW – 26	MARK – 14	LUKE – 22	JOHN – 18
			21 Why askest thou me? ask them which heard me, what I have said unto them: behold, they know what I said. 22 And when he had thus spoken, one of the officers which stood by struck Jesus with the palm of his hand, saying, Answerest thou the high priest so? 23 Jesus answered him, If I have spoken evil, bear witness of the evil: but if well, why smitest thou me? * 24 Now Annas had sent him bound unto Cāi´-ă-phăs the high priest.

232. EXAMINED BEFORE CAIAPHAS AND THE COUNCIL

MATTHEW – 26	MARK – 14	LUKE – 22	JOHN – 18
59 Now the chief priests, and elders, and all the council, sought false witness against Jesus, to put him to death; 60 But found none: yea, though many false witnesses came, *yet* found they none. At the last came two false witnesses, 61 And said, This *fellow* said, I am able to destroy the temple of God, and to build it in three days. 62 And the high priest arose, and said unto him, Answerest thou nothing? what *is it which* these witness against thee? 63 But Jesus held his peace. And the high priest answered and said unto him, I adjure thee by the living God, that thou tell us whether thou be the Christ, the Son of God. 64 Jesus saith unto him, Thou hast said: nevertheless I say unto you, Hereafter shall ye see the Son of man sitting on the right hand of power, and coming in the clouds of heaven. 65 Then the high priest rent his clothes, saying, He hath spoken blasphemy; what further need have we of witnesses? behold, now ye have heard his blasphemy. 66 What think ye? They answered and said, He is guilty of death.	55 And the chief priests and all the council sought for witness against Jesus to put him to death; and found none. 56 For many bare false witness against him, but their witness agreed not together. 57 And there arose certain, and bare false witness against him, saying, 58 We heard him say, I will destroy this temple that is made with hands, and within three days I will build another made without hands. 59 But neither so did their witness agree together. 60 And the high priest stood up in the midst, and asked Jesus, saying, Answerest thou nothing? what *is it which* these witness against thee? 61 But he held his peace, and answered nothing. Again the high priest asked him, and said unto him, Art thou the Christ, the Son of the Blessed? 62 And Jesus said, I am: and ye shall see the Son of man sitting on the right hand of power, and coming in the clouds of heaven. 63 Then the high priest rent his clothes, and saith, What need we any further witnesses? 64 Ye have heard the blasphemy: what think ye? And they all condemned him to be guilty of death.		

233. MOCKING OF JESUS

MATTHEW – 26	MARK – 14	LUKE – 22	JOHN – 18
67 Then did they spit in his face, and buffeted him; and others smote *him* with the palms of their hands, 68 Saying, Prophesy unto us, thou Christ, Who is he that smote thee?	65 And some began to spit on him, and to cover his face, and to buffet him, and to say unto him, Prophesy: and the servants did strike him with the palms of their hands.	63 ¶ And the men that held Jesus mocked him, and smote *him*. 64 And when they had blindfolded him, they struck him on the face, and asked him, saying, Prophesy, who is it that smote thee? 65 And many other things blasphemously spake they against him.	

*John 18:24 — In the Greek, this verse does not appear in the past tense.

234. PETER DENIES KNOWING JESUS *

66 ¶ And as Peter was beneath in the palace, there cometh one of the maids of the high priest:

69 ¶ Now Peter sat without in the palace: and a damsel came unto him, saying, Thou also wast with Jesus of Galilee.

67 And when she saw Peter warming himself, she looked upon him, and said, And thou also wast with Jesus of Nazareth.

56 But a certain maid beheld him as he sat by the fire, and earnestly looked upon him, and said, This man was also with him.

17 Then saith the damsel that kept the door unto Peter, Art not thou also *one* of this man's disciples? He saith, I am not.

70 But he denied before *them* all, saying, I know not what thou sayest.

68 But he denied, saying, I know not, neither understand I what thou sayest. And he went out into the porch; and the cock crew.

57 And he denied him, saying, Woman, I know him not.

71 And when he was gone out into the porch, another *maid* saw him, and said unto them that were there, This *fellow* was also with Jesus of Nazareth.

69 And a maid saw him again, and began to say to them that stood by, This is *one* of them.

70 And he denied it again.

58 And after a little while another saw him, and said, Thou art also of them. And Peter said, Man, I am not.

25 And Simon Peter stood and warmed himself. They said therefore unto him, Art not thou also *one* of his disciples? He denied *it*, and said, I am not.

72 And again he denied with an oath, I do not know the man.

73 And after a while came unto *him* they that stood by, and said to Peter, Surely thou also art *one* of them; for thy speech bewrayeth thee.

And a little after, they that stood by said again to Peter, Surely thou art *one* of them: for thou art a Galilæan, and thy speech agreeth thereto.

59 And about the space of one hour after another confidently affirmed, saying, Of a truth this *fellow* also was with him: for he is a Galilæan.

26 One of the servants of the high priest, being *his* kinsman whose ear Peter cut off, saith, Did not I see thee in the garden with him?

74 Then began he to curse and to swear, *saying*, I know not the man. And immediately the cock crew.

71 But he began to curse and to swear, *saying*, I know not this man of whom ye speak.

72 And the second time the cock crew.

60 And Peter said, Man, I know not what thou sayest. And immediately, while he yet spake, the cock crew.

61 And the Lord turned, and looked upon Peter. And Peter remembered the word of the Lord, how he had said unto him, Before the cock crow, thou shalt deny me thrice.

27 Peter then denied again: and immediately the cock crew.

75 And Peter remembered the word of Jesus, which said unto him, Before the cock crow, thou shalt deny me thrice. And he went out, and wept bitterly.

And Peter called to mind the word that Jesus said unto him, Before the cock crow twice, thou shalt deny me thrice. And when he thought thereon, he wept.

62 And Peter went out, and wept bitterly.

235. FORMAL TRIAL AND CONDEMNATION

CHAPTER 27

WHEN the morning was come, all the chief priests and elders of the people took counsel against Jesus to put him to death:

1a CHAPTER 15

AND straightway in the morning the chief priests held a consultation with the elders and scribes and the whole council,

66 ¶ And as soon as it was day, the elders of the people and the chief priests and the scribes came together, and led him into their council, saying,

67 Art thou the Christ? tell us. And he said unto them, If I tell you, ye will not believe:

68 And if I also ask *you*, ye will not answer me, nor let *me* go.

69 Hereafter shall the Son of man sit on the right hand of the power of God.

70 Then said they all, Art thou then the Son of God? And he said unto them, Ye say that I am.

71 And they said, What need we any further witness? for we ourselves have heard of his own mouth.

236. JUDAS COMMITS SUICIDE

3 ¶ Then Judas, which had betrayed him, when he saw that he was condemned, repented himself, and brought again the thirty pieces of silver to the chief priests and elders,

4 Saying, I have sinned in that I have betrayed the innocent blood. And they said, What *is* that to us? see thou *to that*.

5 And he cast down the pieces of silver in the temple, and departed, and went and hanged himself.

*The three denials by Peter are shown together although they occurred at different times during the early morning hours.

MATTHEW – 27	MARK – 15	LUKE – 23	JOHN – 18
6 And the chief priests took the silver pieces, and said, It is not lawful for to put them into the treasury, because it is the price of blood. 7 And they took counsel, and bought with them the potter's field, to bury strangers in. 8 Wherefore that field was called, The field of blood, unto this day. 9 Then was fulfilled that which was spoken by Jeremy the prophet, saying, And they took the thirty pieces of silver, the price of him that was valued, whom they of the children of Israel did value; 10 And gave them for the potter's field, as the Lord appointed me.			

237. FIRST APPEARANCE BEFORE PILATE

MATTHEW – 27	MARK – 15	LUKE – 23	JOHN – 18
2 And when they had bound him, they led *him* away, and delivered him to Pontius Pilate the governor.	1b and bound Jesus, and carried *him* away, and delivered *him* to Pilate.	**CHAPTER 23** AND the whole multitude of them arose, and led him unto Pilate.	28 ¶ Then led they Jesus from Cāi´-ă-phăs unto the hall of judgment: and it was early; and they themselves went not into the judgment hall, lest they should be defiled; but that they might eat the passover. 29 Pilate then went out unto them, and said, What accusation bring ye against this man? 30 They answered and said unto him, If he were not a malefactor, we would not have delivered him up unto thee. 31 Then said Pilate unto them, Take ye him, and judge him according to your law. The Jews therefore said unto him, It is not lawful for us to put any man to death: 32 That the saying of Jesus might be fulfilled, which he spake, signifying what death he should die.
		2 And they began to accuse him, saying, We found this *fellow* perverting the nation, and forbidding to give tribute to Cæsar, saying that he himself is Christ a King.	
11 And Jesus stood before the governor: and the governor asked him, saying, Art thou the King of the Jews?	2 And Pilate asked him, Art thou the King of the Jews?	3 And Pilate asked him, saying, Art thou the King of the Jews?	33 Then Pilate entered into the judgment hall again, and called Jesus, and said unto him, Art thou the King of the Jews? 34 Jesus answered him, Sayest thou this thing of thyself, or did others tell it thee of me? 35 Pilate answered, Am I a Jew? Thine own nation and the chief priests have delivered thee unto me: what hast thou done? 36 Jesus answered, My kingdom is not of this world: if my kingdom were of this world, then would my servants fight, that I should not be delivered to the Jews: but now is my kingdom not from hence.
And Jesus said unto him, Thou sayest.	And he answering said unto him, Thou sayest *it*.	And he answered him and said, Thou sayest *it*.	37 Pilate therefore said unto him, Art thou a king then? Jesus answered, Thou sayest that I am a king. To this end was I born, and for this cause came I into the world, that I should bear witness unto the truth. Every one that is of the truth heareth my voice. 38 Pilate saith unto him, What is truth? And when he had said this, he went out again unto the Jews, and saith unto them, I find in him no fault *at all*.
		4 Then said Pilate to the chief priests and *to* the people, I find no fault in this man.	

MATTHEW – 27	MARK – 15	LUKE – 23	JOHN – 18
12 And when he was accused of the chief priests and elders, he answered nothing. 13 Then said Pilate unto him, Hearest thou not how many things they witness against thee? 14 And he answered him to never a word; insomuch that the governor marvelled greatly.	3 And the chief priests accused him of many things: but he answered nothing. 4 And Pilate asked him again, saying, Answerest thou nothing? behold how many things they witness against thee. 5 But Jesus yet answered nothing; so that Pilate marvelled.		
		5 And they were the more fierce, saying, He stirreth up the people, teaching throughout all Jewry, beginning from Galilee to this place. 6 When Pilate heard of Galilee, he asked whether the man were a Galilæan. 7 And as soon as he knew that he belonged unto Herod's jurisdiction, he sent him to Herod, who himself also was at Jerusalem at that time.	

238. JESUS BEFORE HEROD

MATTHEW – 27	MARK – 15	LUKE – 23	JOHN – 18
		8 ¶ And when Herod saw Jesus, he was exceeding glad: for he was desirous to see him of a long season, because he had heard many things of him; and he hoped to have seen some miracle done by him. 9 Then he questioned with him in many words; but he answered him nothing. 10 And the chief priests and scribes stood and vehemently accused him. 11 And Herod with his men of war set him at nought, and mocked him, and arrayed him in a gorgeous robe, and sent him again to Pilate. 12 ¶ And the same day Pilate and Herod were made friends together: for before they were at enmity between themselves.	

239. SECOND APPEARANCE BEFORE PILATE

MATTHEW – 27	MARK – 15	LUKE – 23	JOHN – 18
		13 ¶ And Pilate, when he had called together the chief priests and the rulers and the people, 14 Said unto them, Ye have brought this man unto me, as one that perverteth the people: and, behold, I, having examined him before you, have found no fault in this man touching those things whereof ye accuse him: 15 No, nor yet Herod: for I sent you to him; and, lo, nothing worthy of death is done unto him. 16 I will therefore chastise him, and release him.	
15 Now at that feast the governor was wont to release unto the people a prisoner, whom they would. 16 And they had then a notable prisoner, called Bär-ăb'-băs.	6 Now at that feast he released unto them one prisoner, whomsoever they desired. 7 And there was one named Bär-ăb'-băs, which lay bound with them that had made insurrection with him, who had committed murder in the insurrection. 8 And the multitude crying aloud began to desire him to do as he had ever done unto them.	17 (For of necessity he must release one unto them at the feast.)	39a But ye have a custom, that I should release unto you one at the passover:

MATTHEW – 27	MARK – 15	LUKE – 23	JOHN – 18,19
17 Therefore when they were gathered together, Pilate said unto them, Whom will ye that I release unto you? Bär·ăb´·băs, or Jesus which is called Christ?	9 But Pilate answered them, saying, Will ye that I release unto you the King of the Jews?		39b will ye therefore that I release unto you the King of the Jews?
18 For he knew that for envy they had delivered him.	10 For he knew that the chief priests had delivered him for envy.		
19 ¶ When he was set down on the judgment seat, his wife sent unto him, saying, Have thou nothing to do with that just man: for I have suffered many things this day in a dream because of him.			
20 But the chief priests and elders persuaded the multitude that they should ask Bär·ăb´·băs, and destroy Jesus.	11 But the chief priests moved the people, that he should rather release Bär·ăb´·băs unto them.		
21 The governor answered and said unto them, Whether of the twain will ye that I release unto you? They said, Bär·ăb´·băs.		18 And they cried out all at once, saying, Away with this *man*, and release unto us Bär·ăb´·băs:	40 Then cried they all again, saying, Not this man, but Bär·ăb´·băs. Now Bär·ăb´·băs was a robber.
		19 (Who for a certain sedition made in the city, and for murder, was cast into prison.)	
		20 Pilate therefore, willing to release Jesus, spake again to them.	
22 Pilate saith unto them, What shall I do then with Jesus which is called Christ?	12 And Pilate answered and said again unto them, What will ye then that I shall do *unto him* whom ye call the King of the Jews?		
They all say unto him, Let him be crucified.	13 And they cried out again, Crucify him.	21 But they cried, saying, Crucify *him*, crucify him.	
23a And the governor said, Why, what evil hath he done?	14a Then Pilate said unto them, Why, what evil hath he done?	22 And he said unto them the third time, Why, what evil hath he done? I have found no cause of death in him: I will therefore chastise him, and let *him* go.	

240. SCOURGING AND MOCKING OF JESUS

MATTHEW – 27	MARK – 15	LUKE – 23	JOHN – 18,19
			CHAPTER 19 THEN Pilate therefore took Jesus, and scourged *him*.
27 Then the soldiers of the governor took Jesus into the common hall, and gathered unto him the whole band *of soldiers*.	16 And the soldiers led him away into the hall, called Præ·tôr´·ĭ·ŭm; and they call together the whole band.		
28 And they stripped him, and put on him a scarlet robe.	17 And they clothed him with purple, and platted a crown of thorns, and put it about his *head*,		2 And the soldiers platted a crown of thorns, and put *it* on his head, and they put on him a purple robe,
29 ¶ And when they had platted a crown of thorns, they put *it* upon his head, and a reed in his right hand: and they bowed the knee before him, and mocked him, saying, Hail, King of the Jews!	18 And began to salute him, Hail, King of the Jews!		3 And said, Hail, King of the Jews! and they smote him with their hands.
30 And they spit upon him, and took the reed, and smote him on the head.	19 And they smote him on the head with a reed, and did spit upon him, and bowing *their* knees worshipped him.		

241. PILATE PLEADS FOR JESUS

MATTHEW – 27	MARK – 15	LUKE – 23	JOHN – 18,19
			4 Pilate therefore went forth again, and saith unto them, Behold, I bring him forth to you, that ye may know that I find no fault in him.
			5 Then came Jesus forth, wearing the crown of thorns, and the purple robe. And *Pilate* saith unto them, Behold the man!
			6 When the chief priests therefore and officers saw him, they cried out, saying, Crucify *him*, crucify *him*. Pilate saith unto them, Take ye him, and crucify *him:* for I find no fault in him.

MATTHEW – 27	MARK – 15	LUKE – 23	JOHN – 19
			7 The Jews answered him, We have a law, and by our law he ought to die, because he made himself the Son of God.
			8 ¶ When Pilate therefore heard that saying, he was the more afraid;
			9 And went again into the judgment hall, and saith unto Jesus, Whence art thou? But Jesus gave him no answer.
			10 Then saith Pilate unto him, Speakest thou not unto me? knowest thou not that I have power to crucify thee, and have power to release thee?
			11 Jesus answered, Thou couldest have no power *at all* against me, except it were given thee from above: therefore he that delivered me unto thee hath the greater sin.
			12 And from thenceforth Pilate sought to release him: but the Jews cried out, saying, If thou let this man go, thou art not Cæsar's friend: whosoever maketh himself a king speaketh against Cæsar.
			13 ¶ When Pilate therefore heard that saying, he brought Jesus forth, and sat down in the judgment seat in a place that is called the Pavement, but in the Hebrew, Găb′-bă-thă.
			14 And it was the preparation of the passover, and about the sixth hour: and he saith unto the Jews, Behold your King!
23b But they cried out the more, saying, Let him be crucified.	14b And they cried out the more exceedingly, Crucify him.	23 And they were instant with loud voices, requiring that he might be crucified. And the voices of them and of the chief priests prevailed.	15 But they cried out, Away with *him*, away with *him*, crucify him. Pilate saith unto them, Shall I crucify your King? The chief priests answered, We have no king but Cæsar.

242. PILATE RELEASES BARABBAS AND DELIVERS JESUS TO BE CRUCIFIED *

MATTHEW – 27	MARK – 15	LUKE – 23	JOHN – 19
24 ¶ When Pilate saw that he could prevail nothing, but *that* rather a tumult was made, he took water, and washed *his* hands before the multitude, saying, I am innocent of the blood of this just person: see ye *to it*. 25 Then answered all the people, and said, His blood *be* on us, and on our children.	15 ¶ And *so* Pilate, willing to content the people,	24 And Pilate gave sentence that it should be as they required. 25 And he released unto them that for sedition and murder was cast into prison, whom they had desired; but he delivered Jesus to their will.	
26 ¶ Then released he Băr-ăb′-băs unto them: and when he had scourged Jesus, he delivered *him* to be crucified.	released Băr-ăb′-băs unto them, and delivered Jesus, when he had scourged *him*, to be crucified.		16a Then delivered he him therefore unto them to be crucified.

243. JESUS IS MOCKED, LED TO GOLGOTHA AND CRUCIFIED

MATTHEW – 27	MARK – 15	LUKE – 23	JOHN – 19
31 And after that they had mocked him, they took the robe off from him, and put his own raiment on him, and led him away to crucify *him*. 32 And as they came out, they found a man of Çy̆-rē′-nē, Simon by name: him they compelled to bear his cross.	20 And when they had mocked him, they took off the purple from him, and put his own clothes on him, and led him out to crucify him. 21 And they compel one Simon a Çy̆-rē′-nĭ-ăn, who passed by, coming out of the country, the father of Alexander and Rufus, to bear his cross.	26 And as they led him away, they laid hold upon one Simon, a Çy̆-rē′-nĭ-ăn, coming out of the country, and on him they laid the cross, that he might bear *it* after Jesus.	16b And they took Jesus, and led *him* away.

*In Matthew 27:26 and Mark 15:15, the scourging is referring to that already inflicted and recorded in John 19:1.

147

MATTHEW – 27	MARK – 15	LUKE – 23	JOHN – 19
		27 ¶ And there followed him a great company of people, and of women, which also bewailed and lamented him. 28 But Jesus turning unto them said, Daughters of Jerusalem, weep not for me, but weep for yourselves, and for your children. 29 For, behold, the days are coming, in the which they shall say, Blessed *are* the barren, and the wombs that never bare, and the paps which never gave suck. 30 Then shall they begin to say to the mountains, Fall on us; and to the hills, Cover us. 31 For if they do these things in a green tree, what shall be done in the dry? 32 And there were also two other, malefactors, led with him to be put to death. 33 And when they were come to the place, which is called Calvary,	
33 And when they were come unto a place called Gŏl´·gŏ·thă, that is to say, a place of a skull, 34 ¶ They gave him vinegar to drink mingled with gall: and when he had tasted *thereof*, he would not drink.	22 And they bring him unto the place Gŏl´·gŏ·thă, which is, being interpreted, The place of a skull. 23 And they gave him to drink wine mingled with myrrh: but he received *it* not. 25 And it was the third hour, and they crucified him.		17 And he bearing his cross went forth into a place called *the place* of a skull, which is called in the Hebrew Gŏl´·gŏ·thă:
38 Then were there two thieves crucified with him, one on the right hand, and another on the left.	27 And with him they crucify two thieves; the one on his right hand, and the other on his left. 28 And the scripture was fulfilled, which saith, And he was numbered with the transgressors.	there they crucified him, and the malefactors, one on the right hand, and the other on the left.	18 Where they crucified him, and two other with him, on either side one, and Jesus in the midst.

244. SUPERSCRIPTION: "THIS IS JESUS THE KING OF THE JEWS"

MATTHEW – 27	MARK – 15	LUKE – 23	JOHN – 19
37 And set up over his head his accusation written, THIS IS JESUS THE KING OF THE JEWS.	26 And the superscription of his accusation was written over, THE KING OF THE JEWS.	38 And a superscription also was written over him in letters of Greek, and Latin, and Hebrew, THIS IS THE KING OF THE JEWS.	19 ¶ And Pilate wrote a title, and put *it* on the cross. And the writing was, JESUS OF NAZARETH THE KING OF THE JEWS. 20 This title then read many of the Jews: for the place where Jesus was crucified was nigh to the city: and it was written in Hebrew, *and* Greek, *and* Latin. 21 Then said the chief priests of the Jews to Pilate, Write not, The King of the Jews; but that he said, I am King of the Jews. 22 Pilate answered, What I have written I have written.

245. "FATHER, FORGIVE THEM"

MATTHEW – 27	MARK – 15	LUKE – 23	JOHN – 19
		34a ¶ Then said Jesus, Father, forgive them; for they know not what they do.	

246. SOLDIERS CAST LOTS FOR HIS GARMENTS

MATTHEW – 27	MARK – 15	LUKE – 23	JOHN – 19
			23 ¶ Then the soldiers, when they had crucified Jesus, took his garments, and made four parts, to every soldier a part; and also *his* coat: now the coat was without seam, woven from the top throughout. 24 They said therefore among themselves, Let us not rend it, but cast lots for it, whose it shall be: that the scripture might be fulfilled, which saith, They parted my raiment among them, and for my vesture they did cast lots. These things therefore the soldiers did.
35 And they crucified him, and parted his garments, casting lots: that it might be fulfilled which was spoken by the prophet, They parted my garments among them, and upon my vesture did they cast lots. 36 And sitting down they watched him there;	24 And when they had crucified him, they parted his garments, casting lots upon them, what every man should take.	34b And they parted his raiment, and cast lots.	

148

247. FURTHER MOCKING BY THE PEOPLE

MATTHEW – 27	MARK – 15	LUKE – 23	JOHN – 19
39 ¶ And they that passed by reviled him, wagging their heads, 40 And saying, Thou that destroyest the temple, and buildest *it* in three days, save thyself. If thou be the Son of God, come down from the cross. 41 Likewise also the chief priests mocking *him*, with the scribes and elders, said, 42 He saved others; himself he cannot save. If he be the King of Israel, let him now come down from the cross, and we will believe him. 43 He trusted in God; let him deliver him now, if he will have him: for he said, I am the Son of God.	29 And they that passed by railed on him, wagging their heads, and saying, Ah, thou that destroyest the temple, and buildest *it* in three days, 30 Save thyself, and come down from the cross. 31 Likewise also the chief priests mocking said among themselves with the scribes, He saved others; himself he cannot save. 32a Let Christ the King of Israel descend now from the cross, that we may see and believe.	35 And the people stood beholding. And the rulers also with them derided *him*, saying, He saved others; let him save himself, if he be Christ, the chosen of God. 36 And the soldiers also mocked him, coming to him, and offering him vinegar, 37 And saying, If thou be the king of the Jews, save thyself.	

248. WORDS TO THE THIEF

MATTHEW – 27	MARK – 15	LUKE – 23	JOHN – 19
44 The thieves also, which were crucified with him, cast the same in his teeth.	32b And they that were crucified with him reviled him.	39 ¶ And one of the malefactors which were hanged railed on him, saying, If thou be Christ, save thyself and us. 40 But the other answering rebuked him, saying, Dost not thou fear God, seeing thou art in the same condemnation? 41 And we indeed justly; for we receive the due reward of our deeds: but this man hath done nothing amiss. 42 And he said unto Jesus, Lord, remember me when thou comest into thy kingdom. 43 And Jesus said unto him, Verily I say unto thee, To day shalt thou be with me in paradise.	

249. JESUS SPEAKS TO HIS MOTHER

MATTHEW – 27	MARK – 15	LUKE – 23	JOHN – 19
			25 ¶ Now there stood by the cross of Jesus his mother, and his mother's sister, Mary the *wife* of Clē′-ŏ-phăs, and Mary Măg′-dă-lēne. 26 When Jesus therefore saw his mother, and the disciple standing by, whom he loved, he saith unto his mother, Woman, behold thy son! 27 Then saith he to the disciple, Behold thy mother! And from that hour that disciple took her unto his own *home*.

250. DARKNESS FROM THE SIXTH TO THE NINTH HOUR

MATTHEW – 27	MARK – 15	LUKE – 23	JOHN – 19
45 Now from the sixth hour there was darkness over all the land unto the ninth hour.	33 And when the sixth hour was come, there was darkness over the whole land until the ninth hour.	44 And it was about the sixth hour, and there was a darkness over all the earth until the ninth hour. 45a And the sun was darkened,	

251. FINAL WORDS AND DEATH OF JESUS

MATTHEW – 27	MARK – 15	LUKE – 23	JOHN – 19
46 And about the ninth hour Jesus cried with a loud voice, saying, Ē′-lī, Ē′-lī, lä′-mä să-băch′-thă-nī? that is to say, My God, my God, why hast thou forsaken me? 47 Some of them that stood there, when they heard *that*, said, This *man* calleth for Ē-lī′-ăs.	34 And at the ninth hour Jesus cried with a loud voice, saying, Ē′-lō-ī, Ē′-lō-ī, lä′-mä să-băch′-thă-nī? which is, being interpreted, My God, my God, why hast thou forsaken me? 35 And some of them that stood by, when they heard *it*, said, Behold, he calleth Ē-lī′-ăs.		

MATTHEW – 27	MARK – 15	LUKE – 23	JOHN – 19
			28 ¶ After this, Jesus knowing that all things were now accomplished, that the scripture might be fulfilled, saith, I thirst.
48 And straightway one of them ran, and took a spunge, and filled *it* with vinegar, and put *it* on a reed, and gave him to drink.	36 And one ran and filled a spunge full of vinegar, and put *it* on a reed, and gave him to drink, saying, Let alone; let us see whether Ē·lī′·ăs will come to take him down.		29 Now there was set a vessel full of vinegar: and they filled a spunge with vinegar, and put *it* upon hyssop, and put *it* to his mouth.
49 The rest said, Let be, let us see whether Ē·lī′·ăs will come to save him.			
			30 When Jesus therefore had received the vinegar, he said, It is finished:
50 ¶ Jesus, when he had cried again with a loud voice,	37 And Jesus cried with a loud voice,	46 ¶ And when Jesus had cried with a loud voice, he said, Father, into thy hands I commend my spirit: and having said thus, he gave up the ghost.	
yielded up the ghost.	and gave up the ghost.		and he bowed his head, and gave up the ghost.

252. VEIL OF TEMPLE TORN FROM TOP TO BOTTOM

51 And, behold, the veil of the temple was rent in twain from the top to the bottom; and the earth did quake, and the rocks rent;	38 And the veil of the temple was rent in twain from the top to the bottom.	45b and the veil of the temple was rent in the midst.	

253. TESTIMONY OF WITNESSES

54 Now when the centurion, and they that were with him, watching Jesus, saw the earthquake, and those things that were done, they feared greatly, saying, Truly this was the Son of God.	39 ¶ And when the centurion, which stood over against him, saw that he so cried out, and gave up the ghost, he said, Truly this man was the Son of God.	47 Now when the centurion saw what was done, he glorified God, saying, Certainly this was a righteous man.	
		48 And all the people that came together to that sight, beholding the things which were done, smote their breasts, and returned.	
55 And many women were there beholding afar off, which followed Jesus from Galilee, ministering unto him:	40 There were also women looking on afar off:	49 And all his acquaintance, and the women that followed him from Galilee, stood afar off, beholding these things.	
56 Among which was Mary Măg′·dă·lēne, and Mary the mother of James and Jō′·sĕs, and the mother of Zĕb′·ĕ·dēē′s children.	among whom was Mary Măg′·dă·lēne, and Mary the mother of James the less and of Jō′·sĕs, and Să·lō′·mē;		
	41 (Who also, when he was in Galilee, followed him, and ministered unto him;) and many other women which came up with him unto Jerusalem.		

254. JESUS' SIDE IS PIERCED

			31 The Jews therefore, because it was the preparation, that the bodies should not remain upon the cross on the sabbath day, (for that sabbath day was an high day,) besought Pilate that their legs might be broken, and *that* they might be taken away.
			32 Then came the soldiers, and brake the legs of the first, and of the other which was crucified with him.
			33 But when they came to Jesus, and saw that he was dead already, they brake not his legs:
			34 But one of the soldiers with a spear pierced his side, and forthwith came there out blood and water.
			35 And he that saw *it* bare record, and his record is true: and he knoweth that he saith true, that ye might believe.

MATTHEW – 27	MARK – 15	LUKE – 23	JOHN – 19
			36 For these things were done, that the scripture should be fulfilled, A bone of him shall not be broken. 37 And again another scripture saith, They shall look on him whom they pierced.

255. THE BURIAL OF JESUS

MATTHEW – 27	MARK – 15	LUKE – 23	JOHN – 19
57 When the even was come, there came a rich man of Ăr·ĭm·ă·thǣ´·ă, named Joseph, who also himself was Jesus' disciple: 58 He went to Pilate, and begged the body of Jesus.	42 ¶ And now when the even was come, because it was the preparation, that is, the day before the sabbath, 43 Joseph of Ăr·ĭm·ă·thǣ´·ă, an honourable counseller, which also waited for the kingdom of God, came, and went in boldly unto Pilate, and craved the body of Jesus.	50 ¶ And, behold, *there was* a man named Joseph, a counseller; *and he was* a good man, and a just: 51 (The same had not consented to the counsel and deed of them;) he *was* of Ăr·ĭm·ă·thǣ´·ă, a city of the Jews: who also himself waited for the kingdom of God. 52 This *man* went unto Pilate, and begged the body of Jesus.	38 ¶ And after this Joseph of Ăr·ĭm·ă·thǣ´·ă, being a disciple of Jesus, but secretly for fear of the Jews, besought Pilate that he might take away the body of Jesus:
Then Pilate commanded the body to be delivered.	44 And Pilate marvelled if he were already dead: and calling *unto him* the centurion, he asked him whether he had been any while dead. 45 And when he knew *it* of the centurion, he gave the body to Joseph.		and Pilate gave *him* leave. He came therefore, and took the body of Jesus. 39 And there came also Nĭc·ŏ·dē´·mŭs, which at the first came to Jesus by night, and brought a mixture of myrrh and aloes, about an hundred pound *weight*.
59 And when Joseph had taken the body, he wrapped it in a clean linen cloth,	46 And he bought fine linen, and took him down, and wrapped him in the linen,	53 And he took it down, and wrapped it in linen,	40 Then took they the body of Jesus, and wound it in linen clothes with the spices, as the manner of the Jews is to bury. 41 Now in the place where he was crucified there was a garden; and in the garden a new sepulchre, wherein was never man yet laid.
60 And laid it in his own new tomb, which he had hewn out in the rock: and he rolled a great stone to the door of the sepulchre, and departed.	and laid him in a sepulchre which was hewn out of a rock, and rolled a stone unto the door of the sepulchre.	and laid it in a sepulchre that was hewn in stone, wherein never man before was laid. 54 And that day was the preparation, and the sabbath drew on. 55 And the women also, which came with him from Galilee, followed after, and beheld the sepulchre, and how his body was laid.	42 There laid they Jesus therefore because of the Jews' preparation *day;* for the sepulchre was nigh at hand.
61 And there was Mary Măg´·dă·lēne, and the other Mary, sitting over against the sepulchre.	47 And Mary Măg´·dă·lēne and Mary *the mother* of Jō´·sĕs beheld where he was laid.	56 And they returned, and prepared spices and ointments; and rested the sabbath day according to the commandment.	

Saturday

256. GUARDS PLACED AT THE TOMB

MATTHEW – 27	MARK – 15	LUKE – 23	JOHN – 19
62 ¶ Now the next day, that followed the day of the preparation, the chief priests and Pharisees came together unto Pilate, 63 Saying, Sir, we remember that that deceiver said, while he was yet alive, After three days I will rise again.			

MATTHEW – 27,28	MARK – 16	LUKE – 24	JOHN – 20
64 Command therefore that the sepulchre be made sure until the third day, lest his disciples come by night, and steal him away, and say unto the people, He is risen from the dead: so the last error shall be worse than the first.			
65 Pilate said unto them, Ye have a watch: go your way, make *it* as sure as ye can.			
66 So they went, and made the sepulchre sure, sealing the stone, and setting a watch.			

257. WOMEN PURCHASE SPICES TO ANOINT THE BODY

MATTHEW	MARK	LUKE	JOHN
	CHAPTER 16 AND when the sabbath was past, Mary Măg′·dă·lēne, and Mary the *mother* of James, and Să·lō′·mē, had bought sweet spices, that they might come and anoint him.		

IX.   THE RESURRECTION AND FORTY-DAY MINISTRY

Sunday

258. THE RESURRECTION

259. ANGEL ROLLS BACK THE STONE

MATTHEW	MARK	LUKE	JOHN
2 And, behold, there was a great earthquake: for the angel of the Lord descended from heaven, and came and rolled back the stone from the door, and sat upon it.			
3 His countenance was like lightning, and his raiment white as snow:			
4 And for fear of him the keepers did shake, and became as dead *men.*			

260. WOMEN FIND THE TOMB OPENED *

MATTHEW	MARK	LUKE	JOHN
CHAPTER 28 IN the end of the sabbath, as it began to dawn toward the first *day* of the week, came Mary Măg′·dă·lēne and the other Mary to see the sepulchre.	2 And very early in the morning the first *day* of the week, they came unto the sepulchre at the rising of the sun.	CHAPTER 24 NOW upon the first *day* of the week, very early in the morning, they came unto the sepulchre, bringing the spices which they had prepared, and certain *others* with them.	CHAPTER 20 THE first *day* of the week cometh Mary Măg′·dă·lēne early, when it was yet dark, unto the sepulchre,
	3 And they said among themselves, Who shall roll us away the stone from the door of the sepulchre?		
	4 And when they looked, they saw that the stone was rolled away: for it was very great.	2 And they found the stone rolled away from the sepulchre.	and seeth the stone taken away from the sepulchre.

261. MARY MAGDALENE RUNS IMMEDIATELY TO TELL THE APOSTLES

MATTHEW	MARK	LUKE	JOHN
			2 Then she runneth, and cometh to Simon Peter, and to the other disciple, whom Jesus loved, and saith unto them, They have taken away the Lord out of the sepulchre, and we know not where they have laid him.

*When and under what circumstances did Mary and the other women see the resurrected Jesus? For an explanation see note 260.

262. WOMEN ENTER TOMB AND SEE ANGELS WHO PROCLAIM, "HE IS NOT HERE: FOR HE IS RISEN"

MATTHEW – 28	MARK – 16	LUKE – 24	JOHN – 20
		3 And they entered in, and found not the body of the Lord Jesus.	
	5 And entering into the sepulchre, they saw a young man sitting on the right side, clothed in a long white garment; and they were affrighted.	4 And it came to pass, as they were much perplexed thereabout, behold, two men stood by them in shining garments:	
5 And the angel answered and said unto the women, Fear not ye: for I know that ye seek Jesus, which was crucified.	6 And he saith unto them, Be not affrighted: Ye seek Jesus of Nazareth, which was crucified: he is risen; he is not here: behold the place where they laid him.	5 And as they were afraid, and bowed down *their* faces to the earth, they said unto them, Why seek ye the living among the dead?	
6 He is not here: for he is risen, as he said. Come, see the place where the Lord lay.		6 He is not here, but is risen: remember how he spake unto you when he was yet in Galilee,	
7 And go quickly, and tell his disciples that he is risen from the dead; and, behold, he goeth before you into Galilee; there shall ye see him: lo, I have told you.	7 But go your way, tell his disciples and Peter that he goeth before you into Galilee: there shall ye see him, as he said unto you.	7 Saying, The Son of man must be delivered into the hands of sinful men, and be crucified, and the third day rise again.	
		8 And they remembered his words,	

263. WOMEN HURRY TO TELL THE APOSTLES

MATTHEW – 28	MARK – 16	LUKE – 24	JOHN – 20
8 And they departed quickly from the sepulchre with fear and great joy; and did run to bring his disciples word.	8 And they went out quickly, and fled from the sepulchre; for they trembled and were amazed: neither said they any thing to any *man;* for they were afraid.	9 And returned from the sepulchre, and told all these things unto the eleven, and to all the rest.	
		10 It was Mary Măg′-dă-lēne, and Jō-ăn′-nă, and Mary *the mother* of James, and other *women that were* with them, which told these things unto the apostles.	
		11 And their words seemed to them as idle tales, and they believed them not.	

264. PETER AND JOHN WITNESS THE EMPTY TOMB

MATTHEW – 28	MARK – 16	LUKE – 24	JOHN – 20
			3 Peter therefore went forth, and that other disciple, and came to the sepulchre.
			4 So they ran both together: and the other disciple did outrun Peter, and came first to the sepulchre.
			5 And he stooping down, *and looking in,* saw the linen clothes lying; yet went he not in.
		12 Then arose Peter, and ran unto the sepulchre; and stooping down, he beheld the linen clothes laid by themselves,	6 Then cometh Simon Peter following him, and went into the sepulchre, and seeth the linen clothes lie,
			7 And the napkin, that was about his head, not lying with the linen clothes, but wrapped together in a place by itself.
			8 Then went in also that other disciple, which came first to the sepulchre, and he saw, and believed.
			9 For as yet they knew not the scripture, that he must rise again from the dead.
		and departed, wondering in himself at that which was come to pass.	10 Then the disciples went away again unto their own home.

265. JESUS APPEARS TO MARY MAGDALENE

MATTHEW – 28,27	MARK – 16	LUKE –	JOHN – 20
			11 ¶ But Mary stood without at the sepulchre weeping: and as she wept, she stooped down, *and looked* into the sepulchre,
			12 And seeth two angels in white sitting, the one at the head, and the other at the feet, where the body of Jesus had lain.
			13 And they say unto her, Woman, why weepest thou? She saith unto them, Because they have taken away my Lord, and I know not where they have laid him.
			14 And when she had thus said, she turned herself back, and saw Jesus standing, and knew not that it was Jesus.
	9 ¶ Now when *Jesus* was risen early the first *day* of the week, he appeared first to Mary Măg′-dă-lēne, out of whom he had cast seven devils.		
			15 Jesus saith unto her, Woman, why weepest thou? whom seekest thou? She, supposing him to be the gardener, saith unto him, Sir, if thou have borne him hence, tell me where thou hast laid him, and I will take him away.
			16 Jesus saith unto her, Mary. She turned herself, and saith unto him, Răb-bō′-nī; which is to say, Master.
			17 Jesus saith unto her, Touch me not; for I am not yet ascended to my Father: but go to my brethren, and say unto them, I ascend unto my Father, and your Father; and *to* my God, and your God.
	10 *And* she went and told them that had been with him, as they mourned and wept.		18 Mary Măg′-dă-lēne came and told the disciples that she had seen the Lord, and *that* he had spoken these things unto her.
	11 And they, when they had heard that he was alive, and had been seen of her, believed not.		

266. JESUS APPEARS TO THE OTHER WOMEN

MATTHEW – 28,27	MARK – 16	LUKE –	JOHN – 20
*9 ¶ And as they went to tell his disciples, behold, Jesus met them, saying, All hail. And they came and held him by the feet, and worshipped him.			
10 Then said Jesus unto them, Be not afraid: go tell my brethren that they go into Galilee, and there shall they see me.			

267. OTHERS RESURRECTED AFTER JESUS

MATTHEW – 28,27	MARK – 16	LUKE –	JOHN – 20
Ch. 27			
52 And the graves were opened; and many bodies of the saints which slept arose,			
53 And came out of the graves after his resurrection, and went into the holy city, and appeared unto many.			

*For an explanation see note 260.

268. GUARDS ARE BRIBED BY CHIEF PRIESTS

11 ¶ Now when they were going, behold, some of the watch came into the city, and shewed unto the chief priests all the things that were done.

12 And when they were assembled with the elders, and had taken counsel, they gave large money unto the soldiers,

13 Saying, Say ye, His disciples came by night, and stole him *away* while we slept.

14 And if this come to the governor's ears, we will persuade him, and secure you.

15 So they took the money, and did as they were taught: and this saying is commonly reported among the Jews until this day.

269. JESUS APPEARS TO TWO FOLLOWERS AT EMMAUS

12 ¶ After that he appeared in another form unto two of them, as they walked, and went into the country.

13 ¶ And, behold, two of them went that same day to a village called Ĕm·mā´·ŭs, which was from Jerusalem *about* threescore furlongs.

14 And they talked together of all these things which had happened.

15 And it came to pass, that, while they communed *together* and reasoned, Jesus himself drew near, and went with them.

16 But their eyes were holden that they should not know him.

17 And he said unto them, What manner of communications *are* these that ye have one to another, as ye walk, and are sad?

18 And the one of them, whose name was Clē´·ŏ·păs, answering said unto him, Art thou only a stranger in Jerusalem, and hast not known the things which are come to pass there in these days?

19 And he said unto them, What things? And they said unto him, Concerning Jesus of Nazareth, which was a prophet mighty in deed and word before God and all the people:

20 And how the chief priests and our rulers delivered him to be condemned to death, and have crucified him.

21 But we trusted that it had been he which should have redeemed Israel: and beside all this, to day is the third day since these things were done.

22 Yea, and certain women also of our company made us astonished, which were early at the sepulchre;

23 And when they found not his body, they came, saying, that they had also seen a vision of angels, which said that he was alive.

24 And certain of them which were with us went to the sepulchre, and found *it* even so as the women had said: but him they saw not.

MATTHEW –	MARK – 16	LUKE – 24	JOHN – 20
		25 Then he said unto them, O fools, and slow of heart to believe all that the prophets have spoken:	
		26 Ought not Christ to have suffered these things, and to enter into his glory?	
		27 And beginning at Moses and all the prophets, he expounded unto them in all the scriptures the things concerning himself.	
		28 And they drew nigh unto the village, whither they went: and he made as though he would have gone further.	
		29 But they constrained him, saying, Abide with us: for it is toward evening, and the day is far spent. And he went in to tarry with them.	
		30 And it came to pass, as he sat at meat with them, he took bread, and blessed *it*, and brake, and gave to them.	
		31 And their eyes were opened, and they knew him; and he vanished out of their sight.	
		32 And they said one to another, Did not our heart burn within us, while he talked with us by the way, and while he opened to us the scriptures?	
		33 And they rose up the same hour, and returned to Jerusalem, and found the eleven gathered together, and them that were with them,	
	13 And they went and told *it* unto the residue: neither believed they them.	35 And they told what things *were done* in the way, and how he was known of them in breaking of bread.	

270. APOSTLES DISCUSSING JESUS' APPEARANCE TO SIMON PETER

		34 Saying, The Lord is risen indeed, and hath appeared to Simon.	

271. JESUS APPEARS TO TEN APOSTLES AND THOSE WITH THEM

	14 ¶ Afterward he appeared unto the eleven as they sat at meat,	36 ¶ And as they thus spake, Jesus himself stood in the midst of them, and saith unto them, Peace *be* unto you.	19 ¶ Then the same day at evening, being the first *day* of the week, when the doors were shut where the disciples were assembled for fear of the Jews, came Jesus and stood in the midst, and saith unto them, Peace *be* unto you.
		37 But they were terrified and affrighted, and supposed that they had seen a spirit.	
	and upbraided them with their unbelief and hardness of heart, because they believed not them which had seen him after he was risen.	38 And he said unto them, Why are ye troubled? and why do thoughts arise in your hearts?	
		39 Behold my hands and my feet, that it is I myself: handle me, and see; for a spirit hath not flesh and bones, as ye see me have.	
		40 And when he had thus spoken, he shewed them *his* hands and *his* feet.	20 And when he had so said, he shewed unto them *his* hands and his side. Then were the disciples glad, when they saw the Lord.
		41 And while they yet believed not for joy, and wondered, he said unto them, Have ye here any meat?	
		42 And they gave him a piece of a broiled fish, and of an honeycomb.	
		43 And he took *it*, and did eat before them.	

| | | 44 And he said unto them, These *are* the words which I spake unto you, while I was yet with you, that all things must be fulfilled, which were written in the law of Moses, and *in* the prophets, and *in* the psalms, concerning me.
45 Then opened he their understanding, that they might understand the scriptures,
46 And said unto them, Thus it is written, and thus it behoved Christ to suffer, and to rise from the dead the third day:
47 And that repentance and remission of sins should be preached in his name among all nations, beginning at Jerusalem.
48 And ye are witnesses of these things. | |
| | | | 21 Then said Jesus to them again, Peace *be* unto you: as *my* Father hath sent me, even so send I you.
22 And when he had said this, he breathed on *them*, and saith unto them, Receive ye the Holy Ghost:
23 Whose soever sins ye remit, they are remitted unto them; *and* whose soever *sins* ye retain, they are retained. |

272. JESUS AGAIN APPEARS TO THE APOSTLES INCLUDING THOMAS.

| | | | 24 ¶ But Thomas, one of the twelve, called Dĭd′-y̆-mŭs, was not with them when Jesus came.
25 The other disciples therefore said unto him, We have seen the Lord. But he said unto them, Except I shall see in his hands the print of the nails, and put my finger into the print of the nails, and thrust my hand into his side, I will not believe.
26 ¶ And after eight days again his disciples were within, and Thomas with them: *then* came Jesus, the doors being shut, and stood in the midst, and said, Peace *be* unto you.
27 Then saith he to Thomas, Reach hither thy finger, and behold my hands; and reach hither thy hand, and thrust *it* into my side: and be not faithless, but believing.
28 And Thomas answered and said unto him, My Lord and my God.
29 Jesus saith unto him, Thomas, because thou hast seen me, thou hast believed: blessed *are* they that have not seen, and *yet* have believed. |

273. JESUS VISITS AND EATS WITH SEVEN DISCIPLES AT THE SEA OF TIBERIAS

| | | | CHAPTER 21
AFTER these things Jesus shewed himself again to the disciples at the sea of Tĭ-bē′-rĭ-ăs; and on this wise shewed he *himself*.
2 There were together Simon Peter, and Thomas called Dĭd′-y̆-mŭs, and Nă-thăn′-ă-ĕl of Cana in Galilee, and the *sons* of Zĕb′-ĕ-dĕe, and two other of his disciples. |

3 Simon Peter saith unto them, I go a fishing. They say unto him, We also go with thee. They went forth, and entered into a ship immediately; and that night they caught nothing.

4 But when the morning was now come, Jesus stood on the shore: but the disciples knew not that it was Jesus.

5 Then Jesus saith unto them, Children, have ye any meat? They answered him, No.

6 And he said unto them, Cast the net on the right side of the ship, and ye shall find. They cast therefore, and now they were not able to draw it for the multitude of fishes.

7 Therefore that disciple whom Jesus loved saith unto Peter, It is the Lord. Now when Simon Peter heard that it was the Lord, he girt *his* fisher's coat *unto him,* (for he was naked,) and did cast himself into the sea.

8 And the other disciples came in a little ship; (for they were not far from land, but as it were two hundred cubits,) dragging the net with fishes.

9 As soon then as they were come to land, they saw a fire of coals there, and fish laid thereon, and bread.

10 Jesus saith unto them, Bring of the fish which ye have now caught.

11 Simon Peter went up, and drew the net to land full of great fishes, an hundred and fifty and three: and for all there were so many, yet was not the net broken.

12 Jesus saith unto them, Come *and* dine. And none of the disciples durst ask him, Who art thou? knowing that it was the Lord.

13 Jesus then cometh, and taketh bread, and giveth them, the fish likewise.

14 This is now the third time that Jesus shewed himself to his disciples, after that he was risen from the dead.

274. PETER'S LOVE FOR JESUS TO BE MANIFEST BY SERVICE.

15 ¶ So when they had dined, Jesus saith to Simon Peter, Simon, *son* of Jonas, lovest thou me more than these? He saith unto him, Yea, Lord; thou knowest that I love thee. He saith unto him, Feed my lambs.

16 He saith to him again the second time, Simon, *son* of Jonas, lovest thou me? He saith unto him, Yea, Lord; thou knowest that I love thee. He saith unto him, Feed my sheep.

17 He saith unto him the third time, Simon, *son* of Jonas, lovest thou me? Peter was grieved because he said unto him the third time, Lovest thou me? And he said unto him, Lord, thou knowest all things; thou knowest that I love thee. Jesus saith unto him, Feed my sheep.

275. PETER'S DEATH FORETOLD

18 Verily, verily, I say unto thee, When thou wast young, thou girdedst thyself, and walkedst whither thou wouldest: but when thou shalt be old, thou shalt stretch forth thy hands, and another shall gird thee, and carry *thee* whither thou wouldest not.

19 This spake he, signifying by what death he should glorify God. And when he had spoken this, he saith unto him, Follow me.

276. PETER QUESTIONS JESUS ABOUT JOHN'S FUTURE.

20 Then Peter, turning about, seeth the disciple whom Jesus loved following; which also leaned on his breast at supper, and said, Lord, which is he that betrayeth thee?

21 Peter seeing him saith to Jesus, Lord, and what *shall* this man *do*?

22 Jesus saith unto him, If I will that he tarry till I come, what *is that* to thee? follow thou me.

23 Then went this saying abroad among the brethren, that that disciple should not die: yet Jesus said not unto him, He shall not die; but, If I will that he tarry till I come, what *is that* to thee?

277. JESUS APPEARS TO THE ELEVEN IN GALILEE

16 ¶ Then the eleven disciples went away into Galilee, into a mountain where Jesus had appointed them.

17 And when they saw him, they worshipped him: but some doubted.

18 And Jesus came and spake unto them, saying, All power is given unto me in heaven and in earth.

19 ¶ Go ye therefore, and teach all nations, baptizing them in the name of the Father, and of the Son, and of the Holy Ghost:

20 Teaching them to observe all things whatsoever I have commanded you:

15 And he said unto them, Go ye into all the world, and preach the gospel to every creature.

16 He that believeth and is baptized shall be saved; but he that believeth not shall be damned.

17 And these signs shall follow them that believe; In my name shall they cast out devils; they shall speak with new tongues;

18 They shall take up serpents; and if they drink any deadly thing, it shall not hurt them; they shall lay hands on the sick, and they shall recover.

and, lo, I am with you alway, *even* unto the end of the world. Ā'-mĕn.

278. THE ASCENSION

49 ¶ And, behold, I send the promise of my Father upon you: but tarry ye in the city of Jerusalem, until ye be endued with power from on high.

50 ¶ And he led them out as far as to Bethany, and he lifted up his hands, and blessed them.

MATTHEW –	MARK – 16	LUKE – 24	JOHN – 20,21
	19 ¶ So then after the Lord had spoken unto them, he was received up into heaven, and sat on the right hand of God.	51 And it came to pass, while he blessed them, he was parted from them, and carried up into heaven. 52 And they worshipped him, and returned to Jerusalem with great joy: 53 And were continually in the temple, praising and blessing God. Ä´·měn.	
	20 And they went forth, and preached every where, the Lord working with *them*, and confirming the word with signs following. Ä´·měn.		

279. JOHN'S CONCLUDING TESTIMONY

			JOHN – 20,21
			30 ¶ And many other signs truly did Jesus in the presence of his disciples, which are not written in this book: 31 But these are written, that ye might believe that Jesus is the Christ, the Son of God; and that believing ye might have life through his name.
			Ch. 21 24 This is the disciple which testifieth of these things, and wrote these things: and we know that his testimony is true. 25 And there are also many other things which Jesus did, the which, if they should be written every one, I suppose that even the world itself could not contain the books that should be written. Ä´·měn.

NOTE 31. The Feast of the Passover commemorates the angel of death passing over the Israelites when the firstborn of the Egyptians were killed. The subsequent release of the Israelites from Egyptian bondage marked the beginning of the Israelites as a nation. The time of the feast was the month of Abib (later called Nisan) which corresponds approximately with the month of April. By the time of Jesus, the celebration of the Passover had been altered in many ways from the original. It was at the time of the Feast of the Passover that Jesus was arrested and crucified. Also, the length of Jesus' ministry is measured by the number of Passovers. For further information on the number of Passovers and length of his ministry see Note 51.

NOTE 51. The actual feast referred to in John 5:1 is not known. The two most probable are the Feast of Purim or the Feast of the Passover. The Feast of Purim was held one month before the Feast of the Passover. Farrar, p. 283 and Steinmuller, p. 51 call it the Feast of Purim. Robinson, p. 30 calls it the Passover. Most others agree it cannot be known with certainty which feast is referred to. Of further interest is the length of Jesus' ministry. While the synoptic gospels mention only one Passover (Matt 26, Mark 14 and Luke 22) John refers to three by name (John 2:13, John 6:4 and John 12:1). If the feast of John 5:1 is the Feast of Purim, then John 6:4 is probably the Passover of the same year and Jesus' ministry would have been a little over two years. However, if the feast of John 5:1 is the Passover then John records four Passovers and the ministry would be another year longer making it a little over three years.

NOTE 112. It is not known when or from where the Seventy were sent forth. Most harmonists believe the Seventy were sent forth after the Feast of Tabernacles. Those who have Jesus returning to Galilee after the Feast of Tabernacles have the Seventy being sent from Galilee or Samaria. (Farrar, p. 427, Steinmuller, p. 75, Stevens, p. 122) Those who feel Jesus' departure for the Feast of Tabernacles was his final departure from Galilee have the Seventy sent from Judea. (Broadus, p. 110, Robertson, p. 120, Wieand, p. 135) Another approach seems to be more probable. It appears Jesus' departure for the Feast of Tabernacles marked the end of his Galilean Ministry and that he was now going to travel and work Judea and Perea. Since the Seventy were being sent, "...into every city and place, whither he himself would come," (Luke 10:1) it seems logical that he would send them forth "to those cities and places prior to his departure." Further, the "woes" proclaimed against the cities Chorazin, Bethsaida and his own Capernaum (all cities of Galilee) seem to reflect the feelings he must have had as he was preparing to leave these cities which had turned against him after the great works he had done in them.

NOTE 113. "Feast of Tabernacles or 'feast of ingathering,' or 'of harvest,' held in October, marked the completion of the harvest of fruit, oil and wine. For eight days the people lived in booths, in memory of the wanderings in the wilderness. Numerous sacrifices were offered." Dummelow, p. 787. This feast was attended by Jesus six months prior to his death.

NOTE 114. Luke 9:51-56. This journey marks Jesus' departure from Galilee and seems to be a journey of haste to reach Jerusalem before the end of the Feast of Tabernacles. Many harmonists, however, show it to be the beginning of a slow leisurely teaching tour from Galilee after the Feast of Tabernacles. This seems unlikely in light of Luke 10:38, 39 which has Jesus at the home of Martha and Mary probably in Bethany. This must be after the Feast of Tabernacles and therefore supports the idea that Luke 9:51-56 was a hurried trip to Jerusalem. Also, it would be natural for Jesus to visit Martha and Mary as one of his first visits following the Feast of Tabernacles.

NOTE 117. John 7:14-10:21 seems to take place in Jerusalem at the Feast of Tabernacles (October) and shortly thereafter. Notice in John 10:22 it is now winter and Jesus is in Jerusalem for the Feast of Dedication. Then in John 10:24-27 when the Jews asked Jesus if he would tell them plainly if he was the Christ, he replied, "...I told you and ye believed not," "...because ye are not my sheep, as I said unto you. My sheep hear my voice, and I know them, and they follow me." This is an obvious reference to his earlier teaching to them in John 10:4. Then in John 10:40 it states Jesus went away "again" implying he had returned for the Feast of Dedication.

NOTE 124. Luke Problem: "In chapters 10-17 of Luke many sayings and teachings are also given by Matthew and Mark but in other life situations; we must either suppose that Jesus taught numerous truths on various occasions like every other great teacher, or else tear Luke's story into fragments and thus disregard his fine sense of both historical and literary sequences."

"It is not strange that in evangelizing in Judea the same life-situations would arise as had risen previously in Galilee; and so the same questions would be asked and the same answers given.

We know for example that Paul often repeated himself in this way, e.g. in Galatians and Romans, also in Ephesians and Colossians.

In fact all great teachers frequently repeat their most striking sayings, illustrations and teachings.

Besides each one of the Gospels reports Jesus as repeating on different occasions, the same sayings, enunciating the same principles, or using the same illustrations." Wieand, pp. 138 and 146.

NOTE 139. "The Feast of Dedication (lit. 'the Renewal') was instituted by Judas Maccabaeus, 164 B.C., to commemorate the purification of the Temple, which had been profaned by the idolatrous king Antiochus Epiphanes. It was held on the 15th of Kislev (about the middle of December), and on account of the brilliant illuminations was also called 'the Lights'." Dummelow, p. 792.

NOTE 158. A difficult verse to harmonize is Luke 17:11 which has Jesus going to Jerusalem through Samaria and Galilee. It is explained by linking it to John 11:54. After raising Lazarus from the dead, Jesus sought refuge from the Jews by going to Ephraim. Since the Passover was close at hand, Jesus left Ephraim heading north making one final loop through Samaria and into Galilee where he probably joined the many travelers now journeying toward Jerusalem. See Robertson p. 139.

NOTE: 230. The events between the arrest of Jesus in Gethsemane and his deliverance before Pilate the next morning present many difficulties to the harmonist.

Some of the difficulties are as follows:

A. Is John 18:24 out of order and should verse 24 follow John 18:13?

Based upon the above question is the additional problem of whether the interrogation of Jesus in John 18:19-23 was before Annas or Caiaphas. Verse 13 states that Jesus was first led to Annas, father-in-law to the High Priest Caiaphas. Then in verse 19 Jesus is being questioned by the High Priest and one assumes this to be Caiaphas, but at the end of the questioning it appears to have been Annas who then sent Jesus to Caiaphas. Some have concluded that verse 24 is misplaced and should follow John 18:13. In support of this has been the ancient Codex Sinaitucus. Torrey further suggests how verse 24 got misplaced in the copying process (Torrey, p. 329). The more accepted view, however, is to leave John 18:24 where it is. It should be noted that in the Greek, John 18:24 is not in the past tense as it is rendered in the King James Version.

B. Since in all four gospels, Peter and the other disciple followed Jesus to the same place, was it to Annas' or Caiaphas' palace?

Although Matthew 26:57 says Caiaphas, Mark 14:53 and Luke 22:54 say High Priest and John 18:13 says Annas, it appears that all four writers are referring to the same building complex since it is to this place that Peter and the other disciple follow Jesus. This implies, as Farrar (p. 589) suggests that Annas and Caiaphas lived in the same building complex. Since only John mentions the questioning by Annas it is only natural for the synoptic writers to use the word Caiaphas or High Priest in referring to the place where Jesus was taken. Peter is now in the courtyard and it is here that he will make his three denials.

C. Is the trial recorded in Matthew 26:59-66 and Mark 14:55-64 the same trial as Luke 22:26-71?

Benoit (pp. 93-114) presents a very good argument in favor of only one trial held early in the morning. However, traditionally the trials recorded by Matthew and Mark have been thought to be held in the early morning hours before dawn and are referred to as the illegal night trial. Then as soon as it was day, the morning or legal trial was held. Also, Matthew and Mark both imply a second trial in the morning. See Matthew 27:1 and Mark 15:1. This is the view most widely accepted.

NOTE 260. A casual reading of the events on resurrection morning give the impression that John's account is quite different from that of the synoptics. In John, Mary Magdalene appears to visit the tomb alone and very early, and finding the stone rolled away she runs to tell Peter and John who run to see the tomb, and Mary returns with them. After Peter and John leave, the resurrected Jesus appears to Mary telling her to touch him not. Mary then runs to tell the Apostles.

In the synoptics, many women including Mary Magdalene go to the tomb early in the morning. Finding the stone rolled away, they look inside. Angels tell them Christ is risen, the women run to tell the Apostles; the resurrected Jesus meets them on their way and they hold him by the feet and worship him.

Three problems are raised by these two apparently different accounts.

1. Did Mary go to the tomb alone first, or was her visit with the other women?

2. If Mary went to the tomb alone and found it empty (John 20:1) she would not be returning with other women to anoint Jesus' body with spices like the synoptics say she was.

3. If Mary's first visit to the tomb was with the other women, and Jesus appeared to the other women on their way to tell the Apostles (Matt. 28:9, 10), then the appearance to Mary alone at the tomb (John 20:11-18) would not be the first appearance of Jesus like Mark says (Mark 16:9).

I believe these two accounts can be harmonized very smoothly in the following manner: Mary Magdalene's first visit to the tomb (John 20:1) is with the other women and is the same visit recorded by the synoptics (Matt. 28:1, Mark 16:2, Luke 24:1). If Mary had already been there alone and knew of the resurrection she would not be returning with spices to anoint the body and wondering "who shall roll us away the stone." Upon seeing the stone rolled away, Mary immediately left the other women and ran to tell Peter and John (John 20:2). Because she did not stay long enough to see or hear the angels, she believes the body has been taken away. In further support of her visit to the tomb in the company of the other women, notice how she says to Peter in John 20:2, "...and WE know not where they have laid him." The other women now enter the empty tomb and see the angels who tell them Christ is risen. These women now go to tell the Apostles. When Peter and John hear that angels are in the tomb and that Jesus is alive they run to see the tomb. Notice that one of the synoptics (Luke 24:22) parallels John on this point after the return of all the women. Mary Magdalene follows Peter and John because she had not seen the angels or heard their message. Upon their arrival, Peter and John enter the tomb, find the linen clothes, but apparently no angels. Peter and John leave, but Mary lingers at the tomb, still uncertain and wondering at what has happened. It is in this setting that the resurrected Jesus appears to Mary. She then goes and tells the disciples she has seen the Lord.

Matthew 28:9 is the account of Jesus' appearance to the other women. If Mark is correct that Jesus first appeared to Mary Magdalene, then this appearance to the other women must be after his appearance to Mary and not on the return from the tomb early that morning.

MAP OF PALESTINE

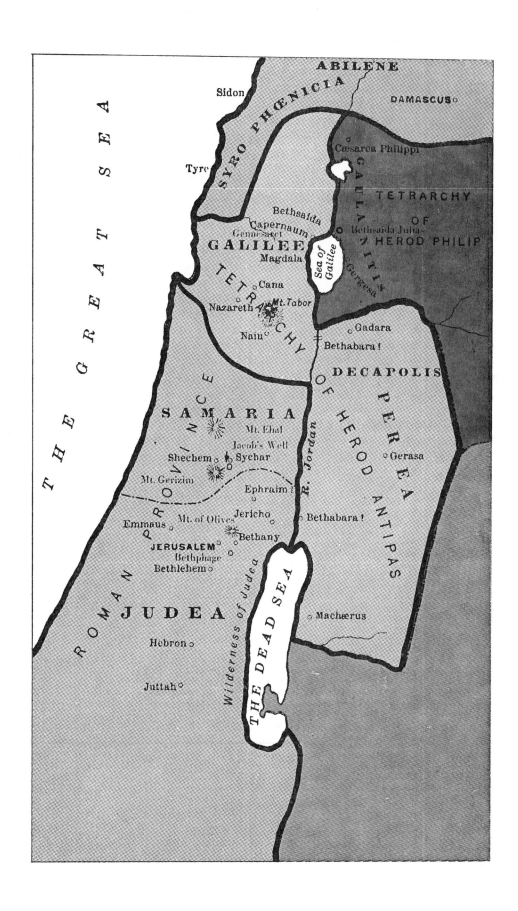

MATTHEW

MARK

LUKE

JOHN

Ch.	Verse	Page	Ch.	Verse	Page	Ch.	Verse	Page
1	1-14	1	9	1-15	78	15	22-27	136
1	15-18	2	9	16-35	79	16	1-15	136
1	19-32	14	9	36-41	80	16	16-33	137
1	33-51	15	10	1-15	80	17	1-20	138
2	1-12	16	10	16-21	81	17	21-26	139
2	13-25	17	10	22-33	90	18	1	139
3	1-4	17	10	34-42	91	18	2-10	140
3	5-25	18	11	1-8	98	18	11-16	141
3	26-36	19	11	9-32	99	18	17	143
4	1-3	19	11	33-51	100	18	18-20	141
4	4-22	20	11	52-54	101	18	21-24	142
4	23-42	21	11	55-57	109	18	25-27	143
4	43-54	22	12	1-3	109	18	28-38	144
5	1-16	28	12	4-11	110	18	39a	145
5	17-35	29	12	12-18	111	18	39b,40	146
5	36-47	30	12	19	112	19	1-6	146
6	1-10	55	12	20, 21	120	19	7-16	147
6	11-20	56	12	22-36a	121	19	17-24	148
6	21-29	57	12	36b-43	122	19	25-27	149
6	30-50	58	12	44-48	121	19	28-35	150
6	51-71	59	12	49-50	122	19	36-42	151
7	1	60	13	1-17	130	20	1,2	152
7	2-10	72	13	18, 19	131	20	3-10	153
7	11-26	73	13	20	130	20	11-18	154
7	27-46	74	13	21-32	131	20	19, 20	156
7	47-53	75	13	33-38	132	20	21-29	157
8	1-13	75	14	1-16	133	20	30-31	160
8	14-33	76	14	17-31	134	21	1,2	157
8	34-54	77	15	1,2	134	21	3-17	158
8	55-59	78	15	3-21	135	21	18-23	159
						21	24, 25	160

BIBLIOGRAPHY

Benoit, Pierre. *The Passion and Resurrection of Jesus Christ*. Translated by Benet Weatherhead. London: Darton, Longman and Todd, 1969.

Broadus, John A. *A Harmony of the Gospels in the Revised Version*. A. T. Robertson. rev. ed. New York: George H. Doran Co., 1920.

Dummelow, J. R. *The One Volume Bible Commentary*. New York: The Macmillan Co., 1966.

Farrar, Frederic W. *The Life of Christ*. Portland, Oregon: Fountain Publications, 1964.

The *Holy Bible,* Revised Standard Version. New York: Oxford University Press, 1962.

The *New Testament,* King James Version. London: Cambridge University Press.

Robertson, A. T. *A Harmony of the Gospels*. New York: Harper and Row, 1950.

Robinson, Edward. *A Harmony of the Four Gospels*. London: The Religious Tract Society, 1875 (?)

Steinmueller, John E. *A Gospel Harmony*. New York: W. H. Sadlier, 1942.

Stevens, William Arnold, and Burton, Ernest DeWitt, *A Harmony of the Gospels for Historical Study*. 12th ed. rev. New York: Charles Scribner's Sons, 1904.

Torrey, Charles Cutler. *The Four Gospels, A New Translation,* Harper and Brothers, 1933.

Wieand, Albert Cassel. *A New Harmony of the Gospels*. Michigan: Wm. B. Eerdmans Publishing Co., 1959.